Wilderness Basics

mountaineers outdoor basics

Third Edition

Hiking | Backpacking

Mountain Biking

By the San Diego Chapter
of the Sierra Club

Edited by Kristi Anderson
and Arleen Tavernier

THE MOUNTAINEERS BOOKS
*is the nonprofit publishing arm of The Mountaineers Club,
an organization founded in 1906 and dedicated to the exploration,
preservation, and enjoyment of outdoor and wilderness areas.*

1001 SW Klickitat Way, Suite 201, Seattle, WA 98134

Published simultaneously in Great Britain by Cordee, 3a DeMontfort Street, Leicester, England, LE1 7HD

Manufactured in the United States of America

Project Editor: Laura Drury
Cover design: Karen Schober
Layout: Mayumi Thompson

Copyeditor: Joeth Zucco
Book design: Peggy Egerdahl
Cover photograph: © Alan Bauer

Illustrators: Benjamin Pease, Robert Frost and Bob Cram; illustrations on page 57, 61, 63, 65, 70, 93, 94, 95, 98, 225, 226 from Cox, Steven M., and Kris Fulsaas, eds. *Mountaineering: The Freedom of the Hills.* 7th ed. Seattle: The Mountaineers Books, 2003.

Leave No Trace, Inc. and The National Outdoor Leadership School are the copyright owners of the material represented in Chapter 2. This abstracted dialog has been approved by Leave No Trace, Inc. and published with their permission. More information, literature, and advice are available at *www. LNT.org* or 1-800-332-4100.

Library of Congress Cataloging-in-Publication Data
Sierra Club. San Diego Chapter.
  Wilderness basics : the complete handbook for hikers and backpackers / by the San Diego Chapter of the Sierra Club ; edited by Kristi Anderson and Arleen Tavernier.— 3rd ed.
      p. cm.
Includes bibliographical references and index.
  ISBN 0-89886-814-9
  1. Outdoor life—West (U.S.) 2. Wilderness survival—West (U.S.) I. Anderson, Kristi. II. Tavernier, Arleen. III. Title.
  GV191.42.W47S54 2003
  796.5'0978—dc22
                            2003021308

Contents

Preface

In an effort to escape the pressures of work and society, people are turning to the outdoors to find a sense of peace and adventure. Wilderness areas are one of the few places left where you can "get away from it all." With a pack on your back, the trail becomes your sanctuary and time slips away while you explore in quiet solitude. After long hikes you'll find it becomes harder and harder to reenter society, for the soul yearns for the tranquility of the trail.

This book is the result of the commitment to and love of the outdoors shared by the leaders and staff of the Wilderness Basics Course. These volunteers have, over the years, taught tens of thousands of adults how to venture safely into and enjoy the wilderness.

The Wilderness Basics Course, under the name of Basic Mountaineering Course, started in San Diego in 1957. It was cosponsored by the Rock Climbing Section of the San Diego Sierra Club and the City of San Diego Park and Recreation Department in response to the perceived need for more in-depth outdoor training. It quickly became apparent that a course book would be needed. Mainly through the efforts of the chief editor, Henry I. Mandolf, the first edition of this book, better known as the "Red Book," was published in 1961.

The book has been revised several times over the years to reflect innovations. Today the trend is toward lighter and more versatile gear that allows the hiker to go farther, faster. This light gear is very practical, as long as the skill and experience level of the hiker is high, but in many instances those levels fall short, leaving hikers in situations beyond their abilities, without the equipment or skill to handle emergencies.

The information contained in this book attempts to raise that skill level, but the hiker also needs practical hands-on experience. This is one of the reasons courses such as the Wilderness Basics Course have become so popular. In these courses, hikers are able to learn in a relaxed classroom environment and also to participate with seasoned hikers in weekend outings structured to increase their hands-on knowledge in the field.

This edition covers a wide variety of subjects that have become increasingly necessary in wilderness travel. Each chapter has been updated to include techniques and equipment that are now available. The Wilderness Navigation chapter now includes detailed information on using the Global Positioning System (GPS). The Foods and Cooking chapter has been completely revised and includes a 4-day sample backpack menu along with an extensive inventory of trail lunches and snack ideas. There are two new chapters: Animal Encounters, with practical ideas on avoiding dangerous contact; and Mountain Biking, expressly for enthusiasts.

While many volunteers contributed to this new edition, if it wasn't for the dedication and persistence of Kristi Anderson, co-editor, this book would have never gone to press. The Wilderness Basics Course would also like to thank Al Hofstatter, Jim Matlock, Bob Feuge, and Skip Forsht, who spent long hours to help keep this edition on track.

As Baba Dioum, a Kenyan environmentalist, once said, "In the end we will preserve only what we love; we will love only what we understand; and we will understand only what we are taught."

I hope you enjoy this book and use its information "To explore, enjoy, and protect the wild places of the Earth."

Arleen Tavernier
Chair, 2003 Wilderness Basics Course

chapter
1

The North American Wilderness: An Introduction

Jerry Schad and Olive Wenzel

Earth, the third planet from the sun, is the mildest and most hospitable of the nine. It is home to more than 6 billion people and millions of species of plants, animals, and insects. It drifts through space like a pale, delicate bubble. It's all we have.

Countless generations have been transforming Earth's environment to satisfy their physical needs and their desire for comfort. Today it's clear that unbridled exploitation of Earth's resources cannot continue without unraveling the planet's life-support systems. People are becoming increasingly aware of the importance of the dwindling number of places called wilderness, where those life-support systems remain intact.

Considerable argument exists about what defines wilderness. Is it a landscape virtually untouched by humans? Can it include places where human beings (Native Americans, for instance) have resided and "peacefully coexisted" for centuries or millennia? Certainly wilderness is not a place so dependent on human intervention—a garden or a golf course or a city park—that it collapses into disarray without constant attention.

Hiking in Hot Spring Canyon, Santa Ana Mountains, Cleveland National Forest. (Photo by Jerry Schad.)

For the purposes of this book, the conception of wilderness is going to be a broad one. Wilderness needs no human presence even though humans may visit on occasion. The focus of this book is that visitation. Almost everyone feels the needs sooner or later, to cast aside the trappings of civilization and escape to someplace wild—if only for a few hours or a few days. You take to the hills for relaxation, inspiration, education, and excitement. And you bring back memories that enrich your life forever.

In the wilderness, you glimpse the world as it once was on a global scale. On mountains, in deserts, and along wild coastlines, your senses drink in simple pleasures: clean air scented with wildflower nectar, muffled silence in an old-growth forest, the blast of icy air off a glacier, the grace of a bighorn sheep moving on stone, the thunder of breakers felt as well as heard.

In cities people usually live apart from the natural environment, with all their needs and wants—food, water, clothing, entertainment, and more—supplied from afar. Traveling in the wilderness, you learn to adjust yourself to fit the environment, not the other way around. In wilderness you discover that everything depends on everything else. You become more aware of the fragility of each component of the natural world and begin to recognize your responsibility as stewards of this remarkable planet.

The "New World" is spacious enough to contain large tracts of natural landscape. Still, urbanization, agriculture, mining, and timber harvesting have encroached upon many easily exploited acres. But plenty of less-accessible, less-hospitable, and, in many cases, stunningly beautiful acres remain relatively untouched, especially in the western United States, much of Canada, and Alaska. And they can remain that way as long as they receive the care and the legal protection they deserve.

The desert is an unfamiliar wilderness to many people. (Photo by Jerry Schad.)

It's hard to speak of the North American wilderness without rattling off a litany of superlatives. Few coastlines around the world surpass the scenic grandeur of the geologically youthful Pacific, where mountains sweep dramatically down to the sea. Our continent contains world-class mountain ranges and peaks in the western half, as well as gentler ranges, such as the Appalachians, which are more remarkable for their rich flora and fauna than for their topography. North America claims the world's tallest trees, the world's most massive trees, and the world's oldest trees. It also features some of the world's lowest, hottest, and driest deserts, and some of the deepest river gorges.

Many of North America's most remarkable landscapes are distinguished by their inclusion in national, state, and provincial parks. A staggering amount of land, particularly in the western United States, including Alaska, falls within the public domain. California, even with its exploding population now approaching 35 million, contains about 35 million acres—about one-third of its total area—of parks and other lands open to public recreation. Huge swaths of public lands exist in Nevada, Utah, Arizona, and Alaska, while substantial tracts have been set aside in Canada and the eastern half of the United States. The national and state parks dotting the Appalachian Mountains from Georgia into Maine would be the envy of most other nations around the world.

Wilderness lovers have worked for decades to improve access to remote areas without damaging them. The 2000-mile Appalachian Trail offers the dedicated walker a sizeable perspective of an entire mountain range. In the West, the Pacific Crest Trail stretches 2600 miles along the roofline of California, Oregon, and Washington. Concepts for other continent-spanning trails are in the works.

It is not only the grand and remote landscapes and famous trails that are worth a wilderness traveler's attention. Plenty of wild areas lie just beyond the fringes of some of the biggest cities. Only 20 air miles from downtown Los Angeles, black bears, bighorn sheep, and mountain lions roam the canyons and crags of Angeles National Forest. A climber living in Denver can take a shot at any of several alpine summits only an hour's drive away. Just over the Golden Gate Bridge from the skyscrapers of San Francisco, serene Muir Woods National Monument beckons those weary of tense city life. Portland, Seattle, and other cities of the Pacific Northwest have abundant opportunities for winter mountaineering on nearby glacier-draped summits such as Mount Hood and Mount Rainier.

Even in America's crowded Eastern Seaboard, semiwild areas such as the Pine Barrens of New Jersey and the Catskill Mountains of New York lie within a 1- or 2-hour drive.

Wherever you find it, the wilderness deserves attention and care. This book was written to help you, the outdoor enthusiast, prepare for wilderness outings. Enjoy the wildlands of North America and at the same time protect both yourself and the environment from injury of any kind.

Bighorn sheep sightings are one of the many joys of wilderness travel. (Photo by Blake Cournyer.)

Outdoor Ethics

Alfred F. Hofstatter and Eugene A. Troxell

Wilderness is where you go to be closer to your roots. As T. K. Whipple wrote in *Study Out the Land,* "All America lies at the end of the wilderness road, and our past is not a dead past but still lives in us. . . . Our forebears had civilization inside themselves, the wild outside. We live in the civilization they created, but within us the wilderness still lingers. What they dreamed, we live; and what they lived, we dream."

The Wilderness Act of 1964 was the first major step of the U.S. Congress to reserve large plots of undeveloped land as federally administered wilderness areas. Before that, certain lands were set aside as "primitive areas," but there were no officially designated and protected wilderness areas. The Wilderness Act defines wilderness as "an area where the earth and its community of life are untrammeled by man, where man himself is a visitor who does not remain. . . . It is a region which contains no permanent [human] inhabitants, no possibility for motorized travel, and is spacious enough so that a traveler crossing it by foot or horse must have the experience of sleeping out-of-doors." Wilderness, by this definition, included most of the earth's surface as

Opposite: *Wilderness areas can become natural playgrounds for the whole family. (Photo by Bob and Ira Spring.)*

recently as 100 years ago. Today as the global human population reaches over *6 billion,* wilderness is rapidly disappearing. Most modern Americans live their entire lives with no real experience of it.

Many, however, still dimly recognize the wilderness as home, and feel comfortable there. After all, the land that "generally appears to have been affected primarily by the forces of nature, with the imprint of man's work substantially unnoticeable," as the Wilderness Act states, is the environment in which all forms of life have evolved over eons.

In the wilderness, it is not uncommon to reach a clear awareness of what you have recently come from, and of what you will soon return to. As John Muir put it, "I only went out for a walk, and finally concluded to stay out till sundown, for going out, I found, was really going in."

Two hundred years ago, a person might cut brush for a campfire, remove tall grasses and saplings to make camp beside a stream, and wash up in the clear, flowing water. A few others might repeat the same actions in the same area in a year's time, with no appreciable harm done. The natural environment has sufficient regenerative power to heal the wounds inflicted by a few people each year. This does not mean there would be no evidence of people having been there. Desert environments heal even the smallest scars very slowly. But if the number of people likely to camp in the same area each year jumps to a dozen, 100, or 1000, the cumulative impact even on relatively stable areas may be well beyond the regenerative powers of the natural environment. Even John Muir, a pioneer in the realm of wilderness ethics, would need to alter his wilderness behavior were he to camp today where he camped a century ago.

As usage of parks and wilderness areas soars, managers are forced to impose unpopular regulations to minimize the cumulative impact of large numbers of people. There will be more of this—permit systems, trailhead quotas, and rules regulating actions as personal as toilet behavior and as sacrosanct as building campfires.

Of course, even if there are no official rules imposed on the area you visit, you should still regulate your behavior. It is important to think of your own impact, as well as the consequences of dozens, or hundreds, of people repeating the same acts.

The staggering numbers of human beings, as well as advanced technology, provide good reasons for rethinking and recasting traditional ethics. Wilderness ethics need to be based upon an awareness of the interconnections among all things. John Muir put it nicely, "When we try to pick out anything by itself, we find it hitched to everything else in the universe." This ethic should enhance, not destroy, the creative process of

Time spent out in the wilderness teaches you to appreciate the delicate balance of nature. (Photo by Al Hofstatter.)

evolution by supporting the web of life. If you temper your actions with concern and tread lightly upon the delicate and beautiful natural world, you can carry that same ethic back into your everyday life.

Land management agencies have set rules and regulations to ensure safety and reduce impact. While it is always important, common sense alone is not sufficient to allow accurate assessment of the cumulative effects of many seemingly inconsequential behaviors. One behavior might not seem destructive until you consider the effect of similar behavior by hundreds of other people. Therefore it is important to be aware of the long-term cumulative effects of your presence in the outdoors, whether a pristine wilderness area or a neighborhood park.

LEAVE NO TRACE SKILLS AND ETHICS

In 1964, when Congress began establishing wilderness areas, it soon became apparent and important to apply special rules to these untrammeled places.

Unfortunately, it soon became obvious that rules, quotas, closures, and stricter regulations were not working. The outdoor recreation boom of the 1960s and 1970s was inflicting damage on wildland environments faster than nature could repair. People were loving the outdoors to death. The land could not recover.

This dilemma can be summed up by the founder of the National Outdoor Leadership School, Paul Petzoldt: "Those of us with a stake in the future of wilderness must begin to develop . . . an agenda which will place a clear, strong, national focus on the question of the responsibility of the wilderness user to the wilderness."

By the early 1980s several federal land management agencies were teaching and fostering "No Trace" educational programs for campers, but a standard and universally accepted program that would apply to all wildland areas was needed. What resulted was the Leave No Trace educational program that promotes skills and ethics to support the sustainable use of wildlands and natural areas. Established in 1994, Leave No Trace, Inc. was the outgrowth of a joint effort between the U.S. Forest Service, National Park Service, Bureau of Land Management, U.S. Fish and Wildlife Service, and the National Outdoor Leadership School. Manufacturers, outdoor retailers, user groups, educators, and individuals who shared a commitment to protect the wildlands joined in the support of Leave No Trace (LNT).

Seven core principles form the LNT education program:
- Plan ahead and prepare.
- Travel and camp on durable surfaces.
- Dispose of waste properly.
- Leave what you find.
- Minimize campfire impacts.
- Respect wildlife.
- Be considerate of other visitors.

These principles can be applied anywhere—in remote wilderness, parks, and even in your backyard—with any recreational activity. Educate yourself and others and adopt the habits and skills that lead to a Leave No Trace culture for your outdoor ethics.

Plan Ahead and Prepare

Regulations. Know the regulations and special concerns for the area you plan to visit. What are the environmental concerns? Is a permit required? What special skills are needed? Is there a group size limitation?

Popular areas. Try to schedule your trip to avoid times of high use. Consider a less-popular wilderness area nearby.

Equipment. Start with the Ten Essentials, and choose your equipment, food, and water based on the weather, terrain visited, and potential emergencies.

Skills. Develop your skills in navigation and first aid.

Tell a friend. Leave an itinerary and map with a friend, as well as a description of your intended route, telephone number of the nearest ranger station, and your anticipated return date and time.

Travel and Camp on Durable Surfaces

Durable surfaces. Use surfaces—trails, expanses of rock, established campsites, gravel, snow, sand, or dry creek beds—that are resistant to impact. This is especially important in desert regions where the scarcity of water and organic soils makes recovery of damaged plants and terrain extremely slow.

Established campsites. Concentrate your activity in established campsites and on trails to minimize the spread of damage to the undisturbed environment. Don't create "social trails" by bushwhacking between campsites or trails. It is best to limit the impact of your visit to established campsites that are worn rather than starting new damage in a new site. When leaving, clean the site and leave it as natural as possible.

Pristine campsites. These lightly used areas do not—and should not—see much human activity; however, you will encounter campsites that indicate prior use. Let nature take its course to recover lightly impacted sites, and seek out durable surfaces. Avoid areas of animal or bird activity (burrows, nests, etc.). Reserve the most durable surface for cooking and eating activity and, if necessary, less durable areas for sleeping. Move your camp daily to avoid causing lasting impacts, and manage your activity to avoid harming the natural features of the site. Vary your routes to water, the bathroom, and the sleeping area.

Departing a campsite. Before leaving, replace rocks, logs, or sticks you have moved. Use a dead branch to rake away footprints. Cover bare areas with pine needles or leaf litter. Make the site less obvious as a campsite so that it can recover.

Distance to water. Establish your camp and latrine at least 200 feet from water sources. In desert areas check the local regulations, as this distance can be as far as a quarter mile to protect the availability of the water to wildlife.

Dispose of Waste Properly

Pack it in, pack it out. This is a familiar mantra to seasoned wildland visitors. Pack out all trash, leftover food, and litter. Human food and garbage can be lethal to animals, so don't bury or burn trash or food scraps. Organic litter such as orange peels, apple cores, or banana peels takes months to decompose and attracts animals that may attack

Crossing a river in Yosemite. (Photo by Skip Forsht.)

your—or someone else's—food supply. Animals then learn to associate food with humans, and they become pests or raiders at camping areas.

Human waste. When disposing of human waste make an effort to avoid polluting water sources, eliminate contact with insects and animals, maximize decomposition, and minimize the chances of social impacts.

If an established outhouse or bathroom is not available, urinate at least 200 feet from water, camps, and trails. (Try not to urinate on plants, as salt-deprived animals will defoliate it to get the salt in the urine.) Deposit fecal matter in a cat hole dug 6–8 inches deep at least 200 feet from water, camps, trails, and drainages. Look for soil that contains organic matter, as the microbes found in the soil break down the feces and pathogens. Where the ground is devoid of organic matter, such as desert sand, dig a shallower cat hole in a sun-exposed spot where the sand will be heated to a temperature that destroys the pathogens. If you cannot retreat 200 feet from the water source (in a narrow canyon with high walls, for instance) pack out fecal matter. Be aware that in some high-use areas it is required that you pack out human waste. Check local regulations and equip yourself properly. Plan ahead to pack out—not burn—used toilet paper, wet wipes, sanitary napkins or tampons, and soiled diapers.

Water for washing. It is best to carry the water to a wash site 200 feet or more away from water sources and camps. Use, if absolutely necessary, minimal amounts of biodegradable soap. Strain dishwater that contains food scraps through a sieve or cloth, put the food scraps into a garbage bag to pack out, and scatter the water (as opposed to pouring it out in one spot). Do the same for gray water from laundry or washing.

Leave What You Find

Artifacts. By observing and not taking, we pass the gift of discovery on to those who follow. Historical and archeological artifacts are protected by many state and federal laws that make it illegal to disturb or remove them. Pretty rocks, feathers, plants, and so on should be left in their natural state—not in your possession. Instead, let photos and memories be your souvenirs.

Avoid spreading nonnative plants and animals. Invasive species of plants, animals, and organisms can cause large scale, irreversible changes in ecosystems. The following guidelines help to prevent the spread of invasive species:

- Don't transport flowers, weeds, or aquatic plants into wetlands.
- Empty and clean your packs, tents, stock trailers, boats, fishing equipment, vehicles, and other gear after each trip.
- Clean dirt out of your boots or tire treads.
- Never discard or release live bait.
- Make sure pack stock and pets are immunized and their coats are free of seeds and harmful pests (ticks).
- Make sure your stock feed (hay, oats) is weed free. Feed your stock only weed-free food for 3 days prior to entering the backcountry.

Minimize Campfire Impacts

Problems of traditional campfires. The natural appearance of many recreation areas has been compromised by the careless use of fires and the demand for firewood. Campfires are beautiful at night, but rings of

soot-scarred rocks overflowing with ashes and partly burned logs, garbage, and trash are unsightly. More importantly, campfires can and do
ignite wildfires.

Many lasting impacts associated with campfires in the backcountry
can be avoided by using lightweight stoves, fire pans, mound fires,
and other Leave No Trace techniques.

Cook on a stove. Carry a lightweight stove and sufficient fuel to cook
all meals. It is much more efficient and your pots will never have soot on
the bottom.

Build a minimum-impact fire. If a campfire is safe, appropriate,
responsible, allowed, and desired:

- Is a fire permit required?
- What are the pertinent campfire regulations and management
  techniques?
- Consider the wind, weather, location, and wood supply. Is it
  safe to build a campfire?
- Where there are no fire rings bring a fire pan or make a mound fire.
- Have a small shovel or trowel and a container of water to
  saturate the ashes or extinguish a spreading fire.

Use an established fire ring or grate. When you are done, leave it
in a cleaner condition than you found it. This encourages those that
follow to use it and not construct new ones.

Use an alternate campfire method.

- A buddy burner or a candle lantern provides a warm flame,
  and regardless of how small, it is a comfort.
- Pan fires are built on about an inch of sand placed in the
  bottom of a metal pan (aluminum roasting pan or trash can
  lid). Scatter the cold ash or pack it out.
- Mound fires are built on a mound of sand, gravel, or soil with
  low organic content. Lay down a small ground cloth and
  collect enough of the mound material to build an 18-to 24-
  inch diameter by 8-inch high flat mound on the cloth. This
  insulates the heat of the fire from scorching the ground. After
  the fire, saturate the ashes and scatter them away from camp.
  Replace the soil to its original site.

Gather firewood. If permitted, use only dead and downed wood.
The sticks you collect should be no thicker than your wrist. These
burn completely as opposed to large logs that usually remain only half
burned. Don't snap branches off trees.

Manage your campfire.

- Never leave a fire unattended.

- Don't put food, food waste, or trash in the fire. Trash can give off toxic fumes and food never completely burns.
- Break up long sticks as needed. Unused long sticks can be returned to the habitat and will look natural.
- Burn wood completely to ash. Stop feeding the fire long before bedtime.
- Saturate the ash until it is cool to the touch, all the way to the bottom of the ash pile.
- Scatter the ash over a wide area away from the campsite.
- Restore the fire site—rocks from a fire ring and soil from a mound fire—to its natural appearance.

Respect Wildlife

Human interaction. Encounters with wildlife inspire tall tales and long moments of wonder. Yet around the world wildlife faces threats from loss, fragmentation, and encroachment of habitat, invasive species, pollution, overexploration, poaching, and disease. We are responsible for coexisting peacefully with wildlife.

Never feed wildlife. It damages their health, alters natural behavior, and exposes them to predators. Animals are adept opportunists. When attracted by an untidy camp kitchen or a handout, they overcome their natural wariness of humans. This can result in you being harassed by pesky marmots or squirrels, or worse, aggressive bears. Prospects of an easy meal also lure animals into hazardous spots such as campsites, trailheads, roads, and villages where they can be attacked by dogs or hit by vehicles.

Store food securely. Check local regulations and suggestions for proper care of your food supply. In areas where there is no threat of bears, simply hanging the food bag to keep it away from rodents and small carnivores should be adequate. In bear country use of a bear canister is strongly recommended, and in some areas it is required. The alternative is to hang your food (see Chapter 10, Animal Encounters, "Food Storage in Bear Country").

Observe wildlife from a distance. Do not follow or approach wildlife. If animals react to your presence, back away and detour your route. Large predators such as bears and mountain lions are dangerous. Check with local authorities as to the correct camping and hiking practices in the area. Always keep children in immediate sight. Remember they are often the same size as animal prey.

Avoid sensitive seasonal times and habitats for wildlife. While mating, birthing, and guarding their young, wildlife can be overly aggressive or stressed.

Wildlife and pets don't mix. It is best to leave pets at home. If you must travel with a pet, check local restrictions. Most national parks prohibit dogs on trails, so check before you go.

Be Considerate of Other Visitors

Respect other visitors. Maintain a cooperative spirit in the wildlands. This protects the quality of everyone's experience. Interactions should reflect the knowledge that you can and do rely on each other in times of need.

Simple courtesies, such as a friendly greeting, wearing earth tone clothing, or stepping aside to let someone pass add to a pleasant experience.

Camping courtesies:
- Don't disturb livestock or equipment of ranchers, anglers, loggers, trappers, or miners. Leave gates as you found them.
- When encountering horses on a trail, move well off the trail and on the downhill side.
- Place your campsite out of sight of trails and other campers.
- Tune in to the sounds of nature. Eliminate or minimize the use of radios, cell phones, or musical instruments.

Adopt this statement as your ethical guide to Leave No Trace: "Those that follow should not regret you were here." (Photo by Al Hofstatter.)

chapter
3

Physical Conditioning

Barbara Amato, Mary Engles, and Carolyn Wood

It's a satisfying feeling to be strong and healthy—to trek up a steep ridge or down a boulder-tossed canyon with confidence. On the other hand, it's not much fun to set out on a hiking or backpacking trip, only to realize partway through that you're hurting or too fatigued to enjoy the rest of the trip. So follow the advice of The Mountaineers and "Never let judgment be overruled by desire when choosing a route or deciding whether to turn back."

Conditioning for wilderness travel is no different than conditioning for any other athletic pursuit. Being physically as well as mentally prepared is an essential ingredient to a fully challenging yet safe experience. One concern novices frequently express is whether or not they will be strong enough to keep up with the group. Adopting an effective program not only builds the necessary physical strength, it also builds confidence. Another important thing to remember is that training should be specific to the activity.

When training for most sports there are compatible and incompatible activities. For example, if you are a weekend skier, then rollerblading is a compatible activity because it trains the same muscle groups. Many cross-training activities provide a break from the same activity, both mentally and physically, so that you stay interested and allow recovery from

A regular fitness program is important preparation for enjoying the outdoors. (Photo by Jerry Schad.)

one activity while continuing conditioning in the other. Running is a compatible activity for hikers, but most of the running should be at an *aerobic* level such as jogging rather than at an *anaerobic* level such as sprinting.

WHAT SHAPE ARE YOU IN?

Wilderness travel involves aerobic exercise. When you exercise aerobically, your heart beats faster and you breathe more rapidly to satisfy the energy demands of your muscles. Aerobic exercise does not consist of short-duration bursts of energy that leave you out of breath but rather longer periods of sustained energy output. In order to improve your aerobic capacity, you need to increase your heart rate and your breathing by running, biking, swimming, rowing, or walking briskly.

Good indicators of aerobic fitness include:

- Resting morning heart rate of 60 beats per minute or fewer
- Stable morning weight
- Stable and repeatable "12-minute test"
- Rapid return to a normal heart rate after exercise

The 12-minute test, originally developed by Dr. Kenneth Cooper in the 1960s, is one yardstick by which you can measure your aerobic fitness. It refers to how far you can walk, run, or jog in 12 minutes (see fig. 3-1).

IF YOU CAN COVER IN 12 MINUTES	YOU ARE IN FITNESS CATEGORY
Less than 1.0 mile	Very Poor
1.0 to 1.24 miles	Poor
1.25 to 1.49 miles	Fair
1.50 to 1.74 miles	Good
1.75 miles or more	Excellent

Figure 3-1: *The 12-minute test.*

It is also good to do an endurance test to set a baseline and then build on it. Another test of condition is a frequency test, which measures how frequently you can repeat an activity at the same level of intensity and duration. According to Don Mann and Kara Schaad in *The Complete Guide to Adventure Racing,* the more frequently you can repeat an activity, the more fit you become.

A still-higher level of conditioning may be required if your goal is to tackle the likes of Mount Whitney, Mount Rainier, or Mount Washington. Your lungs and heart are under greater stress at high altitudes because of the reduced oxygen content in the air. Your training program would include occasional sessions of moderate to vigorous exercise lasting for a number of hours. Long-duration exercise, coupled with frequent, short exercise sessions, helps you attain your highest level of fitness.

GETTING FIT

The recommendations of the American College of Sports Medicine in *Guidelines for Exercise Testing and Prescription* suggest that if you're under thirty-five and free of significant risk factors such as smoking, high blood pressure, elevated cholesterol, or hereditary heart disease, you can begin an exercise program without medical testing. Even so, progress slowly and be alert to unusual signs and symptoms. Beyond age forty-five, you should have a "maximal exercise" (treadmill) test under professional supervision before embarking on any strenuous exercise program.

Contrary to popular belief, you do not have different sets of muscles for different exercise activities. You use the same muscles in different ways and amounts; however, exercise does have a very specific effect on those muscles. The best way to improve your ability to hike up hills is to hike up hills on a regular basis. Not everyone lives in places where this is possible or convenient, but there are alternatives such as jogging, walking briskly, or donning a full day pack and taking a brisk walk.

In the broader arena of activities, any rhythmic action—swimming, skating, bicycling, jogging, rowing, or cross-country skiing—that involves large muscle groups (e.g., the legs) and is maintained for a prolonged period is beneficial. Stop-and-start sports such as tennis, racquetball, and basketball are also effective if maintained for longer periods. The important thing is to do something regularly that increases your heart rate and breathing.

Running on the beach is one way to combine a fitness routine with enjoyment of the outdoors. (Photo by Jerry Schad.)

In *Winning Guide to Sports Endurance,* Scott Tinley recommends using the maximum heart rate as a measure of the intensity of a workout. To calculate your maximum heart rate, subtract your age from 220. Interval training builds speed by training at the maximum heart rate for short intervals. Endurance training conditions for distance at aerobic heart rate levels, or 60 percent of the maximum heart rate for periods of an hour or more.

According to the American College of Sports Medicine, regular and frequent exercise sessions, at least three to five times per week, should consist of 20 to 60 minutes of continuous activity at 60 to 90 percent of your maximum heart rate. Aim for a level of activity that is within your personal training zone. See Figure 3-2 to determine the "training-sensitive" range of your heart rate for these sessions. Your heart rate can be quickly determined by feeling your pulse in your wrist and counting the number of beats for 10 seconds. Multiply the number of beats by six to

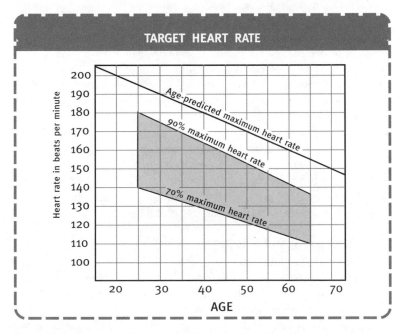

Figure 3-2: *This target heart rate chart assumes that your maximum heart rate is 220 minus your age, and that aerobic exercise (for 20- to 30-minute periods) is most effective in the range of 70 to 90 percent of your maximum heart rate. Your heart rate during aerobic exercise should fall within the shaded area.*

find the number of beats per minute. For example, if you're forty years old, keep your heart pumping between 21 and 27 beats every ten seconds, which corresponds to 126 to 162 beats per minute.

Before you start an exercise program, you'll need to consider any aches, pains, or other problems you're currently experiencing. Some of these may be helped by exercise or stretching and massage, but some may be worsened unless remedial measures are taken. Lower back or knee pain, for example, can be eased by the strength and range of motion gained with exercise, or it may be intensified as a result of a particular kind of action (like running on hard surfaces, going downhill, or twisting your body to put on or take off a heavy backpack) that aggravates a preexisting condition such as weak muscles or mild tendonitis. If you know you have a problem, talk with sports-minded people or with those who have similar injuries to find an orthopedist, sports-oriented physician, or physical therapist who can assist you with a program that addresses your specific problem.

Regardless of problem areas, you'll need to strengthen the large muscle groups of the buttocks, thighs, calves, abdomen, and back to be in peak condition for a backpacking trip. The abdominals are particularly important, as they help support the lower back. And strengthening the shoulder and chest muscles helps you support the dead weight of a full backpack. Use weights or exercise machines. Climb steps or walk inclines at increasing speed to prepare for the elevation gains and losses inherent in mountaineering.

Most sports trainers recommend weight training. According to Scott Tinley, strength training should include eight to twelve repetitions of eight to ten different types of movements, training different major muscle groups twice a week. Weight training increases bone density and replaces muscle mass lost due to normal aging.

Stretching and Massage

While strength training tends to tighten the muscles, stretching improves leg and back flexibility and reduces susceptibility to musculoskeletal injury. Good flexibility also maximizes your ability to climb over rocks, hop small streams, and stretch where you need to with confidence. When out in the wilderness, stretching should be part of your wake-up ritual. Browse through the illustrations in this chapter (fig. 3-3), or use Bob Anderson's book, *Stretching*, as a guide. Anderson's book includes stretching routines designed for a variety of activities. In addition to stretching and massage, yoga is a good way to maintain flexibility.

At times, muscle soreness needs more focused attention, and that's when sports massage comes in. You may prefer to hire a specialist, or, if you are comfortable doing it on your own, apply gentle pressure to the affected area. There is a broad spectrum of techniques, from Swedish massage to acupressure.

Feet First

Your feet deserve some special attention before you begin your program and before you encase them in those hiking boots! Lubricate your skin with lanolin (unless you're allergic), file calluses with an emery board or pumice stone, and keep your nails clean and trimmed.

You should know your foot type before you select a boot. Do you have a high arch or flat feet? Are your feet flexible or rigid? And what kind of terrain will you be hiking? Not every foot or situation demands a stiff, high-top, leather boot.

If your feet are subject to excessive pronation (flattening of the normal arch and inward tipping of the ankle) or other irregularities of motion, you may need an orthotic (shoe-insert) device. A podiatrist or a physical therapist specializing in foot problems can help you solve your problems as well as help with boot selection.

SOME PHYSIOLOGICAL CONSIDERATIONS
Size

Your size affects the length of your stride and your pace. In the United States, the average height for women is five feet four inches and the average height for men is five feet ten inches. If you're shorter than average, your leg length may put you at a slight disadvantage when crossing rough terrain, hopping streams, or scrambling over boulders.

Size and body weight can also affect muscle mass and carrying capacity when backpacking. For a person in good physical shape, figure a load-to-body-weight ratio of one to three (1:3). That means, for instance, that a 180-pound person should carry a maximum load of 60 pounds, and a 120-pound person should carry a maximum load of 40 pounds. This 20-pound difference in pack weight can be significant in planning a trip. If you're a lighter person, you may have to think twice about the personal gear you'll take, and you may not be able to realistically handle the same quantity of community gear that larger or heavier people can carry. Equitable sharing of gear in a group of people of various sizes and abilities doesn't mean that every person must carry the same load.

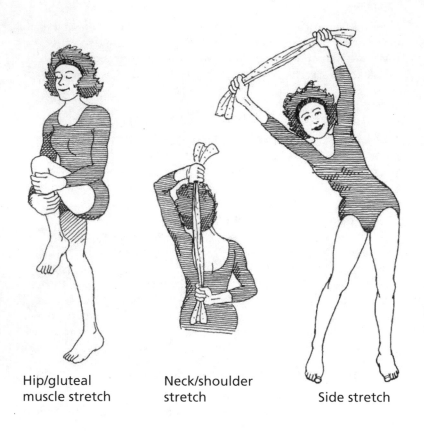

Hip/gluteal
muscle stretch

Neck/shoulder
stretch

Side stretch

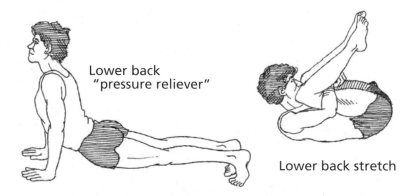

Lower back
"pressure reliever"

Lower back stretch

Figure 3-3: *Various stretching exercises.*

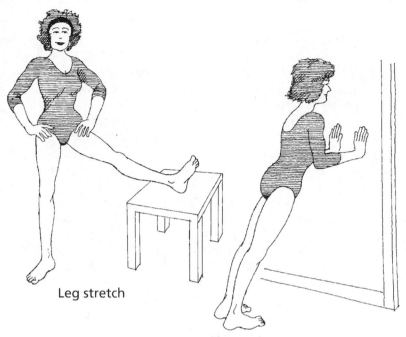

Leg stretch

Calf stretch

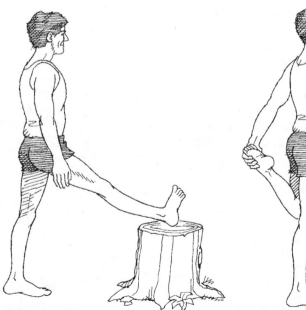

Hamstring stretch

Thigh/quadraceps stretch

Differences between Men and Women

Women tend to have a higher proportion of body fat and a lower proportion of muscle mass than men. Women, because they are generally smaller than men, usually have a smaller heart, less blood volume, and less lung capacity. All of this means that the average woman must work a little harder than the average man for most activities involving motion. It's important to note, however, that a woman's response to physical exercise is equal to a man's, and that improvements in training can far outweigh any differences in the average physical abilities of men and women.

In general, women's bodies do not use oxygen as efficiently as men's. Women have fewer red blood cells per unit of blood, according to Dr. Edward L. Fox in *Sports Physiology*. Red blood cells carry oxygen to the muscles, where the oxygen is used to produce the energy needed for motion. Women are also more likely to have undetected iron deficiencies, even in the absence of anemia. An iron deficiency can delay the removal of lactic acid from the muscles during exercise, which saps energy. Consider having your blood tested for iron deficiency; iron supplements can take care of slight deficiencies.

Since women have wider pelvic structures and looser knee ligaments, they're more prone to alignment problems of the knee cap. Exercises, such as lunges and squats, that strengthen the muscles surrounding the knee are recommended. During the menstrual cycle, certain hormones are released that may cause a general loosening of many of the body's ligaments, resulting in lower back, knee, or arch pain. Since the weight of a pack can aggravate a backache, you may want to use pain reliever, such as aspirin or ibuprofen, to relieve the discomfort.

Many women have the necessary lower-body strength needed to support the weight of a heavy backpack, but they lack the upper-body development that most men have. Upper-body muscles are used particularly when lifting or putting on a pack. Various techniques can overcome any difficulty. For instance, use a rock or tree to prop up the pack when putting it on or taking it off. You can also increase the strength of your upper body through weight training. Even a modest program can yield impressive gains in strength.

Pregnancy

While pregnancy is no reason to avoid wilderness travel entirely, certain considerations deserve mention. Miscarriages, most common in the early stages, and premature labor, in the later stages, can pose serious complications in isolated areas. Before undertaking any wilderness travel while pregnant, be sure to discuss it with your physician.

In the later months of pregnancy, maintaining balance while walking or scrambling may be a problem. A walking stick or trekking poles can be of help. Knee ligaments become looser in late pregnancy, contributing further to instability. Falls, especially on the abdomen, are a serious risk.

Because the pregnant woman provides oxygen to the developing fetus as well as herself, her heart must work harder, even when she's resting. There are more demands on nearly every muscle and organ in the body as well. The pregnant woman must carefully monitor her level of fatigue and scale back any plans for strenuous travel. During the later months, it may be either uncomfortable or impossible to wear a full-size backpack. In that case, a day pack may have to be substituted.

Studies have shown that pregnant women living for long periods at altitudes of 8000 feet and up tend to experience increased blood pressure,

A proper conditioning program will propel you to new heights. (Photo by Jerry Schad.)

problems with breathing, water retention, and swelling of the hands and feet. It is not known if such effects are detrimental for short-duration trips. Certainly, any pregnant woman should carefully monitor herself for any adverse symptoms brought on by high altitude and be prepared to descend to a safer level if necessary. Certain drugs and chemicals commonly used by mountain travelers, including Flagyl for giardiasis, Diamox for high-altitude symptoms, and iodine for water purification, should not be taken during pregnancy.

CONCLUSION

One final note: Be realistic and get into shape prior to the last two weeks before a strenuous trip. Last-minute, rigorous exercise not only depletes your body's energy stores but leaves you too exhausted to enjoy the trip. Instead, do as marathoners do: train vigorously for ten weeks, then ease off for 7 to 10 days before the big event. A short period of rest on top of a good training base will have you exploding from the trailhead.

chapter
4

Trip Preparation

Dave Moser and Marty Stevens

Planning a trip can be almost as much fun as the trip itself. Reading books and spreading maps on the floor gives you a thrill of anticipation. The time and effort you put into your plans results in greater enjoyment and increased safety.

Although most of this chapter applies to overnighters or trips of longer duration, you can benefit by carefully planning even a short day hike. Some of the material below is geared to those in leadership roles. Even if you never take on the responsibility of guiding a large group, you'll profit by and appreciate knowing the detailed planning incumbent on the leader.

RESEARCHING THE TRIP

To help you plan your trip, rely on five primary resources. The first and most obvious resource is your **friends.** Wisdom gained by experience is the best kind. Ask them which areas they liked the best, how difficult each trip was, and whether they would do things differently another time around. If you want a second opinion, ask them for the names and phone numbers of their friends who have visited the same areas.

Of the hundreds of **guidebooks** published for wilderness areas, there's probably at least one just right for the area or region you'd like to visit. Keep in mind, however, that conditions and trails may have changed since the book was written. Note copyright dates and verify information with the local authorities. Also refer to the bibliography or recommended reading lists.

Obtain detailed **maps** of the area so that you can meticulously follow any verbal or printed description of a trip. Road maps, especially county maps, are good for showing major and minor roads leading to trailheads. Topographic maps allow you to visualize in great detail the topography and trails of the area you plan to explore. Different maps show different features of the same area, so try to collect as many as possible. Remember that even the most current maps may not show newer trails and that existing trails can become eroded or overgrown so as to be unusable. Outdated maps are not necessarily useless—they may indicate old mines, defunct trails, historic towns, and other features (left off newer maps) that you may want to explore. A complete research effort might involve a trip to a public or university library for a look at old maps in the historical collection.

Rangers are another excellent source of information; however, before contacting a ranger you should do some homework so you can ask intelligent questions. A cold call to a ranger asking for a good place to hike may waste both your time and the ranger's. When calling, have your maps and guidebooks in front of you. Ask to speak with someone who is familiar with the specific area you plan to visit. You may have to wait for a backcountry ranger to return your call, but the information will be worth the wait. Describe your plans and don't hesitate to ask for additional information or suggestions. In some instances, the ranger may recommend an alternate trail that would better suit your needs.

A very useful and informative resource is the **Internet.** From the Internet you can get detailed information about permits and the quota season; trailheads and trail conditions; passes and peaks; campgrounds, lodging, and dining; reservations; phone numbers for agencies, ranger stations, campgrounds, concessionaires, and permit applications; and links to other useful sites.

But the nicest feature of a website is the convenience of applying for a permit online. Oftentimes the office that has jurisdiction has limited hours, may be closed on holidays and weekends, or is momentarily unmanned when you call. Some useful websites include the U.S. Forest Service, *www.fs.fed.us;* the National Park Service, *www.nps.gov;* and the Bureau of Land Management, *www.blm.gov/nhp.* If you don't know the URL, use a search engine.

If you're the trip leader, it's best to scout the trip in advance to get

Obtain current information about proposed trips from a local ranger. (Photo by James Glenn Pearson.)

firsthand information on road and trail conditions and the availability of water. Make notes on your maps for further reference. You may discover an interesting side trip, or you might end up deciding the trip is not appropriate for the group you intend to lead.

DESIGNING THE TRIP

Designing a trip itinerary is exciting! Using your topographic map, mentally walk along and visualize your intended route. Take the time to study and see elevation gains and losses, the distances to be traveled, the meadows, lakes, forests, and other features. Identify the best over-looks and the best spots for lunch or snack breaks. When choosing campsites, try to visualize where the sun will rise and set. In a similar vein, you may want to plan your trip around a full moon. Or go when there is a new moon to enjoy zillions of stars in an inky black sky.

Rather than having to retrace your steps on a trip, try to design a loop route. Or design a point-to-point trip using a car shuttle or a drop-off-and-pick-up service. With these strategies, you'll enjoy twice as much scenery as you would on an out-and-back trip.

When deciding how many cars it will take to carry people and gear, keep in mind that backpack equipment takes up a lot of space. Most compact cars can carry only two people and two backpacks. If some-one in your group has a van or pickup, consider using it to haul the bulky gear while the participants ride in passenger cars. If you employ a car shuttle for point-to-point trips, remember that everything and everyone may have to fit into half the vehicles.

For a long drive to a distant trailhead, include time for rest breaks or meal stops at least every couple of hours or so. Carry extra water in the car and plan to arrive early enough so you can get plenty of sleep

Maps are essential for successful trip planning. (Photo by James Glenn Pearson.)

before hiking in. If caravanning, CB radios can be very helpful. You can make decisions about when to stop for lunch or whether to take side trips, and you can notify the other drivers if you need to pull over. (Note: In Mexico you need a permit to operate a CB. Call your local Mexican consulate.)

Try to anticipate what the weather will be like on your trip. You should know, for example, that snow flurries can occur above timberline in July and August. Desert winds can hit 50 miles per hour or more anytime. Rivers swollen with snowmelt can be a problem in the mountains in spring and early summer. Sudden rains may turn dirt roads into quagmires of mud. Flash floods can lash the desert and canyon country during the thunderstorm season. Discuss potential hazards when you speak with the ranger. A call to the area's local weather bureau can result in a wealth of information. Hope for the best, but plan for any eventuality.

The amount of water you carry depends on where the nearest streams are in relation to your route and campsite and whether or not they are flowing. Ask the ranger when you call. Decide how you'll treat the water. Some trips may require caches of water (and/or food) placed in advance. These supplies must be well hidden and protected from animals and the elements. Leave a note, with the date indicated, stating that you are depending on these supplies for your survival. If your trailhead is remote, you may want to leave some food and water in your vehicle (except in bear country).

When hiking at altitudes above 6000 feet most people benefit from an acclimation period just before the trip. If you're planning a steep elevation gain on the first day, try to sleep at a high-elevation trailhead the night before. A day or two spent at high altitude usually does the trick. Do some walking or easy hiking so your body adjusts to the thinner air.

To organize all the details of your trip, develop a complete itinerary, starting with the departure. List times and places, and allow a little slack for unforeseen circumstances. Have an alternate trip or route planned in case yours is impossible due to rockslide, fire, damaged bridges, swollen streams, or other unforeseen events. Consider the abilities of the slower participants when estimating times of arrival. Plan to arrive at camp with some daylight left. Much of the pertinent planning data can be summarized on the sample trip planning sheet (fig. 4-1).

PERMITS AND REGULATIONS

The permit system serves several purposes. In some cases it is used to limit the number of people, which helps lessen impacts and guarantees

TRIP PLANNING SHEET

Area_____   Dates_____

Agency	Contacts	Phone	Comments

Road Maps _____   Trail Maps _____

_____   _____

Guidebooks	Dates	Comments

Permit Requirements _____

Maximum Group Size _____   Fires Allowed? _____

Water Availability _____

Weather Bureau Location _____   Phone _____

	DAY										
	1	2	3	4	5	6	7	8	9	10	Total
Destination											
Elevation Gain/Loss											
Mileage											
Hiking Time											
Sun	Rises										
	Sets										
Moon	Rises										
	Sets										

Temp. Range _____

_____

Figure 4-1: *Maximize the enjoyment of your trip by using a planning sheet.*

a better wilderness experience for all. By issuing permits, agencies can advise wilderness users of the appropriate regulations and collect data needed to carry out effective management of the area. Finally, permits allow the authorities to keep tabs on your whereabouts in case of an emergency.

Permit policies vary widely. In most areas permits are free, but some agencies charge a reservation fee. Find out well in advance what the permit policy is for the area you're interested in. Permits are usually obtained by mail or in person, but sometimes permits can be issued by phone or Internet. Guidebooks usually cover the nuts and bolts of permit application, but make sure the information is current.

Quite often, the key to getting the permit you want is to apply early. Permits for the most popular wilderness and park areas may become available only during a limited time several months in advance. Some are granted first-come, first-served on a postmark basis; other permits are granted by lottery. Be flexible about your dates of entry, and try to avoid the most popular days—Fridays and Saturdays, particularly on holiday weekends. Consider group-size restrictions before you invite too many of your friends or accept too many participants. If all else fails, remember that many areas reserve a portion of their permits for people who seek them on the day of entry. You may have a second chance if you missed the first time around (although a lot of your effort in planning can go down the drain if you fail to get one).

Fire regulations vary widely from area to area. In some, campfire permits are required; in others, campfires are banned altogether because of wildfire hazards or a scarcity of firewood. Some jurisdictions allow fires as long as you bring in your own wood. Wild areas may have various fire restrictions imposed on them during the hot and dry summer and fall seasons. During extremely hazardous conditions, visitors may be prohibited from using any open-flame device, or they may be prohibited from entering certain areas. Although campfires are a traditional part of the outdoor experience, they're not always needed for comfort, especially in summer. Campfires draw attention to a small world only a few feet across, while the absence of a campfire opens up to sight and mind the infinite majesty of the night sky.

Some areas require bear canisters, which can be rented or purchased at local retailers that specialize in backcountry gear. Some ranger stations also rent bear canisters, but not on a reservation basis. Call the ranger station during the planning phase of your trip to see if this option is available.

PARTICIPANT INFORMATION

Name _____

Address _____

Age _____ Home Phone _____ Work Phone_____

E-mail_____Regular Exercise Program_____

Recent Trip Experience:

Location	Dates	Reference	Phone

Physical Limitations _____

Allergies _____

Medications _____

Physician's Name_____ Phone _____

Health Insurance Company_____

Policy Number _____

Emergency Contact:

Name_____

Address_____

Phone_____ Relationship _____

Figure 4-2: *The trip leader should have basic information about each member of the group.*

LEADERSHIP CONSIDERATIONS
Choosing Trip Companions

If you're the leader, and you aren't familiar with prospective participants, it's your responsibility to screen them. Each person should
have the proper equipment and skills, be in good physical condition,
and possess the confidence and attitude necessary to handle the trip
without depending unduly on other members of the party. In evalu-
ating a large number of prospective participants, the use of a ques-
tionnaire such as the sample participant information form (fig. 4-2)
is a good idea.

Screen participants initially over the phone, and do more screening
at the planning meeting. Even after someone has been accepted for an
outing, something could come up that would change that status. A
participant's recent injury or illness might be a reason for you to carefully reconsider his participation. It's your duty as leader to continue
screening right up to the beginning of the trip. Dropping an obviously
unqualified individual is fair to the group and to the individual, who
might otherwise end up having a miserable time. If the trip is to be a
backpack over rough terrain, effective screening might include a pretrip day hike over similar terrain. Those who seem to be having trouble
should be kindly informed that the trip is not for them.

Planning Meeting

Planning meetings are effective for almost all trips, especially those
lasting 2 or more days. At the very least, the participants get to know
one another beforehand. During the meeting, the leader explains the
general trip plan and the objectives, including driving route, camp-
ground facilities, hiking route, number of miles to be hiked each day,
elevation gains and losses, hazards, and trail difficulties.

The following details should also be worked out: carpools/drivers,
equipment sharing (tents, stoves, water filters, etc.), cooking groups or a
central commissary (wherein all share the same menu and cooking and
cleaning responsibilities), food purchases and participants' dietary restrictions, and sharing of costs.

All participants must understand what the trip entails, and acknowledge that it's something they want to do. The leader should encourage
questions and discussion. Pass out the following checklists and printed
information:
- Trip description or summary
- Itinerary
- Map of the driving route

- Map of the hiking route (USGS topographic and other government maps can be photocopied without violating copyright laws.)
- List of the required and/or optional maps (if maps aren't provided)
- Water needs
- Equipment checklist
- Important phone numbers; numbers to call in case of an emergency
- List of do's and don'ts (e.g., pack out all toilet paper, bury human waste at least 200 feet from water, do not put anything, including biodegradable soap, into the water, do not feed the animals, etc.)

The more of this the leader puts on paper, the more prepared participants will be before the trip.

At the planning meeting, drivers should be reminded to take along an extra car key, a simple precaution that could save the group countless hours of wasted time. Tell someone else in the party where the extra key is located so they can drive the car if necessary. Or give the extra key to another person to carry. Before leaving, all drivers should have their vehicles checked to be sure they are in good working order.

The leader should remind the group about individual responsibilities. He can hand out a list of special equipment needed, but it's up to every participant to develop his own personal checklist. Everyone is forgetful to some degree, which is why a checklist is a must.

After every trip, add to the list any items you wish you had taken. You'll eventually end up with a very long list—too much for any one trip—but at least you won't overlook anything on future trips. It's also helpful to include the weight of each item so you can make intelligent decisions when it comes time for the inevitable task of eliminating nonessential items that are too heavy or bulky to carry.

Safety

While safety is everyone's business, there are several things the leader can do to assure that trip participants are prepared in the event of an emergency.

Familiarize everyone with the location of the nearest emergency telephones and the appropriate emergency numbers. In addition to 911, this includes the numbers for the local sheriff, ranger, and fire department. An awareness of evacuation routes is invaluable in the event of an emergency.

Leave full written details with someone dependable, such as family or friends, outlining where you are going, when you expect to return, and what to do if you don't return on time. This is vitally important if you'll be hiking alone. You should include phone numbers of the local sheriff and appropriate rangers, vehicle descriptions, and vehicle license plate numbers. Ask them to report you missing if you are not back by a certain time. While it may be a good idea to give a ranger your itinerary, rangers are accustomed to people forgetting to check in when they return.

LAST-MINUTE DETAILS

Some things can't be done until the final day or final hours before the trip starts. Fill up the gas tank and check the oil. Check the weather—call a ranger or the weather bureau nearest the area you're going to visit, or check the Internet. If the weather's been nasty, ask the ranger about trail damage and hazardous stream crossings. Check road conditions by calling your auto club or the highway patrol. On some trips, you're required to sign in and sign out at a ranger station. After the trip, don't forget to sign out! If

A well-planned trip will leave you smiling. (Photo by Arleen Tavernier.)

you don't, you may be responsible for an unnecessary search effort. Finally, if you notice anything during your trip that the authorities should know about, be sure to report it. Those who follow in your footsteps may have a better wilderness experience because of it.

chapter
5

Outfitting

Mike Fry, Bob Stinton, Jim Matlock, Jan Craven, Carolyn Wood,
and Priscilla and Scott Anderson

Life is basic, simple, and clear in the wilderness. It is a minimalist existence of making do with the least possible possessions. This clarity renews weary spirits and reveals simple pleasures neglected in hurried lives.

The experienced wilderness traveler uses basic skills and equipment to keep trips safe and enjoyable. Individuals new to wilderness travel tend to overload on equipment, resulting in heavy packs that tire them and dampen their enthusiasm. This overequipping stems from two forces; the first is the perception that equipment is a quick fix for weak or nonexistent skills. The second is the result of marketing and merchandizing pressure. Both of these pressure the inexperienced traveler to purchase and carry unneeded items.

THE FOUNDATION

Wilderness travel, whether a day hike or multiday trip, requires some basic skills and equipment. Regardless of the length and nature of the trip, experienced wilderness travelers carry the Ten Essentials or an equivalent set of basic items. This concept was introduced in the 1930s in The Mountaineers newsletter—and most recently updated in 2002—as the ten items every wilderness traveler should carry. Though many elements of these essentials do not change from trip to trip, a few items change based on a trip's anticipated demands and weather.

The Ten Essentials: A Systems Approach

1. **Navigation (map and compass)**
2. **Sun protection (sunglasses, sunscreen,** and hat)
3. **Insulation (extra clothing)**
4. **Illumination (headlamp or flashlight,** spare batteries and bulb)
5. **First-aid supplies** (including personal needs and toilet paper)
6. **Fire (firestarter and matches/lighter)**
7. **Repair kit and tools (including knife)**
8. **Nutrition (extra food)**
9. **Hydration (extra water)**
10. **Emergency shelter** (raingear, poncho, or more)
11. New essential—communication (cell phone, two-way radios)

KEEPING THINGS LIGHT

When you carry everything on your back, weight is a major issue. A heavy pack can slow your progress, dampen your enthusiasm, and increase the likelihood of injury. Weight management starts with the big three: pack, tent, and sleeping bag.

How heavy should a pack be or what is the maximum weight an individual should carry? The classic answer is still a pre–World War I army estimate: soldiers should not carry more than one-third their body weight. For example, a 150-pound individual should not carry more than 50 pounds. Since this is rather heavy, others have downgraded the rule to one-fourth of a person's body weight, which is 37 pounds for a 150-pound backpacker. This rule does not factor in the individual's physical condition or the type of terrain and trail conditions. The goal on every wilderness adventure is to maximize enjoyment and minimize discomfort without compromising safety.

To fully understand pack weight it is best to break it down in two categories: consumable and nonconsumable weight. Consumable weight is primarily food, fuel, and water. Food should weigh close to 1.5 pounds (dry weight, no cans) per person per day. This provides about 2400 calories each day. Fuel should be 0.07 quart per person per day if you plan simple meals. Increase it to 0.1 quart for gourmet cooking. If you have to melt snow for drinking water or boil all your water, double the amount of fuel to 0.14 quarts per day. A quart of liquid fuel is the same as 24 ounces of butane. In the case of water, 1 pint weighs 1 pound, and the amount of water you carry depends on

Illumination

Nutrition

Emergency Shelter

Insulation

Navigation

Toiletries

Repair Kit and Tools

Attitude

Flash Light

Something to carry everything in

Figure 5-1: *Items from the Ten Essentials.*

its availability along the trail. Typically the consumable weight is greatest at the beginning of the trip. However, water needs may cause it to fluctuate from day to day.

Nonconsumable weight includes, for example, the backpack, tent, sleeping bag, clothing, and cooking and emergency gear. The key to managing pack weight is addressing the weight of nonconsumable items. A typical pack is about 6 pounds, and the average two-person tent weighs around 7 pounds (when you include poles and tent stakes). The typical sleeping bag weighs in at about 4 pounds. Quick addition brings the total weight of the big three to 17 pounds. The other nonconsumables such as clothing, cooking gear, and first-aid kit can add an additional 5–10 pounds making the nonconsumable pack weight 22–27 pounds.

The big three is where you can cut pounds and ounces. For example, ultralight backpacks, though not as durable as the typical backpack, weigh around 2 pounds versus the 5–6 pounds of a typical backpack. You should also consider a lighter tent and sleeping bag.

After you have taken into account the weight of the big three, look at each item that you plan to carry. For example, don't carry a full bottle of sunscreen; repackage it into a smaller container taking only what you need. Look for multifunctional items: a stuff sack filled with extra clothing can be used as a pillow; extra clothing can be worn while sleeping, allowing you to use a lighter sleeping bag.

Some other ways to keep your load as light as possible:

- Share items such as a tent, stove, cookware, and water purifier with a partner, and divide the common load evenly.
- Hike with a partner who carries the lion's share of the weight and keeps you warm at night.
- Travel where there's abundant water and good weather.
- Purchase the lightest equipment available.
- Ask other wilderness travelers how they trim their pack weight.
- Search "ultralight backpacking" on the Internet.

PRODUCTS

Dozens of companies, large and small, manufacture high-quality wilderness gear. Some design for lighter weight and style as well as function. Check with local stores, catalogs, websites, and read outdoor publications to learn about manufacturers' reputations, the quality of their products, the length of time they've been in business, and their warranties and service capabilities. Check the product labels for specifications, care and cleaning, and guarantees. Ask salespeople if their store offers any guarantees beyond those offered by the manufacturers. After you've made a purchase, follow care directions to keep the gear performing as intended.

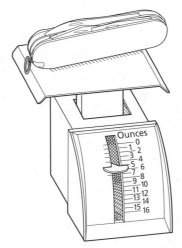

Figure 5-2: *Use a small scale to weigh and evaluate items.*

Product Sources

Where you buy your equipment may be just as important as who manufactures it. Your best bet is to purchase from a source that is reputable, has been in business a long time, offers a product satisfaction guarantee, has knowledgeable salespeople, and offers rental equipment (this is most helpful for a new backpacker).

Fortunately, sports and adventure outfitters tend to attract salespeople who love the outdoors and try out a lot of the equipment they sell. However, ask a few questions about their experience to be sure they aren't too new to the industry. Internet and mail-order outfits may offer considerable savings, but you have to know what you want and how to use it. In addition, scan outdoor magazines and other newsletters and newspapers for bargains. The Internet provides additional sources of information and buying options. Even the trendiest outfitters have periodic sales to clear out excess stock or demo and rental equipment. Not all of your equipment needs to be brand-new. Swap meets, thrift stores, and surplus outlets are all good hunting grounds.

Cost Considerations

When outfitting yourself you may want to prioritize your purchases. The list is short for day hikers—boots (or appropriate walking shoes), day pack, and the Ten Essentials. Accumulating backpacking gear, though, involves major purchases. Fortunately, some of the more expensive items needed for backpacking can easily be borrowed or rented. Personal items such as boots and special clothing are first priority, then sleeping bag, sleeping pad, and backpack. You may be able to share a stove and cookware for some time before deciding what kind to buy. A tent is a key purchase—you may want to rent or share one for a while before investing in your own.

Making your own equipment was once an economical way to ensure excellent quality in your gear. It still is, for some, but equipment prices are low compared to the amount of time it takes to create a finished piece. Most people consider it more fun to spend weekends out hiking rather than laboring over a sewing machine. But do keep your needle sharp for repairing or modifying equipment and clothing. Always bring your sewing kit, ripstop repair tape, and safety pins.

FOOTWEAR

During a typical hiking day, your feet hit the ground 10,000 to 20,000 times (about 2000 steps per mile). Your boots must fit well!

Fortunately, running-shoe technology has spread to hiking boots, and many good choices are available. Lightweight boots are relatively inexpensive and comfortable and provide enough protection for most uses. Choose ankle-high boots with padded ankle collars. Make sure that there is more ankle support than just the padding. A boot can look substantial when it really isn't. Check how solid the lug soles are by pushing in with your thumbnail. The lugs should be solid, not hollow. Hollow lugs wear out extremely fast. Uppers made of nylon or other synthetic materials require almost no break-in, while leather uppers are more rigid.

If you're susceptible to ankle twists or if rougher country dictates the need for more protection against rolling rocks, consider the heavier, all-leather models. Old-fashioned, heavy leather boots are still necessary for most snow travel and for cross-country travel with heavy packs over very rugged terrain. Rigid, plastic boots are appropriate for crampon use when climbing hard snow and ice (see Chapter 15, Winter Mountaineering, "Clothing and Equipment").

Something to consider before purchasing your boots is the possibility of needing more than one pair. In the past, wilderness travelers purchased one pair of boots to meet all their needs. They wore heavy all-leather boots to deal with snow, but on warm summer trips, their feet were sweltering hot. If you only travel on trail during the warm months you are better off purchasing a pair of light, sturdy, well-ventilated boots to keep your feet comfortable. Your boots need to match your travel plans.

For any use, though, the primary consideration is fit. The latest technology is useless if the boots hurt your feet. Some tips for selecting boots:

- Go on a short hike before trying on boots; your feet normally swell some when on the trail. If a hike isn't possible, try on boots later in the day after you've been on your feet for a while.
- Bring along the socks, orthotics, or inner soles you plan to use.
- Look for a retailer with a fit guarantee; the best guarantees allow you to take the boots out on the trail and return them if they don't fit properly.
- Shop at a store with a knowledgeable staff.
- Try on several pairs, and accept none if you have any doubts.
- Go to the footwear department first if you are shopping for other items in addition to boots. When you think you've found the right pair, ask if you can wear the boots in the store while doing your other shopping. The extra time allows you to better evaluate the fit.
- Allow about a half inch of extra toe room. You'll need it for steep downhill hiking when your foot slips forward inside the boot. Swing your foot back, point your toe straight down toward the floor, and kick the floor several times. Can you force your toes to hit the front of the boot? If you can, the boots are too short or not laced tight enough. The back of your heel should slide up and down no more than a quarter inch with each step. Excessive heel movement is an all too common cause of blisters. Excessive heel pressure is just as bad. A quarter inch of movement is a good compromise.

The majority of boots manufactured are patterned on men's lasts, or models of the foot. More and more companies, however, offer boots designed on women's lasts, which are typically narrower, especially in the heel. A snug heel prevents your foot from sliding around in the boot and causing blisters. When shopping for boots, ask the clerk which brands have women's lasts. Don't let anyone suggest you can adapt your feet to men's boots by lacing the boots tightly or adding extra socks.

No boot can be expected to fit perfectly, so consider these possibilities:
- Will the boot stretch as it breaks in, or will your foot break down? (Note: To greatly speed up the break-in period and improve the fit, soak leather boots in water, and then go for a hike.)
- Can the boot be stretched mechanically in the toe or heel cup areas to improve the fit? (Can you locate a shoe repair shop that will do this?)
- Can the heel cup be padded with glue-in pads to reduce heel slippage?

- Can cushioned insoles be added to the boot to make a thin, hard sole more tolerable? (Insoles make the boots feel narrower, which can help if they're too wide.)
- If nothing works, you can always purchase custom-made boots. Look in outdoor magazines for custom boot makers.

Resoling

If you are purchasing an all-leather boot, ask about resoling before you buy. Even the most durable soles wear out with time, often well before the boot upper is significantly worn. Some leather boots can live as many as three lives—at a rather modest additional cost—with resoling. However many of the newer lighter-weight boots based on running shoe designs cannot be resoled because the uppers, the cushioning, and support in the boots break down as quickly as the sole wears. Don't use silicone or petroleum-based products on your leather boots. They can dissolve the glue that bonds the sole. Wax still works well.

Socks

Every pair of boots can benefit from an optimum combination of socks. Start with lightweight polypropylene, which reduces friction and prevents blisters, and use thick wool as your outer layer. Avoid cotton socks—they are cold and abrasive. In general, two thinner socks used together work better than a single thick one. You may need to add an intermediate layer, or use thicker socks, as your boots stretch with age.

Keeping your feet warm in cold conditions is more a measure of how you enclose them than a measure of your boot's weight. You need full circulation to keep your feet warm, so don't pinch your feet by wearing too many socks or by overtightening bootlaces. In subfreezing conditions, vapor barriers (moisture-impervious layers) worn close to your feet can be very effective. A vapor barrier, which can be as simple as a plastic bag, worn outside a thin polypropylene sock keeps foot perspiration from reaching the outer, insulating wool sock layer. Neoprene socks provide both vapor barrier and insulation. Gaiters, designed to keep snow out of boots, also serve to insulate the ankle area. Even when there is no snow, low-top gaiters are useful in keeping sand and dirt out of boots.

CLOTHING SYSTEM

Your clothes must shelter your body from sun, wind, rain, and cold—sometimes all in the same day! Each article of clothing, wet or dry, must continue to function. As you travel, body heat and water vapor (perspiration) need to escape, while wind and rain are repelled.

Almost every year, clothing and fabric manufacturers introduce new high-tech gear and claim everything else is obsolete. Sales clerks and colorful ads push you to spend a fortune on fabrics that wick, breathe, repel, vent, warm, cool, and, of course, flatter. The sad truth, however, is that even the best garment can perform well only in a limited range of conditions.

The well-equipped wilderness traveler needs to assemble a light-weight, compact outfit that will do the job, rain or shine. This is done most effectively through the layering system (fig. 5-3). That is, each item of clothing should work well in any combination, so you can quickly adapt to the demands of the environment (or your own heat output) by adding or subtracting layers of clothing.

Ideally, you need only adjust the outer layer, but at times even the inner layer must be changed. Using thermal underwear as long pants under regular shorts, together with windproof rain pants, can keep you as warm as heavier pants. Combining them eliminates the need for carrying another pair of pants.

Inner layers require different kinds of materials than outer layers. The choices available include:

Cotton. Although comfortable in and fine for warm weather, cotton is not recommended for most cold-weather conditions. Cotton absorbs water readily. When wet, cotton is cold and slow to dry. Combine cold with wet conditions, and it is deadly. Blue jeans (and other heavy cotton items like sweatshirts) seem ideal for outdoor use, but they rapidly drain your body heat when the weather turns soggy. On warm, dry days, though, thin, light-colored cotton shorts, shirts, and bandanas can keep you comfortably cool.

Wool, polypropylene, and polyester. These make good insulating garments and retain much of their insulating ability even when wet. Wool can retain as much as 30 percent of its dry weight in water but is slow to dry. Oiled wool garments absorb less moisture. Synthetics absorb almost no moisture into the fibers and are easier to wring out in case they do get wet. Polyester and polypropylene are versatile fibers and are used in many forms. They can be knitted and used in long underwear or made into fleece and piles for use in shirts, pants, gloves, and hats. Polyester fibers also make up the vast majority of fibers used as synthetic down replacements.

Down. Typically the inner feathers of geese, down is a very effective insulator when dry but is completely useless if wet. It is a poor choice for wet conditions.

Nylon. Lightweight, fast-drying shirts and pants come in a variety of styles and colors. Many of these garments come with SPF (sun protection factor) ratings and provide a lightweight alternative to sunscreen. Tighter woven nylons are used in wind jackets and pants.

Nylon with breathable membranes. Waterproof breathable membranes (formed by specially designed polyurethane coatings or PTFE "Teflon" laminates, such as Gore-Tex) have revolutionized the construction of raingear. These materials contain a thin membrane perforated with tiny pores. In theory, the pores allow water vapor (from perspiration) to pass but resist the passage of liquid water. Unfortunately, the amount of water vapor these materials can pass is about the same amount as that exuded by a person at rest. With increasing activity or in wet conditions, additional venting is needed.

Coated nylon. Water-impervious, nonbreathable, coated nylons are treated with polyurethane, silicone, or PVC, and provide a less-expensive alternative to breathable materials used in raingear. These materials not only block wind and rain but also keep in the moisture generated by the body. This can lead to a build up of moisture in clothing worn under the coated layer. Effective, adjustable ventilation is also necessary.

Vapor-barrier materials. A thin water-vapor-impermeable layer worn next to the skin (or over lightweight undergarments) is most commonly composed of a very lightweight coated nylon. The vapor-barrier layer blocks evaporative heat loss from the skin. This system is most effective at cooler ambient temperatures when you're not very active, or at rest. At higher ambient temperatures or levels of effort these layers become saunas. To be effective, a vapor barrier must cover the majority of the body. Vapor-barrier jackets, pants, and socks are the most common forms. Vapor-barrier sleeping bag liners are also used in extremely cold weather or to extend the range of a lightweight bag.

When building your layering system for active sports in cooler weather, consider the following:

First, or wicking, layer. The purpose of this wicking layer is to provide insulation and transport moisture away from the skin. It normally consists of long underwear, preferably made of polypropylene or polyester, which absorbs little moisture and keeps the skin dry. Cotton should be avoided. Polypropylene has proven itself very effective over the years, but some prefer polyester, which has the advantage of staying a little fresher smelling. For most activities, thin underwear is more versatile than medium or expedition weight. If needed for extreme cold, add a vapor barrier over long underwear.

Figure 5-3: *The layering system.*

Adjustable ventilation is extremely important for any vapor barrier, especially when you are physically active.

Middle layer(s). While the inner layer keeps the skin comfortable, the middle layer provides the bulk of the insulation needed to protect against the cold. You'll likely have to adjust the ventilation to this layer often, as the temperature rises and falls as your activity waxes and wanes.

The experienced wilderness traveler may carry several items to function as middle layers. The simplest may be a long-sleeved, button-up wool, or lightweight fleece shirt. If it is colder this layer may be replaced with either a wool or acrylic sweater or a polyester fleece jacket. If more insulation is needed, the sweater and/or jacket can be worn over the long-sleeved shirt. Fleece pants protect the legs in extremely cold weather or when lounging around camp. Quilted down or synthetic-fill vests or jackets can be used; avoid the ones that include a heavy outer shell. This cuts down on versatility. Remember that down fails if it gets wet and is very slow to dry. But your best insulating layer is your sleeping bag. Save the weight of a layer and go to bed!

Outer or shell layer. Under adverse weather conditions, this layer is extremely important. The outer shell of your layering system blocks wind and sheds rain and snow. Adequate ventilation (like zippered openings) must be provided so plenty of air can reach the middle-insulating layer when needed. The fit should be loose to allow room for all the anticipated inner layers. Coated nylon is inexpensive and very effective in shedding rain, but it requires full-length zippers to ventilate. In addition, some coatings survive only a few machine washings. (Your raingear is washed during each storm! No need to wash in the machine.) A low-cost outer-shell system could consist of wind-repellent (uncoated) nylon pants and windbreaker, plus a two-piece coated-nylon rain suit. Use the coated garments over the uncoated ones in bad weather. (Under warmer storm conditions, you could use the coated layer alone.)

For adequate ventilation, the jacket should have a full-front zipper. Underarm zippers may help, but you'll find it's your back that perspires the most. Pants with full-length leg zippers provide for both ventilation and ease of putting on over boots. Waterproof-layer zippers should be protected by a storm flap that keeps water from blowing or flowing through. A more expensive (but heavier and bulkier) solution is a parka and pants made of Gore-Tex or similar material. This can keep you a little drier but still requires fully adjustable ventilation. You will often find yourself very wet on the inside in warm, wet weather.

When hiking with a backpack, a coated-nylon poncho is sometimes the best solution for rain protection. Ponchos can act like sails in a wind, but you can install and fasten more snaps along the edge of the poncho to run a tighter ship and serve as emergency shelter. Use rain chaps with the poncho to keep your legs dry. Ponchos are more difficult to hike in off-trail because of snagging, and the poncho obstructs your view of footing.

Shop carefully for your outer garments. Some rain and wind shells contain too many pockets, extras, or styling features that simply add to the weight of what should be a lightweight, functional article of clothing. Remember that some outer garments used for rain protection need to be seam-sealed. Others already come with factory-sealed seams.

Small men and women are faced with the challenge of finding smaller sizes of thermal underwear, raingear, and even shorts suitable for outdoor use. Outdoor shops usually do not stock a wide variety of small sizes, since the demand is relatively low. Don't give up, though. Clothing sizes are often notoriously inconsistent. If there's nothing suitable, then talk to the store's buyer about placing a special order. A competent buyer knows which manufacturers offer extra-small clothing and gear. Be prepared to wait some time for your special order. Think twice about accepting a child's size as a substitute.

In addition to the above layers, you also need protection for your head and hands.

Headwear. Did you ever hear the maxim, "If your feet are cold, cover your head"? It's true. In fact, the whole body benefits when you plug the torrent of heat that leaks skyward from the blood-rich vessels of the head. Use a layer system here as well. A lightweight balaclava that covers your mouth (but allows you to breathe) also allows you to recycle warm moisture from your breath. A second hat or knitted cap adds middle-layer insulation. The outer layer is simply the hood of your parka or other shell. It should have enough of a brim (or wear a visor underneath) to keep rain off your face. Pulling the drawstring narrows the opening to your face, helping to prevent heat loss. Taking off headwear is the fastest way to cool off if the weather warms. You'll want to do that first before shedding other layers. When the sun shines brightly, however, don't forget to put your hat back on to protect yourself from the sun's radiation. Some hats provide excellent sun protection. A bandana under your hat also shades your neck and ears.

Handwear. Most knitted gloves and mittens suffice for cold, dry conditions (mittens are warmer than gloves). Wet conditions, though, are a real test for handwear. When you're active, mittens or gloves can easily soak up water, but not enough body heat is delivered to your hands to evaporate it. Waterproof mitten shells are a first defense (don't forget to seal the seams). Inside that, thick wool or pile mittens provide insulation. You may also want to wear a thin pair of liner gloves for tasks that require manual dexterity. Try vapor-barrier protection as well. Plastic bags or disposable rubber gloves work well—you'll be surprised at the difference they can make. Gloves and mittens are easily lost so the almost negligible weight of an extra pair of lightweight gloves is good insurance. Chemical hand-warmer packets (powdered iron in a bag) are excellent for all-day hand warmth in extreme cold.

HOUSING: TENTS AND TARPS

Sleeping under the stars on a clear, bug-free night is a glorious experience. But when there's wind, snow, rain, or annoying insects, a tent is most welcome. In extreme situations, your survival may depend on a sturdy tent. One that's large enough to hold packs as well as people is convenient, but obviously heavier and more expensive. For tents, especially, you'll have to balance the comfort of using a bigger model against the discomfort of carrying it.

Tent costs vary dramatically. Cost is based on materials, quality of construction, design, features, and options. When shopping for a tent, consider the following features and options: weight and size; ease of set-up; ease of entry and exit; ventilation doors, windows, bug screening, and storm flaps; vestibule for cooking and storage; and anticipated seasons of use.

Freestanding tents often weigh more than tents that need to be staked out and must be staked out anyway. Don't count on the weight of your gear to hold down the tent. A sudden wind may blow your unstaked tent into a lake or over a cliff! Dome tents tend to give with the wind and can withstand strong winds if they are anchored properly. But they are usually heavy and only some of their floor space is usable. A double-wall design with a full-coverage rainfly (waterproof outer shell) repels wind and rain but sacrifices ventilation when the fly is up.

Flat tent walls flap in the wind more than curved walls. Tents with a vestibule or awnings keep raindrops from blowing in through the tent door or windows and provide a place to cook in bad weather. The lightest tents usually have no floor. Always pitch a tent (especially a floorless tent) in a spot with good drainage. Almost all tents need to be seam-sealed before use, and every few years after. Don't forget to buy the seam-sealer if it doesn't come with the tent. When comparing manufacturers' specifications, determine if the specified weights include the stakes, poles, repair kit, and stuff sack.

Always set up your new tent at home before heading out. A missing or broken pole could totally disable a tent, and you won't want to spend half an hour reading the directions in camp.

SLEEPING SYSTEM

Comfort on the trail is much different than comfort at home. Your tent doesn't have a heater, so you must rely on a good sleeping bag and sleeping pad. Increase warmth by wearing a knit hat when you sleep, taking a moonlit hike to get your circulation moving, or drinking warm beverages before turning in. A few restless or chilly nights are normal until you discover the right combination of clothing, keeping-warm routines, and sleeping equipment.

Sleeping Bags

The warmth of a bag depends primarily on the amount of loft—the thickness of the insulating layer. The more dead (nonmoving) air there is between you and the environment, the warmer the bag. Another factor is the style, or shape, of the bag. Most efficient are close-fitting bags that keep your body heat close to you. A bag that is too roomy will be colder. Be sure to try on bags when shopping, and purchase a bag that is just your size.

Different styles of baffles—compartments that hold the insulating fill—are available. Their purpose is to distribute the fill evenly. From a practical point of view, there's not too much difference between styles. What matters is that you avoid a quilted bag that is stitched straight through the top and bottom layers, because it lets warm air escape (and cold air in) through the seams.

Mummy bags are the lightest and warmest style. Rectangular bags weigh more but offer more foot room (nice for the warm blooded). (See fig. 5-4.) They're also roomier when two bags are zipped together (or when one bag and a ground sheet are used) for a twosome. Bags used in this fashion must have mating zippers. Semirectangular bags are a good compromise between roominess and warmth. They are open at the top, as opposed to the small hole of a mummy bag, for easier breathing.

Common sleeping-bag features include a contoured hood with a drawstring to keep your head warm, a filled "draft collar" that helps keep shoulders and neck warm, and a "draft tube" over the zipper to prevent leakage of body heat. The lightest weight bags have no insulation in their bottom

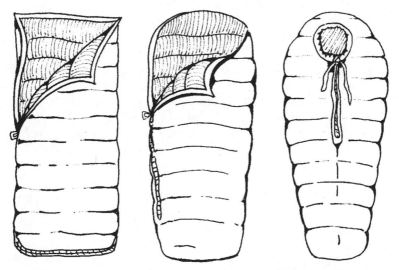

Figure 5-4: *Sleeping bags: Left, rectangular style; Center, semirectangular style; right, mummy style.*

fabric (it just compresses to nothing under your weight anyway) and depend on the sleeping pad for that function.

Summer-weight bags are rated from 40°F down to 20°F, three-season bags are rated from 10°F down to 0°F; and winter bags are rated from -5°F to as low as -50°F. These ratings are of help in comparing bags, but may not guarantee your comfort at those particular temperatures. Outer bags and liner inserts increase the warmth of any bag—not a bad way to go if you want a single bag to cover a broad range of seasonal conditions—and some bags have removable top layers for adjustable loft.

Bags filled with synthetic materials (primarily various forms of polyester such as Lite Loft Polarguard, Quallofil, Hollofil, etc.) are heavier and less compressible but are more reliable than down-filled bags. Cramming a synthetic-filled bag into a stuff sack, washing it, and exposing it to heat in a hot car or the dryer breaks down the fibers. Damaged fibers keep the bag from regaining its loft, and warmth depends on loft. Advantages of synthetic bags are their ability to insulate even when wet, and a lower cost. Synthetic bags are great for extended winter trips, kayaking, and other outings where the bag almost certainly gets damp.

Down bags are lighter and more compressible than synthetic bags of the same loft. They rejuvenate better (but not completely) after laundering, are more durable, but are much more expensive. When wet, they're practically useless, as down is very slow to dry. Some are available with waterproof breathable shells, such as Gore-Tex, to protect them from dew or wind. However these shells increase the bag's weight. Down bags don't need to be cleaned very often, but when they do, they should be professionally laundered. Check with your local outdoor-equipment outfitter, as they may offer this service.

Tips for getting the best performance out of any sleeping bag:

- Always fluff your bag before using it to get the maximum loft.
- Perspiration often condenses on the fibers of the insulating fill during cold weather. Your bag may need some drying time during the day to keep from getting heavier and colder each succeeding night.
- At home, store your sleeping bag by hanging it in the closet; never keep it wadded up in a stuff sack. Make sure it's fully dry before putting it away in an unventilated place.

Sleeping Pads

Sleeping pads are the foundation of your wilderness bed. No sleeping bag keeps you warm on a cold night unless you're thermally insulated

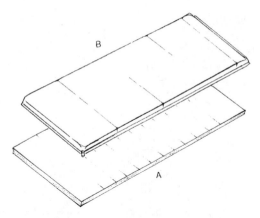

Figure 5-5: *Sleeping pads: A, closed-cell foam; B, self-inflating.*

from the ground. Thick pads have more insulating ability at the cost of greater weight, bulk, and expense. Short pads (48 inches long or so) are fine for summer camping if you don't mind sacrificing a little comfort, while the standard 72-inch pads are best for winter. If you're using a short pad, place some clothing under your lower legs and feet for extra comfort and insulation.

Closed-cell foam pads (fig. 5-5A) are excellent insulators, do not absorb water, and come in several varieties. Some have contours or ridges that help reduce weight while maintaining as much comfort as possible. In general, closed-cell foam pads are the best value in terms of providing excellent lightweight insulation for less money. (Avoid open-cell foam pads like mattress cushions. They're too heavy, water-absorbent, and bulky for backpacking.)

Self-inflating pads (fig. 5-5B) are quite comfortable to sleep on, but they are more expensive and heavier than closed-cell foam pads of the same insulating value. They require more care on the trail to prevent punctures and valve failures (repair kits are available). If you use a ground cloth underneath and avoid punctures they last for years. Any number of soft items can be used as a pillow; tie them up with a bandana.

STOVES AND COOKING EQUIPMENT
Types of Stoves

When choosing a stove, first consider its performance under the conditions—temperature, wind, and elevation—you'll likely encounter during your trip. Also consider the stove's weight, ease of fueling and operation, reliability, and availability of the fuel it uses. To help you choose the right stove, talk to people who use them and to salespeople at outdoor stores. Several outdoor magazines have published comparative information about stoves and reviews of new models. Stoves are classified by the types of fuel they burn.

Liquid fuel. These stoves burn kerosene, white gas (Coleman fuel), unleaded gasoline, and alcohol. In most cases, the fuel reservoir must be pressurized (with a small air pump) and the liquid fuel must be heated in the vicinity of the burner so it can be vaporized for combustion. The start-up procedure, known as "priming the stove," can be quite a ritual for some models. Alcohol will prime the stove more cleanly and without a fireball.

Liquid-fuel stoves are economical to operate and have a high heat output. Most are designed to run on white gas, but a few stoves use two to four different types of fuel (white gas, kerosene, unleaded gasoline, and diesel). That's a good feature if you're traveling to a foreign country where kerosene is available but white gas is not. White gas is very flammable (which is why it's a good stove fuel), burns cleanly, and evaporates quickly when spilled. Kerosene and diesel are less volatile than white gas and slower to ignite and evaporate, but they produce more heat per volume of fuel (same energy per weight). They have a greasy feel, a lasting odor, and a tendency to give off smoke and soot when burning. Some stove manufacturers list unleaded gasoline as usable, but avoid it if you can. It will gum up your stove.

Denatured alcohol (ethanol) is the fuel of choice for homemade stove enthusiasts who use discarded cans to build lightweight stoves. These stoves have no moving parts, making them very reliable. Alcohol burns clean but has the lowest heat output of the liquid fuels (two-thirds of the energy per weight). Avoid methanol for its toxicity and even lower energy/weight. Homemade stoves are more suitable for warming small meals than cooking large meals. There are many home-built designs available on the Internet at lightweight backpacking sites.

Extra stove fuel should be carried in special fuel bottles with tight-fitting caps and special seals. For some models of liquid-fuel stoves, the tank is an integral part of the stove, while for others the stove has no tank but is designed to be connected to a fuel bottle. Some stoves have small tanks (you hope you can finish cooking dinner before running out of gas), while others run full blast for more than 3 hours. Some operate nicely over the entire range from simmer to full heat, while others perform best when operating—and sounding—like a roaring blowtorch.

Canister fuel. These stoves (fig. 5-6) burn propane, butane, a propane/butane mix, or isobutane, all of which are gases at normal temperatures and pressures. Before lighting, the burner of the stove is attached to a nonreusable metal fuel canister. The fuel inside the canister is pressurized, which keeps the gas in a liquid state. It is hard to tell how much fuel is left in a canister (especially from one trip to the next), so carry one or more spare cans, depending on the length of your trip. Propane canisters are much heavier than butane canisters. Butane must be warmed to operate at cold temperatures—you may have to take the canister to bed with you. Most canisters have a built-in valve that allows for detachment from the burner between uses, a few other types are punctured upon installation and must remain attached to the burner until empty. (Spent canisters, of course, must be packed out as trash.)

Using a canister stove is quite simple in warm weather—just light a match and open the single valve. To simmer, close down the valve part of the way. Most of these stoves have less heat output than white gas or kerosene stoves and cost more to operate, but they are easy to set up and use. Make sure your stove and fuel choice operate in the coldest temperatures you will encounter.

Solid fuel. Solid fuels include jellied alcohol (Sterno), waxlike heat tablets, and charcoal. These fuels are very safe to handle, but all have a low heat output. Stoves using these fuels are of limited use in the wilderness.

Stove stability varies quite a bit among models. The bottom of the

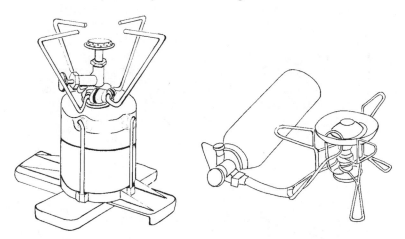

Figure 5-6: *Left, an example of a canister stove; Right, a liquid fuel stove. The canister for the stove on the left must remain attached until empty. The windscreen is not shown.*

stove or the breadth of its tripod legs (its "footprint") determines how stable the stove will be on the ground. Generally, the larger the footprint, the more stable the stove. It is also important to pay attention to the method by which cookware is supported on top of the stove.

Many stoves feature a windscreen that is either part of the stove or an accessory. Some cookware sets are designed to seat into certain windscreens to improve stability and performance. The fuel tank should be below or outside the windscreen. A windscreen, however, should never allow the fuel tank to overheat. Because all stoves are very sensitive to wind, a windscreen should be considered a mandatory piece of stove equipment.

Fueling the Stove

All stoves must be considered dangerous, but with a little knowledge and common sense, it is possible to minimize this danger. The most important thing to do is understand how your stove works—**READ THE INSTRUCTIONS.** Some models have instructions printed on the stove itself. Test the stove's operation at home (outside) to see that it works properly before taking it on a trip.

Precautions and tips for fueling a stove:

- Never refuel a liquid-fuel stove when the stove is hot.
- Use care when pouring liquid fuel into the stove. Use a small funnel or a pouring cap and add fuel slowly. Check the level in the tank and don't overfill. A filter funnel helps keep the fuel and your stove clean.
- Leave an air space above the fuel. Don't fill all the way to the top.
- Refuel away from flame sources.
- Don't refuel inside a tent or building.
- Check the fuel level before lighting the stove to ensure that you don't run out while you're cooking.
- Replace the cap on both the fuel bottle and the stove before lighting the stove.
- When attaching a canister to a canister-type stove, be careful. The screw threads should be easy to turn (don't cross-thread the fittings), and the gasket surfaces must be clean.
- After the canister is attached, make sure it doesn't leak (listen for a hissing noise). Make sure the on-off valve is closed and the canister is tightly attached.
- Puncture-type canisters must not be removed unless empty.
- Never throw an empty canister into a campfire.
- Always store fuel bottles away from cooking area to avoid combustion.

Using the Stove

Operating a stove can be simple and easy but hazardous if done improperly. By observing these guidelines, you can prevent accidents and end up with a warm meal:

- Avoid cooking inside a tent. A burning stove consumes oxygen and gives off deadly carbon monoxide gas. If you are forced to cook inside, open the door flap and vents to let plenty of fresh air inside. Some tents have a covered vestibule that can be used. If possible, prime and light the stove outside and carefully bring it in after the stove is operating properly. Caution: Many stove bases get hot enough to melt nylon and foam pads. They also frequently flare up when being lit.
- Make sure that the stove is in a safe place and is on a stable, level surface.
- Place a pan on the stove to check stability before lighting.

Know how to operate your stove before setting out into the wilderness. (Photo by James Glenn Pearson.)

- For canister stoves, light the match and hold it next to the burner before turning on the gas. Never leave a burning stove unattended.
- Insulate the warm bottom of the stove from the snow with a piece of plywood or high-temperature plastic.
- Remove the key (if your stove has one) that operates the flame adjustment during stove operation before it gets too hot to touch.
- Carry spare parts, tools, cleaning needles, and instructions on how to repair your stove. Clean openings regularly.
- If your stove has a pump, oil it before each trip.

Cookware

Economize, but don't skimp, on your cookware and utensils. One pot and perhaps a small kettle may suffice for one or two people, but fancier meals may require the use of two pots. Backpacking pots are made of aluminum, stainless steel, or titanium. Some now come with a nonstick surface and heat-absorbing, black exteriors.

Some cook sets consist of two pots nestled together with handles that fold down, or no handles at all (a pan grip is used) and a lid that also serves as a fry pan. You can also modify ordinary pans by removing or shortening their handles.

It is very helpful to have your cookware marked with common intervals of volume measurement (1 cup, 2 cups, 3 cups, etc.). If your pots are not already marked, do it yourself with a hammer and screwdriver.

If you're cooking only for yourself, simply eat from the pot or pan. Otherwise, each person needs a cup or bowl to eat from. As a minimum for utensils, use a pocketknife for cutting food and a spoon for eating. A fork is nice but not necessary. A cook group needs a large spoon for stirring and serving.

The stainless steel "Sierra Cup" has been popular with backpackers for years. It is easy to clean and nests with a bowl, however, it is easy to spill and allows liquids to cool quickly in cold temperatures. An insulated plastic cup, with or without a lid, keeps your beverage or soup hot for a longer period of time, but it is bulkier. Any cup can have its volume measured and marked at home.

A few other useful items: Wide-mouth plastic bottles marked at quarter-cup intervals are handy for mixing beverages, pancake batter, and pudding. A small wire whisk takes the place of your mixer back home. Don't forget a small can opener (if you have cans), a measuring cup (if nothing else you have measures volume), aluminum foil (for a variety of uses), a spatula, and a wooden spoon. A bandana can serve as a mini-tablecloth, dish towel, hot pad, and more. For cleaning up, you'll need a pot scrubber. Some people just use very hot water without soap for washing dishes, but if your food is particularly greasy (the bears will love you), you may want to use a small amount of biodegradable soap and wash well away from water sources.

PACKS

There are numerous choices of packs for the wilderness traveler:
- Fanny pack (often too small, but 1000-cubic-inch models are available)
- Small day pack (for short hikes)
- Full day pack (for longer hikes)
- Extra-large day pack (sometimes called a "day-and-a-half pack")
- External-frame or internal-frame backpack (for overnights)

The backpack you choose greatly affects how much you enjoy the sport. Fit and style are as personal with backpacks as they are with shoes. What works great for one person may not work for you. Another person's reject may be just what you need.

Correct fit is important. Never buy a pack without trying it (or a similar rental) first, preferably on an overnight trip. Select the right size for your body frame, load it up with 30 pounds, and walk, climb up and down, tip, turn, and twist. You've found a winner if the pack feels like an extension of your body, moves with you, and doesn't poke or gouge. After prolonged use, you shouldn't have excessively sore spots on the collar, hips, or elsewhere.

When you try out a backpack, understand that the perceived load may vary by as much as 10 pounds, depending on how you distribute items inside. Place the heaviest items in the bottom, close to your back. Don't hang anything out from the back of the pack. Adjust the waist and shoulder straps to distribute weight more or less evenly between shoulders and hips. Other desirable features include padded shoulder straps, a padded waist or hipbelt, load leveler straps, and a sternum strap (this is tightened across your chest to relieve pressure on your shoulders). Packs tend to leak through the seams and sometimes the material itself, so you may want to buy a waterproof pack cover and/or waterproof stuff sacks to protect your gear.

Internal- and external-frame backpacks (fig. 5-7) are quite different from each other. Internal-frame packs have vertical stays (curved, rigid structural members) inside the pack sack. Internals are relatively compact and should fit snugly against your body. They're designed to hold sleeping bags, and sometimes tents and pads, inside. Adjustable straps compress the load and keep it from shifting. If properly designed and adjusted, internal-frame models feel more balanced. Drawbacks include generally higher cost, heavier weight, more difficulty in getting at your gear (in top-loading models, particularly), and less air circulation for your back. Internal-frame packs are currently very popular.

The rigid, exposed frame structure on an external-frame pack keeps the load slightly away from your body, allowing more air circulation. These packs need fewer adjustments. Sleeping bag, pad, and tent strap onto areas provided for them on the frame, and most other gear fits inside the pack's many pockets. Some have a metal hip support as part of their suspension system. External-frame packs are easier to load and may handle heavy loads (50 pounds or more) better than most internal-frame packs, but gear strapped on the outside tends to snag on branches and rocks. Most external-frame packs are lighter but bulky—they can take up more space in the trunk of a car.

As of this writing, manufacturers of both styles are working to blend the best features of each. The latest internal-frame models have divided compartments for easier loading, and they now handle heavier loads with more comfort. The newer external-frame packs are becoming less boxy and more contoured to enhance stability, while maintaining their carrying volume. Ultralight backpacks are becoming more comfortable and easier to pack. Some use a sleeping pad as the "frame."

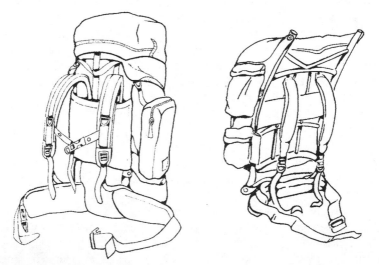

Figure 5-7: *Frame packs: Left, internal frame; Right, external frame.*

For recreational (as opposed to expedition) backpacking, you'll need a pack capacity of 4000 to 6000 cubic inches in an internal-frame pack (which holds sleeping bag and possibly tent and pad) and 3000 to 3500 cubic inches in an external-frame pack. Don't be tempted to buy too much backpack (what you choose to put in your pack always seems to exceed the capacity anyway). Choose the size that fits your needs most of the time. You can always use add-on pockets for additional space, or rent a larger pack when you require extra capacity.

If your search turns up more than one suitable model of backpack, consider individual characteristics or special features like weight, color, extra pockets, ice ax loops, tie-on patches, and versatility (some packs, for example, have top pockets that can be detached and used as a day pack or fanny pack).

Once you've made your choice, ask that your pack be fitted properly. The structural members of both internal- and external-frame packs should be carefully adjusted to fit the size and contours of your body.

Women choosing a backpack should look for a pack frame that arches away from the head and buttocks. A pack designed for a man's slimmer hips and buttocks tends to tilt forward on a woman, bumping her in the head with each step. A pack designed for a woman is also shorter between the waist and shoulders, has contoured shoulder straps (to keep the pack riding closer to her narrower shoulders), and has a suspension that allows most of the weight to be carried on her hips. The last factor is important because it takes advantage of a woman's lower-body strength and relieves pressure on her shoulders.

Day Packs

For day hikes or peak climbs, you'll need a small pack. With regular day packs, most weight is carried on the shoulders (waist belts and sternum straps are stabilizers); with fanny packs, the weight is on the hips. For a summit bid, you may need a pack holding as much as 2000 cubic inches of necessary equipment such as raingear, extra clothing, food, water, a first-aid kit, and other essentials. On any pack, look for good construction, nonmetal zippers and fasteners (to reduce binding), padded straps, and reinforcements where the straps are sewn in. Cordura material and leather reinforcement make for a heavier but more durable pack. Compressibility is a very important feature if the smaller pack has to fit inside a backpack.

A large daypack (3000 cubic inches) can be used for multiday backpacking if you strap your bedroll on the outside. The pack is then small enough to use as a day pack. This can save 4 pounds or more.

FOR DAY HIKES

Wear or carry in pockets

- ❑ Long pants
- ❑ Polypropylene shirt
- ❑ Long-sleeve, light-colored shirt
- ❑ Wool sweater
- ❑ Hat with brim
- ❑ Bandana or handkerchief
- ❑ Hiking shoes or boots
- ❑ Socks—liners and wool socks
- ❑ Sunscreen
- ❑ Sun-protective lip balm
- ❑ Sunglasses
- ❑ Water bottle (in a belt bag)
- ❑ Swiss army knife with file and scissors
- ❑ Compass
- ❑ Wallet or plastic bag with driver's license, credit card, health insurance info, emergency phone numbers, money, coins for phone

Carry in your day pack

- ❑ Shorts
- ❑ Hooded rain jacket and pants
- ❑ Wool hat and mittens
- ❑ Large trash bag (for emergency shelter)
- ❑ Lunch and snacks (along with extra food for delays or emergencies)
- ❑ Water or electrolyte replacement drink
- ❑ First-aid kit
- ❑ Nylon cord
- ❑ Closed-cell foam sit pad
- ❑ Maps
- ❑ Pencil and paper
- ❑ Flashlight with extra batteries and spare bulb
- ❑ Whistle
- ❑ Lighter or waterproof matches, and candle
- ❑ Toilet bag to carry toilet paper, trowel, plastic bags

- ❑ Ditty bag for personal items (*e.g.*, comb, hand lotion, hair barrette, tweezers, moleskin, pain-relief tablets, towelettes)

FOR BACKPACKING TRIPS

Add the following to the day-hike list on the left. Select gear and quantities appropriate for your planned trip.

- ❑ Frame backpack (also take along a day pack if you will be day hiking away from camp).
- ❑ Tent
- ❑ Sleeping bag
- ❑ Sleeping pad
- ❑ Ground cloth
- ❑ Stove
- ❑ Cook pots
- ❑ Cup, bowl, utensils
- ❑ Hiking stick
- ❑ Water bottles
- ❑ Water purification (filter, disinfectant tablets, or extra fuel for boiling water)
- ❑ Food and beverage powders
- ❑ Larger first-aid kit
- ❑ Safety gear (rope, ice ax) as needed
- ❑ Long underwear
- ❑ Parka
- ❑ Gaiters
- ❑ Mitten overshells
- ❑ Lightweight shoes or booties (to wear in camp)
- ❑ Toothbrush
- ❑ Biodegradable soap
- ❑ Glacier glasses (for snow)
- ❑ Insect repellent

Note: Not all of the items listed here are essential for all trips. Some trips require less equipment and some trips require more.

Figure 5-8: *Use an equipment list to make sure you bring everything you need. This list can be adjusted for different types of trips.*

chapter
6

Foods and Cooking

Pauline Jimenez, Priscilla and Scott Anderson,
and Carolyn Wood

John Muir, founder of the Sierra Club, wrote, "My meals were easily made, for they were all alike and simple, only a cup of tea and bread."

The choices of what you eat in the wilderness and how you prepare it have never been broader. You can emulate John Muir and subsist quite comfortably on a variety of uncooked foods. Or, bring along a few tools and ingredients to whip up a great feast at the end of each day.

NUTRITION BASICS

Some people think backpacking is a good way to lose weight, or they may try fasting in the wilderness for health or spiritual benefits. There's nothing wrong with a low-calorie diet on layover days or days with moderate exercise, but wilderness travel demands more calories. If you rely only on the energy from your body's fat reserves, you are setting in motion an inefficient and dangerously uncomfortable process. This is especially true if you're far from civilization or if an accident or delay occurs.

A low-calorie diet doesn't work with strenuous, long-duration exercises like hiking and backpacking. If you're on a medically supervised liquid diet program, consult your physician to determine how to adjust

Mealtime is a chance to share company, food, and recipes. (Photo by Pauline Jimenez.)

your program. If you know you have special nutritional requirements, take them into account. For instance, a pregnant woman may need to double her protein intake and increase her consumption of milk products. A person with diabetes may need to bring hard candy to be used for medical emergencies (see Chapter 16, Wilderness First Aid, "Diabetes"). No one should use the wilderness for weight loss—do it at home.

The number of calories you need depends on your size, your metabolism, the length of the trip, the weather, and the activities planned. For a short, leisurely trip you may only need to raise your caloric intake over the normal amount by 10 to 20 percent. For long, strenuous trips lasting more than a few days, you may need 50 to 75 percent more calories. Uphill backpacking can burn 500 or more calories per hour.

Poor nutrition can decrease your endurance, cause actual muscle loss, and limit your body's ability to repair itself after a hard day of hiking. It can also affect morale and decision-making skills. When out in the wilderness, it helps to be conscious of how *carbohydrates, proteins, fats,* and other nutrition components keep your body fortified.

Carbohydrates are the staple of a hiker's diet and come in two forms. The first are simple carbohydrates such as sugar, honey, jam, candy, and fruit. Since most of these are metabolized quickly, they're beneficial when consumed during or after strenuous exercise, a small amount at a time. During larger meals, combine them with other foods. Never eat a high-sugar snack just before exercising unless it is combined with other foods. Sugar stimulates insulin production which absorbs blood glucose and decreases your endurance.

The second are complex carbohydrates. These high-nutrient foods include whole-grain products (e.g., cereals, rice, breads, and pastas) and starchy vegetables (e.g., potatoes, peas, and beans). The energy from complex carbohydrates is stored in the liver and muscles as glycogen. You have enough stored glycogen to last through about 1½ hours of vigorous exercise. To keep your body working effectively, replenish these reserves with frequent snacks throughout the day. Fifty to seventy percent of your total daily calories should be carbohydrates.

Be sure to eat carbohydrates, some protein, and drink something within 30–60 minutes after you stop hiking. Missing that timing can have consequences. If you forget to eat or skip some meals, you may "hit the wall" within only a few hours. When this happens, it usually takes more than 24 hours to restore glycogen reserves, and recovery for tomorrow's hike will be slow. Even with frequent snacks and meals, your glycogen reserves can be somewhat depleted, so stoke them up again during your evening meal. Foods like pasta fit the bill nicely. Half of your daily calories should come from complex carbohydrates.

Protein is best eaten regularly in small amounts because it is either used immediately for muscle renewal and repair or it is stored as fat. You need protein to help fight disease; to build, repair, and maintain body tissue; and to keep your brain cells thinking and your blood flowing. Complete proteins (e.g., animal products such as jerky or canned meat, fish, eggs, and powdered milk) contain all essential amino acids. Complex carbohydrates eaten the same day also pair their amino acids to form complete proteins. Complete protein partnerships are dairy/grains (e.g., cereal with milk); grains/legumes (e.g., beans and rice or peanut butter and whole-grain bread); and legumes/seeds (e.g., peanuts and sunflower seeds in trail mix). About 15 percent of your daily calories should be from proteins.

Fats provide more energy per ounce, keeping you satisfied longer than either carbohydrates or proteins, but they take longer to digest. It is best to include the majority of your day's fat in the evening because it is easier to digest when at rest. When eaten at dinner, fats keep you from becoming hungry during the night and help you stay warm. Increase fat consumption slightly when dealing with extreme cold or long-distance trekking, but be aware that fats eaten in large quantities at high altitudes may cause indigestion. Good sources include butter, margarine, nuts, cheese, meat fat, and oil. Under normal conditions, fewer than 30 percent of your daily calories should be from fats.

Vitamins and minerals enable your body to make the best use of the food you eat. Eating a variety of foods is the best way to ensure that you get all the vitamins and minerals your body requires. If you are uncertain, you may want to take a vitamin and mineral supplement.

Fiber is important because it prevents constipation. Fiber is found in whole grains, fruits, and vegetables.

Fluid intake can become critically important with strenuous exercise. Most of us have experienced the discomforts of cotton-mouth, dizziness, weakness, and headaches when exercising heavily on hot days. These conditions are symptoms of dehydration—the loss of water and minerals from the body. Dehydration impairs your judgment and coordination, and it makes you more vulnerable to altitude sickness, hypothermia, and heat stroke (and of course death). Lost body fluids must be replaced by drinking water or other fluids and by eating sodium- and potassium-rich foods such as soy sauce, tomato juice, cheddar cheese, beans, spinach, raisins, potatoes, oranges, bananas, and milk. Always remember that *water* is the most important thing you can take on a hike or backpack.

Before you start, drink 8–16 ounces. Then drink about 10–12 ounces every half hour while you are hiking. In general, you should consume 1 gallon of water or other fluids per day. In the desert or with heavy exertion you may need much more, but in cool or wet conditions you may need less. With experience, you'll learn what your body requires.

Remember that thirst comes *after* your body begins to dehydrate, so it is not the best indicator of your needs. Drink small amounts at frequent intervals rather than at one long gulping session. Drink regularly and often, and never ration your water.

For vigorous hikes lasting longer than an hour, you need to replace carbohydrates as well as fluids. Unlike water, some sports drinks can replace both. The drinks that work best during exercise contain 13–21 grams of carbohydrates per cup. Those with more carbohydrates slow digestion and can cause cramping, nausea, bloating, and diarrhea during exercise. Those with fewer won't provide enough fuel to your muscles fast enough. Check the ingredient list for sugars (e.g., sucrose, fructose, glucose, and maltodextrin). Avoid those with a high concentration of fructose because this can slow hydration and upset your stomach. Some fructose is fine, but make sure it is not the first or only sugar listed. Sports drinks should also include sodium, potassium, minerals, and electrolytes. The small amount of sodium (less than that found in sweat) encourages you to drink more and helps you retain water to prevent dehydration. Choose a drink with 100–110 milligrams of sodium and about 30 milligrams of potassium per 8-ounce serving.

Other beverage choices include herbal tea, hot chocolate, powdered instant breakfast, fruit crystals, soups, and broths. Coffee drinkers should be aware that caffeine is a diuretic, which increases the output of urine, and a vasodilator, which increases the chances of frostbite. It is a stimulant that increases heart rate and causes blood pressure to rise. However, caffeine withdrawal may spoil your trip. Consider limiting yourself to one cup of coffee, which you can count as a half cup of fluid.

Alcohol is an even stronger diuretic than coffee. It dehydrates you and decreases your appetite. Taken in excess, it generates a feeling of warmth for a short time, but it actually promotes a net loss of heat in cold conditions and makes you more vulnerable to hypothermia. Alcohol impairs your judgment, balance, coordination, and awareness. These effects are multiplied at high altitude. Excessive alcohol consumption puts you at risk in an environment that magnifies mistakes and misjudgments.

TYPES OF FOOD

Deciding whether you should take *fresh, frozen, dehydrated, freeze-dried,* and/or *canned foods* depends on how many days you plan to travel and how much weight you want to carry. Your meals will be more appetizing if you incorporate a variety.

Fresh and frozen foods are the healthiest foods you can bring, but most of them spoil easily and weigh a lot. They are great for weekend trips but less practical for longer trips. Homemade breads, energy bars, and cereal mixes keep for days or weeks and also have high energy-to-weight ratios. By making your own foods in advance, you control the ingredients, and eliminate or reduce additives such as preservatives.

Canned foods expand your choices because they do not spoil. However, the weight of the packaging is a consideration on longer journeys (remember that you'll have to pack out the empty cans). Certain flavorful items that enhance your versatility in meal planning are available in small cans.

Freeze-dried foods offer good alternatives for longer trips because they are lightweight, convenient, and almost never spoil. They are widely available at grocery stores, camp supply stores, by mail order, and on the Internet. Some are laced with chemical additives, but many companies offer healthier alternatives. Freeze-dried foods tend to be expensive, may need longer cooking times than the package indicates, and have small portion sizes. Large packets (four 8-ounce servings) usually only feed two people. Consider these as entrées, not a whole meal. Round them out with soups and desserts. The foil packaging does not burn in a campfire, so be sure to carry out the trash. Some specialty foods, such as freeze-dried strawberries or precooked, freeze-dried beans, are well worth the cost.

Dehydrated food can be bought as prepackaged meals (turkey tetrazzini, beef almondine, etc.) or as individual-item packages. A disadvantage of some dehydrated foods is that larger chunks can be slow to rehydrate. Presoaking helps because the food hydrates in your pot instead of pulling fluids from your body while it sits in your stomach. Start the soaking process several hours before making camp by mixing the dehydrated food with water in a carefully sealed container or wide-mouth water bottle.

You can dehydrate your own food at home. The process is fairly simple and can be done in an oven, but better results are obtained from a food dehydrator. If you spend a lot of time in the wilderness and want "home" taste at minimum cost, the investment can be deliciously worth your money. You can home-dry fruit leather, sauces, chilies, salsas, thinly sliced fruits and vegetables, jerky, stews, and even whole meals. Dehydrated food gives you variety, nutrition, your own choice of ingredients, and homemade taste. Commercial freeze-drying processes remove about 96 percent of the moisture, whereas home dehydration removes about 90 percent. That's not bad, considering the money you save for the little time invested and the control you have over what goes into the food.

Wild foods foraged along the trail can supplement your diet. However, this requires specialized knowledge of plants and their uses.

Learning about nonpoisonous and edible plants and gathering them in the right areas can add a new appreciation of nature's bounty and beauty. Foraging takes time and work, and you may not locate what you want when you want it. Always check with the local rangers first to see if harvesting wild plants is legal in the area you plan to visit. In many parks, cutting or picking any plant is illegal. Even if foraging is permitted in the area you're visiting, consider the effects of overharvesting and limit your gathering to what the environment can tolerate. If huge quantities of people visit an area, it likely cannot tolerate even minimal foraging, due to sheer numbers. Under no circumstances should you gather endangered or rare plants, nor should you gather plants for commercial sale.

WHAT TO TAKE

On weekend trips, you can eat almost anything. Nutrition is not a major concern, except that you must take in enough calories to cover your energy expenditures. Trips longer than 3 days require more planning regarding nutrition and weight. With dried foods and those naturally low in water content, and with removal of cardboard packaging and moderately careful menu planning, the average hiker can eat to repletion on 2 pounds of food per day. With more precise planning, 1½ pounds of dry weight per person per day is usually enough. With experience, you will learn what your body requires.

Planning meals can be time-consuming until you develop a repertoire of recipes. It is important to create a menu and then check off each item as you purchase it and pack it. To decide which foods will fit your trip, consider the following: *water, climate, itinerary, preparation time, variety and taste,* and *cost.*

Water. Be sure to study a map of the area where you intend to camp to locate water supplies. Determine whether you'll have to make do with one or more dry camps, where you carry in your water, or if you'll need to spend time melting snow to make water. An important factor affecting your selection of food is the amount of water you'll have to carry, since water is heavy and bulky. Remember that 1 gallon of water weighs 8.3 pounds. Never underestimate your need for food and water. Carrying a few extra pounds is far better than suffering dehydration or hypothermia.

Climate. Heat reduces your appetite but increases your water needs. In hot weather, avoid excess salt, which makes your heart work harder. Extra salt (salt tablets) is only needed with profuse sweating (over 4 quarts in 1 day) coupled with inadequate calorie intake. Except in extreme conditions, high-salt soups, sports drinks, or pretzels will provide all the salt you need. Cold increases your need for calories and extra, quick energy, so it's a good idea to eat small carbohydrate snacks frequently. Hot foods and liquids are more appetizing in cold conditions and help you stay warm.

Itinerary. Think about your estimated mileage and elevation gain/loss for each day. For a short, leisurely trip, you may only need to raise your calorie level slightly. But weeklong, strenuous trips with a heavy pack may require 500–1000 more calories per day. Depending on the terrain, incline, pack weight, and hiking speed, backpackers can easily burn 400 calories or more per hour. Consider known conditions. Will you be carrying your backpack to move camp every day? Is the trip cross-country or on trail? Are there technical challenges such as boulder-scrambling? These factors not only affect your caloric needs, but the time and energy you have available for meal preparation.

Preparation time. One-pot meals are the best choice if the trip is very strenuous, if you don't want to spend a lot of time cooking, or if only one stove is available. Simple, quick meals are always appreciated when people are cold, tired, and hungry. Always pack at least one meal that requires little or no effort for situations like these. On rest days or where wood fires can be built, you might make a fancier meal. For example, pancakes contain minimal water and are efficient in the ratio of weight to calories. If you're not going anywhere and you're camping in paradise, who cares if breakfast lasts until lunchtime?

Variety and taste. Well-balanced meals should give you plenty of variety. Remember that there is no single food that meets all of your nutritional needs. Play with colors, textures, and flavors to ensure that your nutritional needs are met. If your food is tasteless and boring, eating will be a chore, not a joy.

Cost. Keeping costs down is another consideration when preparing a trip menu. Perhaps you would put this high on your importance list, but food cost should never be the primary factor in choosing what is right for a trip. If a trip seems expensive, you should consider whether or not you should go, not how little food you can bring to survive.

EATING STYLES

Depending on your preference, meals can be quick and require minimum preparation, allowing maximum time on the trail. Or, meals can be more elaborate, with several courses and substantial time required for preparation and cleanup. On a longer trip, you may want at least one such meal, where decadent enjoyment is a welcome break from many short snacks during long days of hiking.

Neither type of meal, or variations in between, is better than the other—it's a matter of choice, and you can do both on the same trip. Remember that advance preparation at home can save hours in the wilderness, where you lack the conveniences of a modern kitchen and a nearby grocery store.

Types of Meals

A substantial **breakfast** is important. It gives you much of the energy you'll need for the first half of your day's activity. Generally, this meal should consist of carbohydrates (both simple and complex) to get you going and some protein or fat to help sustain you for several hours. A whole-grain cereal, served hot or cold and mixed with dried fruit, powdered milk, and water, is a good choice. Round out your meal with a beverage to make sure you are fully hydrated before starting the day's activities.

Lunch may not be a square meal, but instead intermittent snacking on high-carbohydrate, low-protein, low-fat foods that digest quickly, such as grain products, beans, vegetables, and fruit. You can bring a premade rice or bean salad, or if time is limited, you may decide to base your midday meal on whole-grain breads or crackers with spreads such as jam, honey, and peanut butter. A common trail snack is GORP, or good old raisins and peanuts. Today, GORP comes in a variety of combinations of nuts, seeds, small crackers, dried fruits, and candies. Most prepackaged trail mixes are loaded with fats. You may wish to create your own combinations.

Energy bars and gels are also becoming common trail foods. For hiking, opt for bars with no more than 8–10 grams of protein and 4 grams or less of fat per every 230 calories. High fat content slows digestion and makes you feel nauseous. Also, choose bars with 5 grams or less of fiber because too much may also slow digestion and trigger the urge to defecate. Make sure to consume at least 12–16 ounces of water for each bar you eat. Energy gels typically weigh about 1 ounce per packet and are very portable. Choose packets that contain 70–100 calories and 17–25 grams of carbohydrate. Remember to drink about 8 ounces of water for each gel packet you swallow. Gels may contain caffeine, and for some people, these can have a laxative effect.

One energy bar or two gel packets per hour (30–60 grams of carbohydrate) is about right. Keep in mind that no single bar or gel supplies the wealth of nutrients found in whole foods. These foods should be

TRAIL LUNCH/SNACK IDEAS

For backpacking, about 50 percent of your daily calories should come from lunch and snacks. Of these, 60–70 percent should be from carbohydrates such as whole grains, fruits, and vegetables. Aim for a variety of textures and tastes.

BREADS & GRAINS	FRUITS & VEGETABLES	DAIRY PRODUCTS
Bagels, pitas, sesame bread sticks, English muffins, hard rolls, flatbreads, tortillas, cornbread	Fruit leathers, dried fruits (peaches, pears, apricots, cranberries, pineapple, mangos, raisins, figs, dates), chocolate-covered raisins	Hard cheeses (string cheese, cheddar, Parmesan, Gouda)
Pretzels, crackers, pilot biscuits, rye crackers, Wheat Thins, saltines, Pringles	Fig bars, fruit bars	Hard-boiled eggs
Pasta salad (made with oil, _not_ mayonnaise), couscous/tabouli salad	One piece of fresh fruit (apple, orange, banana) OR one canned fruit (peaches, apricots, etc.)	Powdered milk (add ⅓ cup plus 1 cup water to granola, etc.)
Animal crackers, graham crackers	Bean salad sprinkled with sesame seeds, bean and cheese burrito	Yogurt
Trail breads (fry-breads, pancakes, biscuits, bannock)	Carrot salad, fresh vegetables (broccoli, carrots, cauliflower, cabbage, green beans, Chinese pea pods, small zucchini, jicama, celery, bell peppers)— store in paper, _not_ plastic	
Granola, cereals	Precooked baked potato with butter and brown sugar, or relish, cheese, bacon bits, etc. (Try a sweet potato or Yukon Gold. Seal well so it doesn't leak.)	

Figure 6-1: *Trail lunch/snack ideas.*

ANIMAL PROTEINS	SPREADS & DIPS	MISCELLANEOUS
Jerky	Bean spread, hummus, pesto, olive oil	Recovery drinks and powders *(e.g. Gatorade, Cytomax, Gookinaid)*, boxed fruit juices, instant breakfast, hot Jello, tea
Salami	Honey packets	Hard candy, lemon drops
Condensed mincemeat *(this comes in a box, not the kind in a jar)*	Jam packets, fruit spread, apple butter	Trail mix *(ideas: melba toast, croutons, goldfish crackers, mini pretzels, nuts, corn nuts, dried fruits, sesame sticks, pumpkin seeds, sunflower seeds, Rice/Wheat Chex, M&Ms, granola, shredded coconut, raisins)*
Sardines	Nut and seed butters (i.e. peanut butter, tahini)	Chocolate bars, malt balls, gummi bears, gourmet jelly beans, M&Ms
Canned tuna or chicken, Vienna sausages, bacon bits, devilled ham *(Water packed. Choose only one can per trip; eat immediately after opening.)*	Cream cheese packets, mayonnaise and/or mustard packets *(These keep for 2–3 days if protected from heat and the seal is not broken.)*	Energy bars *(best ones have 40 grams carbo-hydrates, 8–10 grams protein, less than 5 grams fat)*
Foil packet of tuna (e.g. Starkist in sunflower oil)	Salsa	Fruitcake, pound cake, Pop Tarts, Twinkies, cookies

only one of the kinds of snacks you bring, and they are not meant to take the place of regular meals. You can get the same carbohydrate value from a banana, four graham crackers, or four fig bars.

Since about half your daily food allotment should be for lunch and snacks, and most need to be portable hiking food that is not cooked in camp, coming up with a varied menu for this part of the day can present challenges. See Figure 6-1 for ideas.

Dinner should include carbohydrates, protein, and fats for your body to digest while you sleep. This is also the time to replenish the salts and liquids you have lost during the day. Start with a hot beverage or soup (unless it's a warm evening where something cool might be more refreshing).

To conserve fuel and save time, try one-pot meals. Choose a carbohydrate base (pasta, rice, grains) and then build a full meal with additional ingredients for protein, fat, and flavor (such as canned or dried chicken, dried vegetables, butter or margarine, and a dehydrated soup or sauce mix). Hearty soups (such as minestrone, bean, beef, barley, or chicken) are also good choices. Add instant potatoes, rice, crackers, cheese, or bread to round out these meals.

Add spices and seasonings to enhance the flavor of prepackaged meals, or sprinkle curry to liven up a rice dish. Add onion flakes to stew. Sprinkle a little sage and basil in the butter or oil before cooking freshly caught trout. Last, but not least, top the meal off with a satisfying dessert and enjoy a social gathering around the campfire.

Always pack a small amount of "emergency food." Take foods that keep well and need little or no cooking, in case you run out of fuel, there is bad weather, or a member of your group is sick or hurt. Your emergency supplies might include jerky, granola bars, trail mixes, dried fruits, and additional dehydrated, prepackaged meals. Don't pack foods that are too tasty, or you may be tempted to dig into them unnecessarily. Wrap the food up tightly, store it in the bottom of your bag, and forget about it. Use the same batch of emergency food for multiple trips, as long as it remains fresh enough.

Menu Planning

To simplify menu planning, create a chart with the trip days, the meals required for each day, itinerary notes, and space to list the foods for each meal (see sample menu, fig. 6-2). Your ideas will include which meals are eaten on the way to and from the trailhead, whether certain meals need to be eaten hot or cold, whether you are snacking on the move or stopping for a "real" meal, etc. Consider

SAMPLE MENU

This menu is for a summer backpack in the Sierra Nevada at 9000 feet (pleasant daytime weather around 70°F with possible thunder showers, night lows just above 35°F, with readily accessible water. The itinerary is for an easy backpack on trail, setting up a base camp, and rambling day hikes on trails with no technical difficulties.

	Breakfast	Lunch/Snacks	Dinner
Thursday	*Eat at home*	*Purchase en route*	*Purchase en route, sleep at trailhead*
Friday	*Cold breakfast to get on the trail fast* Granola mixed with 1 cup water and ⅓ cup powdered milk, dried fruit and nuts, hot cocoa, water	*Eat on the move* Prebaked sweet potato (with butter and brown sugar), jerky, dried apricots, salty trail mix, sports drink, water	*Set up camp* Freeze-dried entrée or pasta with sun-dried tomatoes, pine nuts, powdered sauce, breadsticks, brownies (made at home), hot tea
Saturday	Powdered eggs with rehydrated hashbrowned potatoes, rehydrated fruit compote, instant chai (spiced tea with powdered milk)	Couscous salad (made with hot water at breakfast), pita bread, string cheese, salty trail mix, fig bars, sports drink, water	Instant miso soup, one-pot shrimp dish (canned) with spiced couscous (instant soup packet) and toasted almonds, heated pita bread, fortune cookies (packed carefully in your pot), hot tea
Sunday	*Hardest hiking day* Hot whole-grain cereal (fortified with dried fruit bits, nuts, and powdered milk), hot tea, water	Peanut butter and crackers (or whole-grain bagel with low-fat cream cheese), raw carrot, fruit leather, sweet trail mix, energy bar, sports drink, water	Instant hot broth, quesadillas, salsa (rehydrated), beans and rice, instant chocolate pudding (if you have a snow bank to chill it on) or instant hot tapioca with cinnamon, hot cocoa
Monday	*Break camp, hike out* Instant potatoes with smoked sausage and cheese bits, instant hot broth	*Eat on the move* Sweet trail mix, oatmeal-raisin cookies, jerky, energy bar, dried apricots, sports drink, water	*Purchase en route*

Emergency Food: One packet of sports gel, instant corn chowder, instant potatoes with salt, pepper, and one pat of butter, shelled sunflower seeds, (hard candies e.g., Lifesavers).

Figure 6-2: *Sample backpacking menu.*

both nutritional value and weight, and remember to pack a little extra food for emergency situations.

Cut the weight you carry by forming a "cook group" with people who share the same menu or cook their evening meal together. This system has less duplication of cooking equipment, and the weight is distributed among those who eat the food. Since most backpacking pots hold only about 6 cups of liquid and most stoves are made for this size pot, cook groups of two to four people usually work quite well. With a larger group, consider arranging a "central commissary," where two or three stoves and several large pots serve up to fifteen people, and cooking and cleanup chores are rotated among the members of the group.

Meal planning also involves equipment considerations. How will you measure the amount of water you need to cook your dinner? Do you have a bandana or metal gripper to lift the pot when it is hot? For group cooking, do you have a ladle or clean cup so no one needs to dip dirty dishes into your pot? Find out how much fuel your stove requires and what size pot you'll need. Remember that 3 quarts of food won't fit in a 6-cup pot.

SHOPPING AND PACKAGING

Once you have planned your meals, create a shopping list. Check each item off as you get it and again as you pack it for the trip. There are a variety of places to shop: supermarkets, natural food stores, and ethnic food stores. Camping stores, mail-order catalogs, and the Internet (e.g., Adventure Foods, AlpineAire Foods, The Baker's Catalogue, Spices, Etc.) are good sources for dehydrated foods and meals.

Before you start, decide how much food you need, what containers work best, and how you will organize your foodstuffs to make them easily accessible. Remove all unnecessary store packaging to minimize weight. (Some crackers travel best in their boxes; canned meats, of course, are best left in their cans.) Measure and pack ingredients for individual meals together in a labeled plastic bag, and don't forget to include instructions. If your entire food supply ends up too heavy, then examine the heaviest items. Ask yourself if the portion size is right, if there is something lighter that could be substituted, or if a lighter container is available. Most of the containers you'll need are probably around the house already:

Bags. Most food items can be repackaged in plastic bags. Bags are economical, convenient, light, and reusable, but they don't meet every backpacking need. For example, freeze-dried products are often packaged in foil packets, which are moisture-tight and also serve as good containers for rehydrating.

Plastic bottles and jars. Dry seasonings can be packaged in pill containers or small plastic bottles. Use wide-mouth plastic jars and other plastic storage containers when necessary, but keep these to a minimum, as they are bulky. Be aware that plastics can absorb odors,

Snow camping requires extra fuel to melt snow for water. (Photo by Pauline Jimenez.)

flavors, and oils from the contents, which may foster bacteria, so you need to thoroughly clean these containers between trips. Make sure that the lids are leak-proof. If the contents are a liquid or powder, it is good insurance to put the plastic container in a plastic bag to contain any possible leakage.

Squeeze tubes. Reusable squeeze tubes (as opposed to squeeze bottles) are great for semiliquid or semisolid foods such as honey, peanut butter, jam, and mustard. Squeeze tubes are filled from an open end that is then sealed tight by a plastic clip. They can be obtained at camp supply stores, by mail order, and on the Internet.

Egg cartons. Plastic egg cartons come in sizes that hold as few as two and as many as a dozen eggs. Use one to carry fresh eggs but place it in a plastic bag—just in case. (If you plan to use fresh eggs very early on the trip, break them into a plastic bottle at home. To keep eggs cool and away from direct sunlight, pack eggs deep in your pack and use them within the first 24 hours of your trip.)

Repackaging and grouping your food supply takes some time at home, but it shortens time and effort once you're on the trail. For the final organization of your food, employ either of these two methods:

Package by common meals (the "three bag" method). Select a different-colored stuff sack for each type of meal—breakfast, lunch/snack, dinner—and another sack for coffee, tea, sugar, and condiments and seasonings that could be used during any meal.

Package by day (the "series method"). Group all breakfast, lunch, and dinner foods for a given day in the same sack. You'll still want to keep a separate bag for items that could be used during any meal.

THE WILDERNESS KITCHEN

Now that you're out in the wilderness, your planning and preparation at home pays off. After a long day, you can still eat as well as you might at home.

Take time to pick out a cooking area that is well away from your tent and at least 200 feet away from any water source or established trail. Look for a flat, wind-protected location to place your stove. A large, flat rock or rock ledge, or a low area next to a large fallen tree works well. If the soil is sandy or soft, or if you're camping on snow, you may need to put some support under your stove to steady it. Avoid digging trenches, breaking branches for firewood, or charring nearby rocks or soil. Your goal is to leave behind no sign that you were there.

Remember to *wash your hands* before handling and cooking food.

Dirty hands are one of the most common ways that illnesses are spread in the backcountry: fecal-oral transmission. Fecal-borne pathogens get into your system through direct contact (even using toilet paper leaves germs on your hands), indirect contact (letting someone with contaminated hands dip into your bag of trail mix instead of shaking it into their hand), contact with insects that have rested on feces, and through contaminated drinking water.

The best way to reduce the risk of contamination is to wash your hands and to use clean cooking and serving implements. The best camp soaps are both *biodegradable* and *germicidal* (e.g., Klenz Gel Blue), but they are hard to find. The majority of biodegradable soaps (e.g., Campsuds or Dr. Bronner's Magic Soap) don't kill germs, and many germicidal soaps (e.g., Betadine or Hibiclens) are not biodegradable. One option is to use a biodegradable soap and after your hands are dry, use a tiny amount of antibacterial hand sanitizer. Never use soap directly in any water source, and keep in mind that biodegradable means that the soap *eventually* decomposes, not that it has zero impact.

After you've established your kitchen site and washed your hands, find a safe, comfortable place to sit. Read the package directions or mentally run through the cooking steps to decide what needs to be done first. Make sure the water you need is handy, and locate your matches and flashlight before dark. Set out the ingredients and equipment you need before you start cooking.

For *freeze-dried* and *dehydrated* foods, read the instructions carefully. These foods can be quite inedible if not properly rehydrated. Presoaking of some foods may take 50 to 60 minutes, so allow enough time. Food that has been shredded, grated, or powdered usually takes a short time; whole pieces take longer. The higher the water temperature, the shorter the time it takes to rehydrate.

High-altitude cooking is always slower because the higher the elevation, the lower the boiling temperature of water (see fig. 6-3). Some packaged-food instructions give cooking-time adjustments for various altitudes. For foods that cook in 20 minutes or less at sea level, add 1 minute of cooking time for each 1000 feet of elevation. For items that take more than 20 minutes at sea level, add 2 minutes of cooking time for each 1000 feet of elevation. This means that cooking time for most boiled or simmered food doubles around 10,000 feet. You may want to keep notes on the cooking time of your favorite foods for reference on future trips. Remember to take extra fuel if you'll be cooking a lot at high altitudes.

Elevation	Temperature
Sea level	212°F
5,000 feet	203°F
10,000 feet	194°F
14,000 feet	187°F

Figure 6-3: *Boiling temperature of water at various altitudes.*

When you're ready, start up the stove and heat some water. Hot water is always needed—for preliminary hot drinks or soup and for your main course or courses. While you enjoy your meal, you may want to keep your stove busy heating water for more hot drinks, dessert, and dishwashing. After everyone has eaten, store all food immediately to discourage animal visitors.

Cleaning up is quite simple and should also be done immediately. For some foods, plain hot water is sufficient. For meats, greasy foods, or those that stick to cookware, the use of biodegradable soap is recommended. Water used for washing (dishes or people) should be scattered well away from camp and at least 200 feet from any body of water. Before you dispose of dishwater, strain it to catch any loose food particles, and then pack them out.

Pack out everything—paper products, plastics, aluminum, orange peels, apple cores, egg shells, and the like. Garbage in or near a camp is unsightly and trains animals to become camp thieves. Most non-food garbage degrades very slowly, and some food garbage takes months or years to rot away in a cold and/or dry environment.

It may be impossible to stop hungry critters from visiting your campsite at night. As a safeguard, remove all food from your backpack and leave all the pockets unzipped. If an animal can't get access to the contents of a pocket that smells of food, it usually chews or tears into it. Hanging your food in bags several feet above the ground may be effective against bandits such as rodents and raccoons. In bear country, carry your food in protective bear canisters or use bear boxes if they're provided. Otherwise, certain hanging techniques work best (see Chapter 10, Animal Encounters). In any case, never keep food in your tent, and to discourage any visitation at all, keep your camp clean and free of garbage.

Ah, smell that night air! Feast your eyes on the stars! Bon appetit!

chapter
7

Wilderness Navigation

Nelson Copp and Ted Young

More and more Americans are discovering the beauty and tranquility of parks and trails, and the fun of wilderness camping and travel. Many people are seeking more remote trails and cross-country routes without a good command of the navigation techniques and skills that make such outings safer, more predictable, and more rewarding. Navigation requires relatively little in the way of equipment. It's primarily a mental effort that keeps a person constantly aware of position, direction, and speed of travel. Like the mental effort required in driving an automobile, it requires plenty of practice but gets easier with time.

In normal life, you're continually faced with challenges of navigating. You're probably quite accustomed to using navigation tools and cues such as road maps, street signs, and verbal directions. Wilderness navigation is simply an extension of the same routefinding skills you use in the civilized world. Instead of signposts and road maps, you use a topographic map, a compass, the physical features of the land, and even a Global Positioning System (GPS receiver).

Since cues indicating precise location are not always visible in the wilderness and you won't be meeting other travelers very often, you have to get used to being a little uncertain about your exact position from time to time. This does not mean you'll be "lost," but rather somewhere in transit

The locations of most benchmarks (survey markers) are shown on topographic maps. (Photo by Jerry Schad.)

between one known position and the next. The more you practice reading the lay of the land, the more comfortable you'll be in the wilderness.

THE TOOLS OF NAVIGATION
Maps

Topographic maps are almost always best for navigation purposes. These are scale maps with a unique feature—contour lines indicating elevations above (or in some cases below) sea level. Topo maps also show bodies of water and watercourses, vegetation types, named geographical points of interest such as mountain peaks, and man-made features. A skilled user of a topo map is able to clearly visualize the topography by carefully studying the patterns made by the contour lines.

Topo maps published by the U.S. Geological Survey (USGS) can be purchased at backpacking and map stores, or directly from the USGS. Private publishers often use USGS maps as a base and update the man-made features, such as roads and trails.

Other maps, such as road maps or trail maps without contour lines, may be of some use for navigation as long as they are drawn to scale. Also useful to some degree are shaded relief maps, giving some rough indication of the topography.

All topo maps are printed with the direction of true north toward the top of the map. From any place on earth, true north is the direction toward the geographic north pole—the north end of the earth's spin axis. Magnetic north, on the other hand, is the direction toward the magnetic north pole, which is located some distance away from the geographic north pole in northern Canada. For any place on earth, there's a correction called magnetic declination that expresses the angle

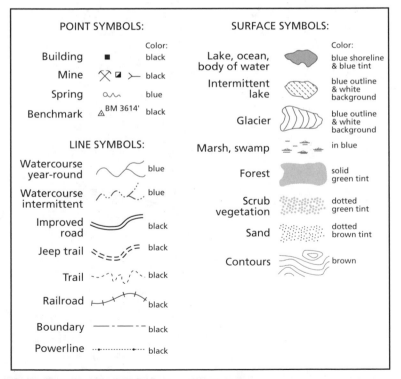

Figure 7-1: *Some symbols used on USGS maps.*

from the direction of true north to the direction of magnetic north. For North America, magnetic declinations range from about 20 degrees east to 22 degrees west. If you aren't using a compass, the magnetic declination is of no use; if you are using a compass, then knowing declination is essential. USGS topo maps come in two types: 7.5 minutes (scale 1:24,000) in which 1 inch on the map equals about 2000 feet, and 15 minutes (1:62,500) in which 1 inch on the map equals about 1 mile. (The "minutes" refer to minutes of arc in latitude and longitude: 7.5 minutes covers 0.125 degree, while 15 minutes covers 0.25 degree of latitude and longitude.) It takes four 7.5-minute maps to

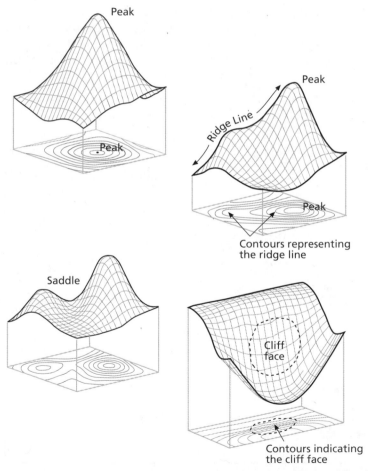

Figure 7-2: *Two- and three-dimensional representations of landscapes.*

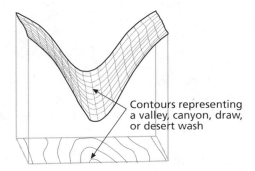

Contours representing
a valley, canyon, draw,
or desert wash

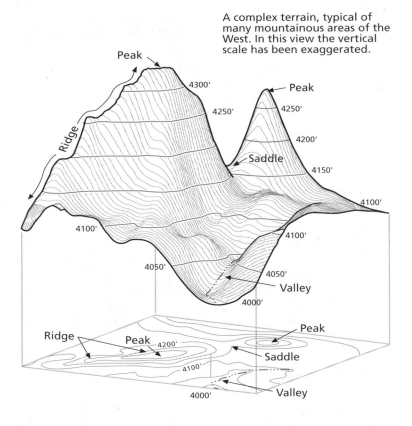

A complex terrain, typical of
many mountainous areas of the
West. In this view the vertical
scale has been exaggerated.

Peak

4300'

4250'

Peak

4250'

4200'

Ridge

Saddle

4150'

4100'

4100'

4100'

4050'

4050'

Valley

4000'

Ridge

Peak

Peak

4200'

Saddle

4100'

Valley

4000'

cover the same area shown on one 15-minute map. Knowing the map scale, it is possible to calculate the distance between any two points along a line or curve. For example, if a route on a 7.5-minute map measures 8.3 inches, simply multiply this length by approximately 0.38 mile/inch, which equals a distance of approximately 3 miles.

Quite often a route spans several maps. Each USGS topo has the names of adjacent maps (usually eight of them) printed on the sides and corners. (Provisional topo maps indicate all adjoining maps at the bottom.)

Figure 7-1 provides a close look at the symbols appearing on USGS topo maps. There are four classes of map symbols: point, line, surface, and contour.

Contour lines, typically printed in brown ink on topo maps, are imaginary lines of constant elevation. If you could actually see these lines on the earth, they would curve around the terrain but always remain level. The elevation difference between adjacent contour lines on the map is called the contour interval. Depending on the type of terrain and the scale of the map, the contour interval can vary from 200 to 20 feet or less. A map with a contour interval greater than 80 feet is generally not very useful for critical navigation. Visualizing the terrain represented on a topo map involves understanding the patterns of the contour lines. Figure 7-2 shows several types of terrain and the corresponding contours.

Although topo maps reflect a great deal of information about the terrain, it is impossible to show every detail. Certain features too small to be detected in the pattern of contour lines may be insurmountable to the traveler. On a map with a contour interval of 80 feet, for example, a cliff or waterfall 60 feet high may not be shown at all if it happens to fall between contour lines. On a map with 40-foot contours, cross-country travel over a gently sloping hillside may appear simple, but not so if the slope is strewn with 10- or 20-foot-high boulders.

Some features on topo maps are necessarily vague. A vegetation pattern indicating forest may represent anything from scattered trees to a dense redwood forest. The pattern indicating scrub vegetation could mean scattered bushes or impenetrable chaparral. A desert wash (a brown stipple pattern on the map) could be filled with anything from sand to boulders. Streams indicated by a thin blue line could be 1 foot wide or 50 feet wide.

Always take note of a map's publication date and the information in fine print at the bottom. The fine print may indicate that the map area was surveyed several years before the map was actually published. Significant changes may have occurred since then. Landslides or simple neglect may have obliterated roads and trails, buildings may be reduced

Good navigation skills will lead you to peak wilderness adventures. (Photo by Arleen Tavernier.)

to nothing but half-buried foundations, and vegetation may have changed as a result of a fire, logging activity, or urban development.

Compass

The compass has developed over many centuries from a simple direction finder to a sophisticated tool. In most modern versions used for navigation, the compass needle (a small, bar-shaped magnet) turns freely while suspended in a circular housing filled with a transparent liquid. The liquid quickly damps out oscillations in the needle's rotation whenever the compass is moved or adjusted in any way.

There are many different types of compasses, but for map and compass work in the field, you should use an orienteering compass (fig. 7-3). In this design the circular housing is transparent and rotates on a transparent plastic base. The perimeter of the housing is inscribed with the cardinal directions (north, east, south, and west) and a 360-degree scale, typically in 2-degree increments. Inside the housing is an orienting arrow for taking readings and a rotating needle. The north-pointing end of the needle is usually painted red, and there's a prominent arrow on the base that can be used to indicate direction of travel or the direction to a prominent land feature.

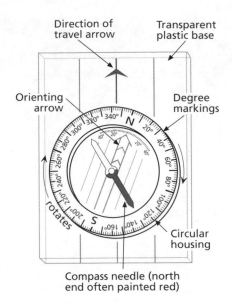

Figure 7-3: *Parts of an orienteering compass.*

In some compasses, the needle's north end is coated with phosphorescent paint, allowing readings to be made at night. Most compass base plates include a small ruler in inches or centimeters to facilitate measuring distance on maps and have a 1:24,000 scale for measuring distance directly on a 7.5-minute map. More expensive compasses include a built-in mirror that helps you make more accurate sightings.

Global Positioning System

The GPS is a satellite-based navigation system that can pinpoint your position anywhere on earth. The GPS uses the signals from twenty-four satellites circling the globe, and by locking onto these signals a GPS receiver can triangulate both your horizontal and vertical positions. GPS units have an accuracy of about 7–15 meters horizontally and about 35 meters vertically.

GPS receivers work at night and in any weather, but the GPS satellite signals cannot penetrate buildings, heavy vegetation, rocks, or other dense objects. Narrow canyons, cliffs, or tall buildings may interfere with the signals and prevent your receiver from obtaining a position location. If this type of interference happens, move away from these areas so your receiver has a direct line of sight to the sky and the

GPS satellites. The GPS receiver runs on batteries, which are affected by cold weather, so always carry spares.

Many models of GPS receivers are available that provide information such as position in terms of coordinates and elevation, direction and distance to waypoints, speed and direction of travel, and estimated time of arrival. Some GPS receivers also display street maps and topographic maps to help you determine position and route. The GPS receiver can be used by itself without a map or as a navigational aid to confirm the position on the map. Use your GPS unit as an additional tool to complement your map and compass rather than relying on it solely.

Altimeter

In hilly or mountainous areas where navigation is critical, an altimeter can be a useful third tool. Altimeters are really barometers calibrated to measure altitude. They can be used to fix your position relative to the contour lines on a topographic map. Altimeter readings are affected by changes in the weather, so it's important to calibrate an altimeter's reading whenever you arrive at a point of known elevation.

NAVIGATION BY MAP

Considering all the information a map contains, it alone may be all you need to determine your location and plot your course. This works particularly well when distinct features such as roads and trail junctions, peaks, passes, or uniquely shaped lakes are within view. This map-alone method of navigation, however, is not effective in bad weather or low visibility. In those cases, a compass or GPS receiver is often necessary as well.

The locating process begins with aligning the map so that it corresponds to the landscape in view and ends with fixing your exact location on the map. You're ready to begin if you can identify features seen on the land with their printed representations on the map. Rotate the map until the features are in the same relative position on the map as they are in view around you.

For example, if you recognize a peak in front of you and a known river junction just below on your left, the map should be rotated and aligned so that when it is held between you and the peak on the horizon, the peak on the map lies in front of you, while the river junction on the map appears to the left but closer than the peak. Then find the spot on the map where the river junction is at the same angle to the left of the peak as is the river junction in your view. That's your approximate location. To further refine your position, look for other nearby

Figure 7-4: *Locating your position by map alone.*

distinctive features. Are you standing on top of a ridge, somewhere along the slope, or in a valley? Is there a meadow or a lake in view? Are there any other high points around you that may help to fix your position? Can you see a bend in the stream and find that bend on the map?

Once you have located yourself, mark your position and keep the map within easy reach or carry it in front of you as you travel so that you can periodically relocate yourself. If you're carrying the map, you may want to encase it in a large, transparent plastic envelope to protect it from rain, perspiration, and abrasion.

NAVIGATION BY COMPASS

Basic compass skills involve setting, taking, and following bearings. A compass bearing is simply the angle, as measured by your compass, between the direction of magnetic north (the direction a compass needle points) and the direction of an object or destination. As suggested by the scale on your compass's circular housing, bearing angles increase eastward from north, that is, they increase to your right.

Setting a Bearing

Let's say a friend tells you her favorite fishing hole is on a magnetic bearing (compass bearing) of 60 degrees from a certain parking area.

Without a compass, you might have only a vague idea of which direction to hike after you park your car. But if you set a bearing of 60 degrees on your compass, simply follow the direction-of-travel arrow on the base of the compass to head in the right direction.

To set that 60-degree bearing, hold the compass flat in the palm of your hand and turn the circular housing until the 60-degree mark lines up with the direction-of-travel arrow on the base plate (fig. 7-5A). On some compasses, the arrow is labeled Read Bearing Here.

Turn the entire compass until the north end of the needle lines up with the orienting arrow in the circular housing (fig. 7-5B) (the red end of the needle now points to N on the housing).

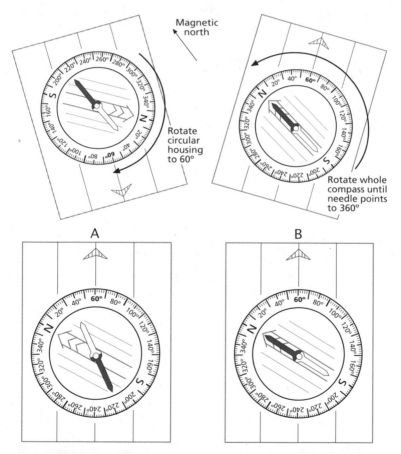

Figure 7-5 A & B: *Setting a bearing.*

Your compass is now oriented to magnetic north, the direction-of-travel arrow is pointing toward the fishing hole, and you are facing in the direction you want to go. Soon you'll learn how to successfully follow that bearing.

Be aware that nearby metallic objects, such as mechanical pencils or pens, a pack frame, a metal watch or ring, or a car can affect the pointing accuracy of a compass needle. Always take compass measurements away from these kinds of objects. A compass can also be rendered useless in certain areas where large amounts of iron-bearing rock are present.

Taking a Bearing

"Taking" a bearing is the opposite of setting a bearing. In this case, you can see where you want to go, but you don't yet know what the bearing angle is. For example, let's say your goal is to reach a peak visible in the distance. You can see a good route straight ahead and you realize that much of the time you'll be hiking in a forest where your view of the peak will be obscured. First you need to take a bearing on the peak.

To take a bearing, hold the compass in your hand with the direction-of-travel arrow pointing toward the peak (fig. 7-6). You may want to hold the compass near eye level to sight more accurately, but remember to keep the compass level. With the direction-of-travel arrow fixed on the peak, turn the housing until the orienting arrow in the circular housing lines up with the north end of the needle. In effect, you are setting up a measurement of the angle between magnetic north (the

Figure 7-6: *Taking a bearing.*

direction of the needle's north end) and the peak (the direction indicated by the direction-of-travel arrow).

As you walk through the forest, refer to your compass often to maintain your course (fig. 7-7). The degree reading on the compass is not really important, as long as you don't rotate the compass housing along the way. Just keep the needle lined up on the orienting arrow, and the direction-of-travel arrow points your way. Still, it's a good idea to memorize or jot down the degree reading in case your compass housing is accidentally reset.

Following a Bearing

In the previous example, you took a bearing on a peak. You're now ready to start hiking through the forest. Since the bearing is already set on your compass, all you have to do is hike in that direction. But how easily can you follow this bearing? What happens if you must skirt obstacles like dense brush or large boulders? To answer these questions you must learn how to select intermediate points.

Before you start hiking, turn the compass until it is oriented toward north (don't turn the circular housing or you will change the bearing

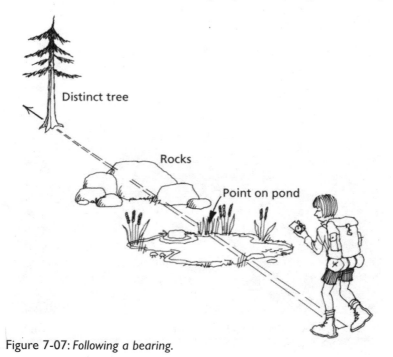

Figure 7-07: *Following a bearing.*

you set earlier). The magnetic needle lines up with the north arrow on the housing and the direction-of-travel arrow on the base plate points in the direction of your hike to the peak.

Now look for an object in the near distance that is between you and the peak, such as a distinctive tree or a pile of rocks. This is your first intermediate point. Walk toward the intermediate point as directly as you can. Moving a little to the left or right to avoid obstacles will not make you lose your original direction. Just keep heading, on average, toward the intermediate point. You should not have to check your compass again until you reach it.

Let's assume that at the first intermediate point you can't see the peak. Easy—just orient your compass to north again, and look along the direction-of-travel arrow. Then pick out a second intermediate point in that direction of travel to which you can hike without losing your way. Continue leapfrogging in this manner until you reach your goal.

Backsighting

Now and then you may lose sight of your next intermediate point. To make sure you are still on the right course, use the technique of backsighting to find the previous point.

Challenging cross-country requires accurate land navigation skills. (Photo by Ted Young.)

Turn around and reorient your compass by lining the south end of the needle with the north end of the orienting arrow (since you are looking 180 degrees back). Now the direction-of-travel arrow points back toward the previous intermediate point. If it does not, move in a direction either left or right until it does. Now you are on the correct bearing again. It's good practice to backsight often to make sure you stay on course. It also helps you to recognize the terrain for the trip back if you plan to return using the same route.

Back Bearings

Let's say you've spent an enjoyable hour on the summit, and now you want to return to your car. You never took a bearing on the car, in fact you can't even see the car. How do you get back? Your car is just 180 degrees from your original bearing. There are two techniques to use to get back.

In the first method, you find the angle that is 180 degrees from your original bearing (if your original bearing is less than 180 degrees, then add 180 degrees to it; if your original bearing is more than 180 degrees, then subtract 180 degrees from it). Reset the housing to this new bearing, orient your compass, and start the journey back (see fig. 7-8).

In the second method, you leave the original bearing set, but orient your compass by aligning the south end of the needle with the orienting arrow (which indicates north).

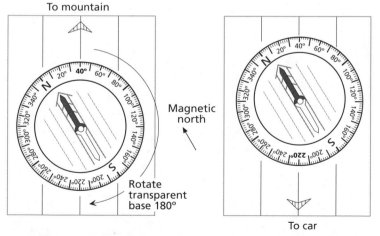

Figure 7-8: *Back bearings: In the diagrams above, 180 degrees was added to the original bearing of 40 degrees to produce a back bearing of 220 degrees.*

Navigating around Obstacles

Using intermediate points to reach a goal is nice, but sometimes there are obstacles you can't easily sidestep. You might encounter some obstacle you'd rather not try to climb over that also blocks your view of the next intermediate point. You could walk around it, but you're afraid that would throw you off course.

One fairly exact solution to this dilemma is to navigate on a right-angle course (fig. 7-9). First determine whether going to the left or the right will be easier. Orient the compass, and face your original bearing. Notice that the near and far ends of the base plate are perpendicular to your original bearing; this will be your new direction. Start walking in this new perpendicular direction, either left or right, as far as you need to, counting your paces as you walk.

Let's say you had to walk 100 paces to the right to get a clear shot past the hill. Orient the compass again and walk in your original direction to a point beyond the hill. Then turn left (in this case) and follow a course 100 paces back to your originally projected course. Reorient your compass and continue toward your next intermediate point.

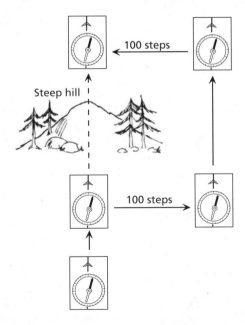

Figure 7-9: *Navigating a right-angle course around an obstacle.*

An Exercise in Compass Navigation: Following a Circuit

This circuit exercise gives you and your friends some practical experience in taking and following bearings. First, find a rather large, open outdoor area with at least a few obstacles (fig. 7-10). Pick out five or ten points on the landscape that can be linked together in a more-or-less circular course. It's more interesting if some of the points can't be seen from the starting point.

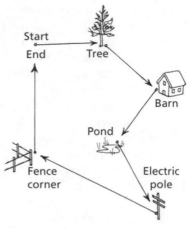

Number and describe the points on a sketch map and give everyone a copy. The object is to take bearings on each successive point, and

Figure 7-10: *Circuit exercise.*

to navigate to each successive point using compass techniques. Each participant should record the measured bearing on each leg of the circuit. After completing the circuit, the participants can compare their bearings and discuss any problems.

NAVIGATION BY GPS

Basic GPS navigation skills involve storing positions as waypoints or landmarks in your GPS receiver, traveling to waypoints, and determining the direction and distance to waypoints. Before leaving the trailhead always save the current position as a waypoint in case you have trouble finding your way back.

As you travel along your route, save waypoints now and then to allow yourself to backtrack if needed. These can be distinctive features like trail junctions, stream crossings, lakes, or saddles. GPS waypoints default to numbers that are difficult to remember, so be sure to give your waypoints distinctive names so they will be easy to distinguish later.

Storing a waypoint. The most common use of a GPS receiver is to store specific positions as waypoints or landmarks. For example, a favorite fishing spot or the location of a secluded campsite or even a spot you have never visited. Waypoints are stored by entering the position coordinates by hand from a map, by using a specific button or function that saves your current position, or if your GPS receiver is capable, by downloading waypoints from a computer with mapping software installed. The latter method is highly recommended when planning your trip at home. Mapping software allows you to easily create and name waypoints and create routes for easier navigation. You can also upload waypoints and routes from your GPS receiver to your mapping software at the conclusion of a trip for future use.

Distance and direction. Once you have waypoints saved in your GPS receiver, determine the direction and distance from your current position to a given waypoint. Many GPS receivers have a Nearest Waypoints list that displays the distance and direction to waypoints near your current position. Note that distances represented on your GPS receiver are straight lines and you have to account for variations in the route or elevation you actually travel.

Traveling to a waypoint. To travel to a waypoint stored in your GPS receiver, use the GoTo feature available in most GPS receivers. This function allows you to select a specific waypoint, and the GPS receiver will display a direct path to the location. Once GoTo is enabled, a navigation screen provides guidance using a compass or a highway that indicates the direction to travel and provides corrections if you steer off course. En route to a waypoint, a trip information screen displays your speed, heading or bearing, elevation, and estimated time of arrival, just to name a few. You must be moving for this data to be accurate.

Routes. Navigation using routes allows you to create a sequence of waypoints linked together in "legs" that guide you to your final destination. Simplify routes using your GPS receiver by automatically switching to the next leg as you approach each waypoint. You can also reverse a route to backtrack to your original starting point. Routes can be created as you travel by including selected waypoints, or prior to the trip on a computer with mapping software and transferred to your GPS receiver.

Track log. Many GPS receivers have a "track log" feature that automatically saves points at regular times or distance intervals as you travel. You can then navigate, usually back to your starting point, without marking waypoints.

NAVIGATION BY MAP AND COMPASS

The needle of a compass points toward the earth's magnetic north pole, but from most places on the earth, this is not quite the same direction as the earth's true north pole. Since maps are drawn with true north at the top, the magnetic bearings you've been setting and taking will be skewed a little, relative to directions on the map. The difference in degrees between true north and magnetic north directions as measured from any given location on the earth is the *magnetic declination.*

If you are using a compass merely as a direction finder independent of a map, then declination is unimportant. When using a map and a compass together, however, you'll have to take declination into account.

On topographic maps, magnetic declination is usually indicated at the bottom left. The symbol includes a vertical line pointing toward a star representing true north,

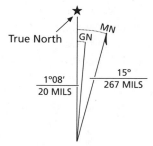

UTM GRID AND 2003 MAGNETIC NORTH
DECLINATION AT CENTER OF SHEET

Figure 7-11: *Magnetic declination symbol.*

and an arrow labeled "MN" indicating magnetic declination. Figure 7-11 shows a magnetic declination of 15 degrees east of true north.

Once you know the declination for your map, you may apply either of two methods for orienting your map correctly:

Compass-oriented map method. First place your map on a flat spot. Orient it by looking at the features around you and comparing them to the map. Then rotate the compass's circular housing to line up the orienting arrow with the direction-of-travel arrow on the base plate. Place the long edge of the base plate along the left or right border of

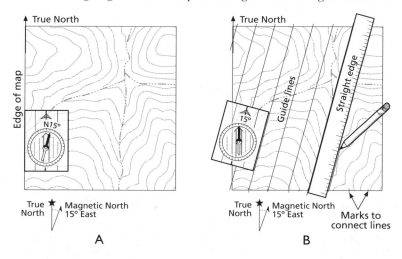

Figure 7-12: *Orienting the map: A, compass-oriented map method; B, parallel declination lines method.*

the map, with north pointing to the top of the map (don't use any vertical lines drawn inside the map area, since they can represent roads or boundaries that may not go precisely north and south).

For east declinations (for example, everywhere in the western United States), turn the map and compass together (see fig. 7-12A) until the needle points to the number of degrees on the circular housing that matches your declination. Your map now has its vertical dimension oriented to true north, and its orientation is also correct relative to the landscape around you.

Parallel declination lines method. Adding parallel declination lines to a map simplifies navigation technique when using that map in the field. It's much easier if you draw the lines on your map at home before your trip. In addition to your compass, you'll need a sharp pencil and a long ruler or straightedge.

Turn the compass housing until the scale reads the same value as your declination (this example assumes your declination is 15 degrees east). Place your map on a flat, hard surface and rotate the entire compass until the orienting arrow on the housing lines up with the border of the map. The long edge of the base plate and the direction-of-travel arrow are now lined up with the correct declination. (Double-check this by making sure they are angled in the same direction as the declination arrow on the bottom of your map.) Place the straightedge along the long edge of the base plate and draw a straight line the entire length of the map. Starting from this line, mark 1-inch increments along the top and bottom edges of the map. Then use the straight-edge to connect each pair of these marks until your map—or at least the area you'll be hiking in on the map—is covered with parallel declination lines (see fig. 7-12B).

Map orientation is very simple using this method. Rotate your map so that the parallel declination lines are also parallel to the direction of your compass needle. Make sure the north end of the compass needle points toward the top of the map, not the bottom.

Setting a Bearing

Let's assume you want to hike to a small lake you see on the map (fig. 7-13). You'll need to set a bearing on the lake from your present position and then follow that bearing.

If you are using the compass-oriented map method, lay the map on a flat spot and orient it to true north as described earlier. Place one of the back corners of your compass base plate on your current (known) location on the map. This point acts as a pivot. Hold this corner down

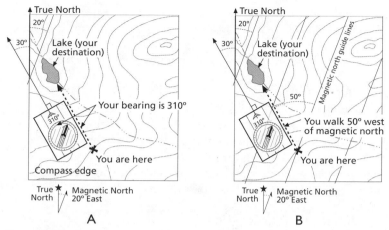

Figure 7-13: *Setting a bearing: A, compass-oriented method; B, parallel declination lines method.*

with your thumb and rotate the entire compass until the front corner on the same side of the base plate is in line with your destination. The long edge of the base plate should now be making a line between the two points. Holding the base plate in this position, rotate the circular housing until the orienting arrow on the housing lines up with the north end of the needle. You have now set your compass to the correct bearing from your location to the lake. The number of degrees is not important. As in Figure 7-13A, just follow the direction-of-travel arrow on your oriented compass to navigate to the lake.

For the parallel declination lines method, follow the first few steps described above, but rotate the circular housing until the orienting arrow on the circular housing lines up with the declination lines drawn on your map. When using this method, always ignore the magnetic needle when you're working on the map. In this case the declination lines you have drawn represent magnetic north. The direction of the needle is not important when matching the circular housing to the map. (In Figure 7-13B, a magnetic declination of 20 degrees is assumed.)

Following a Bearing

Now that you have successfully set the bearing to the lake, you are almost ready to start hiking. First choose the best route to your destination. If you start hiking without checking the route, you may end up having to climb steep hills or hike through dense vegetation. So take a few minutes to plan your route, using that wonderful tool—a map.

Take note of any obstacles you may detect on the map and mark them. Then plot your course, which may or may not be a direct route. To avoid tough spots, pick out intermediate points, take their bearings from the map, and plot a crooked course, with bearings noted for each leg.

Aiming Off

If a destination is not large, like a small lake hidden in the trees, you could walk right past it. To reduce that possibility, try to find on the map a prominent stream or an obvious road or trail touching or passing near the lake. If you find some feature like that, aim slightly off the target lake so that you cross the more obvious feature sooner or later. When you get there, you'll know which way to turn to find the lake (fig. 7-14).

Checking Your Location

A good way to keep track of your position, especially during critical navigation, is to frequently recheck your position relative to nearby landmarks and update your position on your map. You can do that by keeping your thumb on your current position on the map at all times, or by making a series of pencil marks on the map.

If, for whatever reason, you do lose track of your position on the map, use the triangle-of-error technique to rediscover your location (fig. 7-15). First choose three identifiable points both in the surrounding terrain and on the map. The closer the points are to you, the better. Take a bearing on the first point and leave it set on the compass. Transfer it as a

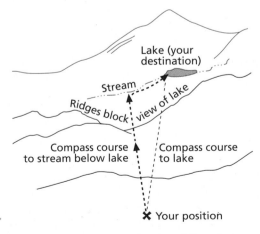

Figure 7-14: *Aiming off: Aim left of the lake, then follow the stream to the lake.*

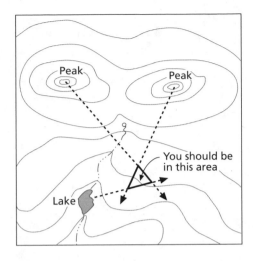

Figure 7-15: *"Triangle of error" technique.*

line on the map by placing one of the front corners of the compass on the point, holding it with your finger, and pivoting the entire compass until the orienting arrow either lines up with the north end of the needle, if you are using the compass-oriented method, or lines up with the parallel declination lines you drew on your map.

Draw a line from the first point back along the long edge of the base plate and extend it beyond where you think you are. Repeat these steps for the next two points. The three lines should converge to a small triangle, and you are somewhere inside the triangle!

If the triangle seems inordinately big, then you've erred in taking or plotting a bearing, or you may have misidentified one of your points, either on the map or on the landscape. If this happens, check your bearings and try it again.

After getting at least a general fix on where you are, it may be useful to do a second triangulation on closer landmarks (if you can identify any) to determine your location more precisely. Once you have a better fix, you may be able to determine your location to a precision of just a few yards by examining the contour lines on your map and recognizing around you the features they represent.

Taking Cross Bearings

Suppose you want to hike to a hidden spot, say a desert mine you noticed on the map, which is some distance away from an easily traveled

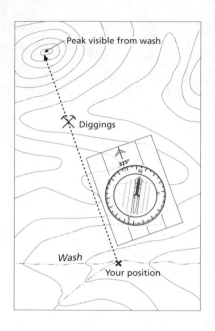

Peak visible from wash

⚒ Diggings

325°

N

E

S

W

Wash

Your position

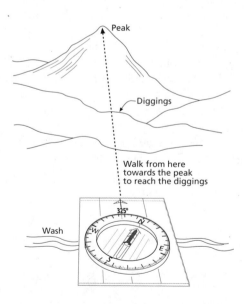

Peak

Diggings

Walk from here
towards the peak
to reach the diggings

325°

N

E

S

W

Wash

Figure 7-16: *Taking cross bearings.*

linear feature like a straight wash. Let's further suppose there are no distinguishing features along the wash to indicate the best place to turn off. But the map shows the mine lying between a distant peak and the wash (fig. 7-16).

Draw a line connecting the mine and the peak and extend it backward to where it intersects the wash. Using your compass, take a bearing of this line on the map. This is the bearing you want to follow when you reach the right spot in the wash. Set this bearing on your compass.

Then, as you walk down the wash, stop often and point the direction-of-travel arrow on the base plate toward the hill, as if you were going to take a bearing (*do not* rotate the circular housing). See if the north end of the needle lines up with the orienting arrow. If not, keep walking. As you continue, a place will be reached where the needle lines up with the orienting arrow. You're now on the bearing line you drew on the map. Turn and head toward the mine by following the direction-of-travel arrow.

NAVIGATION BY MAP AND GPS

Navigation using a map and a GPS receiver involves two basic operations: translating GPS position coordinates (your current position or any other stored waypoint) from the GPS receiver to a location on the map; and translating physical locations on the map (your destination or any other point along the way) into coordinates that can be used in the GPS receiver.

GPS receiver setup. There are a number of setup options in your GPS receiver that affect how your receiver operates and displays information. Some of the settings, including the datum and coordinate system, depend upon the map you are using and must be set correctly. Others such as distance and elevation units and declination mode are based on user preference. To use your GPS receiver with a compass, it is best to set your receiver to use magnetic headings. Contour intervals and distance units are normally set to feet and statute miles (unless your map uses the metric system).

Map datum. In order to use your GPS receiver with a map you need to make sure the GPS datum matches that of your map. A datum is a reference system that ties your GPS receiver to the map and is printed on the bottom of your topo map. Most topo maps in the United States and Canada use the North American Datum 1927 Continental, or NAD27 or NAD27 CONUS for short. Some newer maps use NAD83 or WGS84. Make sure you change the datum in your GPS receiver setup to match that of your map or your positional information will be incorrect by as much as a mile.

Coordinate system. Maps use a geographic coordinate system in the form of a grid to define specific locations. The coordinate system can be angular, expressed as latitude and longitude, or rectangular, expressed as Universal Transverse Mercator (UTM). USGS topographic maps use

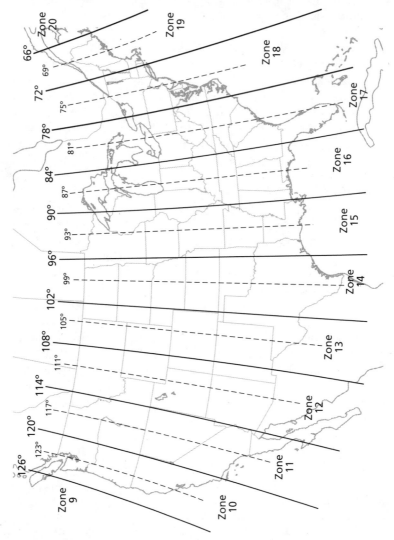

Figure 7-17: *The UTM zone coverage of the United States.*

both systems and your GPS receiver can handle either. Latitude and longitude tick marks and UTM grid tick marks are found on the sides of topo maps. UTM marks are usually colored blue. Make sure to match the coordinate system you will be using with that in your receiver setup.

The UTM grid system makes using a GPS receiver with topo maps very easy, introduces less distortion than latitude and longitude, and provides a rectangular grid with constant linear distance in all directions. Each UTM coordinate is expressed in terms of meters east and meters north of a given reference point. There are sixty UTM grid zones numbered from west to east and a number of latitude band letters measured from south to north. As shown in Figure 7-17, the United States ranges from zone 10 on the West Coast to zone 19 on the East Coast. The latitude bands range from R in south Florida to U at the Canadian border.

A UTM coordinate has two sets of numbers such as 0559264 and 3652428. The first set of numbers represents a measurement of east-west position within the zone in meters. It is called an "easting." The second set of numbers represents a measurement of north-south position within the zone in meters. It is called a "northing." The standard topo map has UTM grid lines spaced every kilometer or 1000 meters.

UTM coordinates are often abbreviated when they appear on maps to make them easier to read. For example the UTM coordinate 0559264mE and 3652428mN would have the thousands and tens of thousands of meters (third and fourth digits) in enlarged bold type and truncated to one kilometer resolution, becoming 0559 and 3652. The easting value is always given first and the northing second. Before starting out on your trip· it is helpful to draw lines connecting these UTM tick marks horizontally and vertically. The resulting 1000-meter squares make it easier to do the following steps.

Translating GPS coordinates to the map. One of the primary operations you perform is translating GPS position coordinates (your current position or any other stored waypoint) from the GPS receiver to a physical location on the map. As mentioned above, this is easy using the UTM coordinate system.

To locate your position on the map if your GPS receiver reads 11S 0559264mE and 3652428mN, look on the bottom or top edges of the map for the blue UTM grid tick mark with the numbers 0559. Then look on the left or right side of the map for the blue UTM grid tick mark with the numbers 3652 (the enlarged bold numbers indicate the thousands and tens of thousands of meters). The intersection of these two lines marks the lower left corner of the 1000-meter square you are in. Then using the last three numbers of each coordinate, measure meters

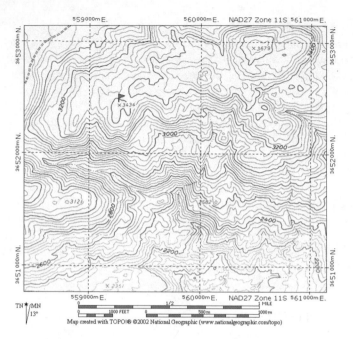

Figure 7-18: *Finding a location on a map using UTM coordinates.*

"right" and meters "up" to find your exact position (within the accuracy of the GPS receiver). In this example, the position is 264 meters right and 428 meters up. Anywhere you go, the rule for UTM is always "read right then up." Plastic templates are available with 1000-meter scales along the edges that overlay these squares to make it easy to find your exact position.

Translating map coordinates to the GPS receiver. To translate a map coordinate (your current position or another location) to the GPS receiver you need to reverse the previous procedure—determine the coordinate values (UTM or latitude/longitude) from the map and enter them in your receiver using the waypoint entry mode.

Locate the position on the map that you want to transfer to the GPS receiver and then look on the top or bottom sides of the map for the blue UTM grid tick mark closest to, but to the left of, the position. Then look on the left or right sides of the map for the UTM mark closest to but below the position. The intersection of these two lines marks the lower left corner of the 1000-meter square the point is in. Next, read meters "right" and "up" to find the exact location. Proceed to the waypoint entry screen on your GPS receiver and enter these coordinates.

SPECIAL TECHNIQUES

The techniques discussed so far are basic ones you will use again and again. There are several other techniques to be aware of for special situations.

Using Baselines

Aiming off, discussed earlier, involves intersecting a baseline, like a road or stream, and then following this baseline to the destination. In the last example (of cross bearings), you were hiking down a wash looking for a bearing line to a distant peak. When you reached the bearing line, you simply had to walk in that direction to reach the mine. There were really two baselines in that example—the wash itself and the imaginary bearing line connecting the wash, the mine, and the peak.

Imagine you've found the spot where the bearing intersects the wash and you're heading toward the mine. But after an hour you haven't found the mine and you want to head back to the wash. There are actually two baselines you can rely on (see fig. 7-19). Recheck the bearing on the peak, which is one of your baselines. Move either left or

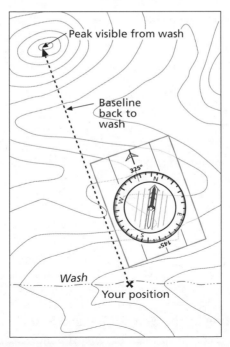

Figure 7-19: *Using baselines.*

right until you line up with that bearing and are on that baseline. Now simply walk in the reverse direction, picking intermediate points along the way if needed, until you hit the wash.

The other baseline—the wash—is even easier to find. You know it's behind you when you're facing the hill, so turn around and walk away from the hill. You will soon find the wash and can return to your starting point (if you know which way to turn when you reach the wash).

Always be aware of the location of at least one baseline—a stream, a road, or some other fairly linear feature—before you start your excursion.

Finding a Favorite Spot Again

There are other applications for the triangle-of-error technique that are useful in pinpointing a location. Imagine you are hiking in the desert and come across a beautiful Indian-made *olla* (clay vessel). You don't want to disturb it but would like to inform a ranger of its exact whereabouts. There are no distinguishing landmarks nearby, only some hills. So how can you find this spot again? You guessed it—using your compass take bearings of at least three of the hills and mark the location on your map using the triangle-of-error technique or record the location with your GPS receiver.

Dead Reckoning

When visibility is poor, it is often wiser to stay put until conditions improve. However, there may be circumstances in which it is essential to keep moving. You may not have the opportunity ahead to confirm your position very often because of darkness or fog. In this situation, you may use the technique of dead reckoning. While you are still certain of your position, find your destination on the map and mark a number of easily distinguishable points along the way. Draw lines between each of these points, take their bearings, and write them next to each point.

Set the first bearing on your compass and start walking, using intermediate points. If conditions are really bad, you may have to count your paces to determine how far you have gone. Continue doing this from point to point. This technique is risky, since you can easily lose the thread of your course. If you do, try to retrace your footprints back to the last known location. This is one occasion when the GPS is extremely useful in that it is unaffected by darkness or bad weather.

Navigating by the Sun, Moon, and Stars

Carrying a compass is a necessity on any trip in the wilderness. There are, however, a few tricks to use that will make you feel like an explorer.

The path of the sun can be used as a general direction indicator. For example, at middle latitudes in the Northern Hemisphere, the sun always lies toward the south at midday. Therefore your shadow points north at approximately 12:00 P.M. (noon) standard time, or 1:00 P.M. daylight time. On the summer solstice (in late June), the sun rises roughly in the northeast, passes high overhead in the south at noon, and sets in the northwest. On the winter solstice (in late December), the sun rises roughly in the southeast, passes low in the south at noon, and sets roughly in the southwest. During the equinoxes (in late March and late September), the sun rises due east and sets due west.

A good technique, if you're patient, is to put a stick in the ground and mark the point at the end of its shadow (fig. 7-20). Do this several more times at intervals of 10 or 15 minutes. A line connecting these points will be generally east-west; a line perpendicular will be generally north-south.

If you have a watch with sweep hands, use it to find rough directions. Make sure the watch is set for standard time (not daylight savings time) and face the sun. Move your body to point the hour hand to the horizon below the sun. South will be roughly halfway between the hour hand and 12 o'clock on your watch. This works because the sun moves only 15 degrees in an hour, while the hour hand moves 30 degrees. During the months near the summer solstice, this does not work well near the middle of the day.

During late afternoon, another interesting feat is to use your hand to estimate the time before sunset. Hold your hand at arm's length with fingers parallel to the horizon, and count the number of fingers between the horizon and the sun (fig. 7-21). Each finger represents about 10 to 12 minutes. You can also determine how long the sun has been up in the morning using the same method. Since this technique depends upon your latitude, you may want to experiment first; check how long it takes the sun to traverse one finger-width.

Like shipboard navigators, you can also use the stars to indicate directions. The stars move across the sky in the same direction as the sun, east to west. So stars that climb in the sky are somewhere

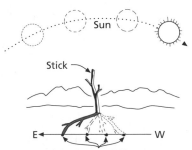

Ends of shadow at different times

Figure 7-20: *Using the shadow of a stick in the ground to determine general north-south direction.*

near east, and stars that sink are somewhere near west. Polaris (the North Star), however, hovers in the northern sky all the time.

Find Polaris by first looking for the Big Dipper. A line extended through the two outermost stars of the Big Dipper's bowl points to Polaris (fig. 7-22). When the Big Dipper is not visible, Cassiopeia usually is. The top of Cassiopeia's W-shaped form points toward Polaris. A further hint is that Polaris's altitude, or angle above the horizon, very nearly matches an observer's north latitude. An observer at Yellowstone National Park (latitude 45 degrees north), for example, would locate Polaris halfway up in the sky.

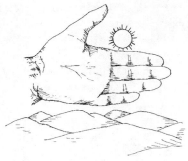

Figure 7-21: *Time until sunset is 10–12 minutes for each finger above the horizon.*

From simple day hikes to longer wilderness trips, it's important to keep your sense of direction and maintain an awareness of where you are. Carry a map and a compass when you travel in unfamiliar areas, and refer to your map often. With practice, navigational skills become everyday habits.

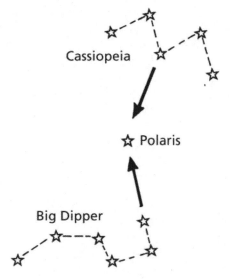

Cassiopeia

☆ Polaris

Big Dipper

Figure 7-22: *Finding Polaris using the Big Dipper or Cassiopeia.*

chapter
8

The Weather

Mark Mauricio and Keith Gordon

Unpredictability in weather forecasting has repeated itself for thousands of years, and scientists now consider meteorological systems to be inherently chaotic and unpredictable. Although the course and flow of chaotic systems cannot be predicted with absolute certainty, they do follow probable outcomes over short periods of time. Since the behavior of meteorological systems follows probable outcomes, with a little bit of knowledge, you can begin predicting the daily weather with a certain sense of confidence and reliability. As your knowledge of weather systems increases over time, your predictions become more reliable, and you can use this knowledge to be better prepared and to travel safely in wilderness settings.

The atmosphere consists of a mixture of various gases that are held close to the earth's surface by gravitational attraction. Ninety-seven percent of the air that envelopes the planet lies within 18 miles (29 km) of the earth's surface, but it is densest at sea level and rapidly thins with increasing elevation. Virtually all of the weather takes place in the lowest layer of the atmosphere, called the troposphere, which ranges from 5–6 miles (8–10 km) above the earth at the poles to about 10 miles (17 km) at the equator.

The temperature of the air within the troposphere decreases at a

At higher elevations, clouds become an extension of the mountaintop landscape. (Photo by Bob and Ira Spring.)

fairly constant rate of 3.5°F per 1000 feet (6.5°C per km) as altitude increases from the earth's surface. This uniform decrease in temperature is known as the standard lapse rate. This rate in the decline of the air temperature as altitude increases, however, can vary by geographic location and season. In addition, air that is rising or being lifted may cool at a rate of more than 5.5°F per 1000 feet.

Knowledge of the standard lapse rate can be very useful in helping to estimate the temperatures you may experience while hiking when weather conditions are dry and stable. If you know the elevation and the expected high and low temperatures in the town at the base of a mountain, you can estimate the temperatures at the mountain's peak. If the town is situated at 2000 feet and the high and low temperatures are predicted to be 75°F and 45°F respectively, then the peak of the 10,000-foot mountain should be about 28°F cooler than the town (the 8000-foot difference in the elevations multiplied by the lapse rate of 3.5°F per 1000 feet) and only warm up to about 47°F. If you plan to camp at 8000 feet, you can expect the nighttime temperatures to drop down to about 17°F. Conversely, if you're hiking down into the Grand Canyon from the north or south rim, you need to be prepared for warmer temperatures as you hike down to the canyon floor. Take note, however, that if weather conditions are fairly clear but unstable, the lapse rate can be as high as 5.5°F per 1000 feet.

PRESSURE SYSTEMS AND WINDS

Radiant energy from the sun is the earth's primary source of heat. The surface of the earth and its atmosphere, however, do not heat and cool in a uniform fashion. This creates both pockets and masses of heated air that continue to expand and rise in relationship to the surrounding air. This air continues to rise and cool until the temperature of the rising air equals the temperature of the air that surrounds it. Masses of rising air exert less pressure upon the earth's surface and are associated with low-pressure centers. In turn, pockets or masses of cool air create areas where the air is descending. This descending air warms as it flows downward toward the earth's surface. Masses of descending air exert

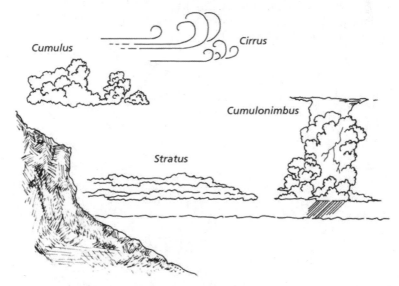

Figure 8-1: *Stratus (layered) clouds are formed by gentle lifting of warm, moist air. Cumulus (lumpy, billowy) clouds are formed by vertical air currents. Rain, hail, or snow can fall from these in heavy showers. Cirrus (wispy) clouds are the high, gossamer-like formations of tiny ice crystals that often precede the passage of a storm front. Cumulonimbus are huge, towering clouds formed by strong updrafts. The friction from air movements within these clouds builds up the electrical charges that are released as lightning. These clouds can unleash great torrents of rain or hail, but they are short-lived.*

more pressure upon the earth's surface and are associated with high-pressure centers. Air from high-pressure centers flows toward low-pressure centers to replace the air that is being lifted. This movement of air allows heat to be transferred from one place to another. You experience the horizontal movement of this air as wind.

Air pressure, also known as atmospheric or barometric pressure, is measured in inches of mercury. In the metric system, barometric pressure is measured in millibars. At sea level the atmospheric pressure is close to 29.92 inches of mercury (1000 millibars). This figure is known as the standard sea-level pressure. Measurements above the standard sea-level pressure are designated as high pressures. Measurements below 29.92 inches of mercury are considered low pressures. Low-pressure centers are commonly associated with unstable, cloudy, or stormy weather conditions. Large billowing clouds can form in these systems (fig. 8-1) and bring rain, sleet, and snow. High-pressure centers are associated with cool or cold weather and dry, stable conditions.

Figure 8-2 is a typical example of a weather map of the United States

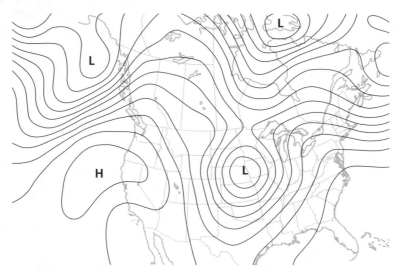

Figure 8-2: *Think of this weather map as a kind of topo map in which the contour lines (isobars) denote equal pressures across the surface of the earth. Generally, air moves from highs (H) to lows (L) across isobars, but the earth's rotation induces a clockwise circulation around a high, and a counterclockwise circulation around a low. Just as on a topo map, the closer the contour lines, the steeper the pressure gradient. The steeper the gradient, the faster the winds.*

and Canada that depicts high- and low-pressure systems at a given point in time. The lines on the map are known as isobars and connect geographic locations of equal barometric pressure. The highest barometric pressure readings are found in the center of a high-pressure system and progressively diminish as you move away from this center. The opposite occurs in low-pressure systems. Strong winds occur in areas where the isobars are crowded closely together. Weak winds occur in areas where the isobars are spaced widely apart from each other. The centers of high-pressure systems are very calm.

Due to the earth's rotation on its axis, air does not flow directly from a high-pressure system to a low-pressure system. Instead, a force known as the Coriolis Effect causes the air to be deflected to the right. This deflection causes the air in high-pressure systems to circulate in a clockwise fashion around and diverging from its center, and the air in low-pressure systems to circulate in a counterclockwise fashion and converge toward the center of the low. In the Southern Hemisphere, the Coriolis Effect causes the air to flow clockwise in low-pressure systems and counterclockwise in high-pressure systems. This movement of air led to the development of Ballot's Law, which states that a person standing with their back to the wind in the Northern Hemisphere will have a low-pressure system on their left and a high-pressure system on their right.

LOCAL WINDS

Local winds are generated by the influences of surface irregularities in the surrounding geographic terrain rather than by the influence of large pressure systems. A sea breeze occurs along a coast during the daytime when the land heats up at a faster rate than the ocean. This unequal heating causes the air to rise over the land and have a lower barometric pressure than the nearby ocean. Since air flows from areas of higher pressure to replace the rising air in areas of lower pressure, the air begins to flow from the ocean toward the land giving the coastal communities some relief from the heat. The opposite occurs at night as the land cools down at a faster rate than the nearby ocean, creating a land breeze that flows toward the ocean.

Mountain and valley winds operate in a similar fashion to the land and sea breeze. Mountain winds are created when the sides of the mountains are heated more intensely than the valleys. This causes the air to rise from the mountainsides toward the summits, with the air from the valley flowing upward to replace the rising air. During the evening, the mountainsides cool more rapidly than the valley causing a reversal in the direction of the wind.

Drainage, or katabatic, winds occur as a result of gravity influencing the flow of cold air as it moves from an area of higher elevation to a lower area. This typically occurs in winter when cold air accumulates on a high plateau or valley and then begins to spill over the divides and passes to lower elevations. These winds can be very strong and cold. Since gravity guides these winds to flow through the lowest-lying points in a valley or canyon, setting up your camp above and off the low-lying valley floor can keep you out of the flow of this frigid air, especially if the wind flow is very weak.

The dry, warm chinook winds of the northwestern United States and the foehn winds of Europe occur when strong winds pass over a mountain range and are swept down the lee slopes of the mountain range. These winds dry and warm rapidly and may cause snow to quickly melt and soil moisture to evaporate. They are quite turbulent, as the upper air is swept downward and mixes with the air below it.

The Santa Ana winds in southern California are caused by regional barometric pressure differences. Typically, there is a Pacific high west of California that causes the air to flow toward the east and inland over the western states. If a high-pressure system develops over one of the southwestern states like Nevada, and a low-pressure system develops off the southern California coast, the air flow reverses its direction sending warm, dry winds from the interior toward the ocean.

CLOUDS, PRECIPITATION, AND STORMS

Water vapor is an invisible gaseous form of water that resides in the troposphere and is colorless and odorless. It enters the air through the evaporation of water that is exposed on the earth's surface, such as an ocean, lake, or even moist soil. Some water vapor also enters the atmosphere through the transpiration of plants. The amount of water vapor present in the air is highly variable by season and from one location to another. Since warm air is capable of holding more water vapor than cold air, up to 4 or 5 percent of the air in the warm tropical climates of the earth may be composed of water vapor. During the winter, the air of the polar regions of the earth is so cold that virtually no water vapor is present.

Water vapor changes from a gaseous state to a liquid state through a process called condensation. When this occurs in the atmosphere, a visible cloud begins to take form consisting of billions of tiny droplets that are so small that they remain suspended in the air. Condensation can only occur when the temperature of the air cools down to the dew point and the air is saturated or incapable of holding any more water vapor. As the air cools below the dew point, the tiny droplets may freeze and form ice crystals within the cloud.

Raindrops form when at least a million tiny droplets coalesce into a mass too large to remain suspended in the air yet large enough to fall and strike the earth. Rain, snow, sleet, and hail are commonly referred to as precipitation and only occur when a large mass of air is being lifted to higher elevations and cooled below the dew point. This lifting occurs through convection, orographic lift by mountains, or by weather fronts.

Convectional lifting occurs when a surface area is heated more rapidly than the area adjoining it. This in turn heats the air and creates an updraft in which the warmer, lighter air rises in a tall column. If the air rises and cools to a temperature below the dew point, a cumulus cloud begins to form. These clouds take on a cauliflower shape and have a flat bottom where condensation occurs. If the convectional currents are strong, a cumulonimbus cloud or thunderstorm may develop, bringing heavy rain or hail.

Precipitation from orographic lifting occurs when an air mass laden with water vapor is forced to flow up and over a mountain range. As the lifted air is cooled below the dew point, precipitation occurs. Heavy rain and thunderstorms can also be associated with orographic lifting (fig. 8-3). Once the air passes over the range of mountains, it descends and becomes warmer and drier, creating a rain-shadow effect in which a dry climate is formed. The deserts of the American Southwest are an example of this rain-shadow effect.

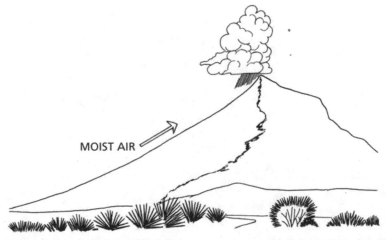

MOIST AIR

Figure 8-3: *Orographic lift.*

A front is a term that refers to the line of contact where two dissimilar air masses are separated from one another. Precipitation from weather fronts occurs as a result of air being lifted within traveling low-pressure systems. Clearing weather occurs as a high-pressure system follows behind it. These low-pressure systems typically travel at an average speed of 25 to 30 miles per hour (40 to 50 km per hour) and have a diameter between 500 and 1000 miles (800 to 1600 km). In North America, the Polar Jet Stream—a swift current of air that flows between 30,000 and 40,000 feet (10,000 to 12,000 m) and can reach speeds of more than 250 miles per hour (450 km per hour)—meanders in a broad curving track over the continent and plays an important role in directing the path of the low pressure systems. The Polar Jet Stream also generally demarcates the boundary between the cold polar air mass and the sub-tropical humid air mass from the lower latitudes.

A warm front occurs when warmer air moves into a region of cold air and replaces it. The warm air rises above the denser cold air and creates the typical sequence of clouds that is shown in Figure 8-4. The wispy cirrus clouds composed of ice crystals can sometimes be seen as far as 1000 miles ahead of the surface edge of the warm front. This can give you as much as a 2-day warning of the advancing front. The air of the warm front tends to form flat, layered stratiform clouds as the air is lifted and cooled below the dew point. Warm fronts typically produce a light steady rain or snow.

A cold front occurs when a region of warm air is displaced by colder air. The colder air mass remains in contact with the ground as the cold front wedges under the warmer and lighter air, forcing it to rise (fig. 8-5). Cold fronts are associated with strong atmospheric disturbances and have the potential to produce heavy rains or snow. A fast-moving cold

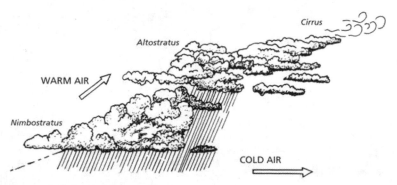

Figure 8-4: *Approaching warm front.*

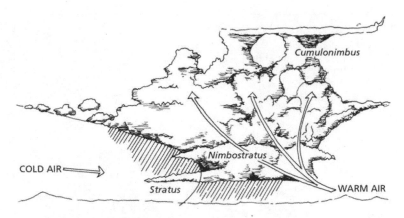

Figure 8-5: *Approaching cold front.*

front can sometimes rapidly lift the warmer air creating a line of thunderstorms or a squall line in advance of the front. Precipitation from a cold front, however, is relatively brief with cold, crisp, clear skies and scattered fair weather cumulus clouds following the wake of the front. This crisp, cold air can become very hazardous for unprepared hikers, as subfreezing temperatures may prevail, especially at night.

A cold front does not typically give you a lot of advance warning, but you will probably notice the increase in dark cumulus clouds. If you are carrying a barometer, you will notice that the barometric readings are steadily falling. In addition, you'll find that as the cold front approaches, the winds will be generally coming from the southwest. Once the front has passed, the winds shift and start flowing from the northwest. There may still be some precipitation associated with the front, but the end should be near.

A cold front generally moves faster than a warm front. If a cold front overtakes and converges with a warm front, the warm air mass is lifted entirely off the ground, forming an occluded front. The weather associated with an occluded front can be very complex, yielding the worst qualities of both warm and cold fronts.

A stationary front occurs when the surface position of a front fails to move. This occurs when the flow of air on both sides of the front is almost parallel to the front. The clouds and precipitation associated with a stationary front are very similar to the weather associated with a warm front.

Figure 8-6 displays the various symbols that are used to display the different types of fronts that can be found on a weather map. There are two cold fronts with their icicle-shaped barbs on the map. One of the

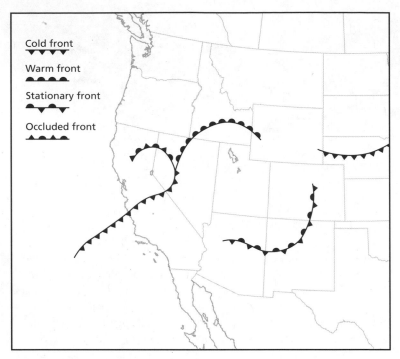

Figure 8-6: *Symbols used on weather maps for various types of fronts.*

cold fronts is moving across central Nebraska while the second cold front is moving southeast across California. A warm front symbolized with round barbs is extending across Nevada, Idaho, and the western edge of Wyoming. An occluded front is symbolized with icicle-shaped barbs and rounded barbs on only one side of the line representing the front. An occluded front extends from central Nevada to northern California. A stationary front has sharp and rounded barbs on opposite sides of the line representing the front, and can be found extending across Arizona, New Mexico, and Colorado.

FOG

Fog is a type of stratus cloud that lies close to the ground. Radiation, or tule, fog forms at night when the temperature of the air near the surface of the ground falls below the dew point. It usually forms on cold, clear nights when there is little or no wind. Radiation fog typically forms in valleys and can persist for days when conditions are stable and there is very little mixing of the air.

Advection fog occurs when warm moist air flows over a cold or snow-covered surface. Advection refers to the horizontal movement of air. Advection fog commonly occurs off the California coast when warm moist air flows across the cold coastal currents and causes the water vapor to condense. The fog simply flows with the sea breeze and is then carried onshore.

Upslope fog forms when humid air gradually moves up a steep mountainside or a gently sloping plain. The air cools due to its slow upward movement and condenses into fog. This type of fog can become very thick in mountainous areas and makes navigation very difficult, as visibility is reduced to just a few feet. Hikers in the Great Plains states may also experience this type of fog. If the air temperature is already near the dew point, fog forms as the air slowly moves westward from the Mississippi River toward the Rocky Mountains.

Steam fog occurs when cool air moves over a warmer water surface. Water vapor that has evaporated from the water surface strikes the cool air and immediately condenses. This commonly occurs over lakes and rivers during fall and early winter, giving the body of water a steaming appearance.

WEATHER INFORMATION

Two of the most readily accessible sources for weather information are newspapers and television. The information in newspapers becomes dated fairly quickly, as it is several hours old by the time the newspaper is delivered. Television news weather forecasts are timelier than newspapers, but they tend to be short and lack details. In addition, the weather report may be given by someone who knows very little about the complexities of weather. Cable television, however, typically carries a weather channel that broadcasts information continuously throughout the day. And most PBS-affiliated television stations broadcast a program called *A.M. Weather.* Airplane pilots are the target audience for this program that typically airs weekdays at 6:00 or 7:00 A.M., and it tends to be more technical than most people need. However, it is an excellent and reliable source of information.

The Internet has also allowed weather information to become readily available in your home. Wireless laptops can now access the Internet in a number of locations, including airports and restaurants that provide wireless access points. There are a number of websites that can give you basic weather information, but the National Weather Service (*www.nws.noaa.gov*) tends to be the best source.

The National Oceanic and Atmospheric Administration maintains a network of radio stations that broadcast weather conditions. Reports are updated every 4 hours, and broadcasts are transmitted on the VHF FM band between 162.40 and 162.55 MHz range. These transmissions can be picked up with any weather radio but signals can be difficult to pick up in mountainous terrain.

As your knowledge of weather increases, you'll become much more adept at predicting the weather and weather conditions. You'll also be better at critically examining weather reports that you see and hear. If the weather is going to be warm with pleasantly cool nights, shed pounds from your backpack by bringing lighter gear and clothing. You'll also feel secure in the knowledge that you will still be safely prepared for the wilderness setting. Desert hikers who keep track of winter weather are commonly willing to bravely drive through stormy mountains to experience the beauty, warmth, and sunshine of the desert. Listen and learn more about the weather around you, and you'll be hiking safer, smarter, and better enjoying your wilderness experiences.

Cumulus clouds over Utah's Grand Staircase. (Photo by Jerry Schad.)

chapter
9

Wilderness Travel

Mike Fry, Bob Feuge, Nelson Copp, Donald B. Stouder,
and Carolyn Wood

The qualities of wilderness areas are preserved when travelers leave no trace of their passage and are degraded when abused in any of dozens of ways, some of them not too obvious. You can only justify your use of a wilderness area for recreation when you strive to leave no trace.

LEARNING NEW SKILLS

Inexperienced people often don't ask questions or attempt to participate in making trip decisions because they may believe everyone else already knows the answers. Actually, being a novice means you need to ask questions about anything you don't understand. Don't hesitate to speak to the leader about a pace that's too fast, or when you need to stop to adjust your pack or clothing. Taking care of such needs immediately, rather then delaying, saves time in the long run.

Don't leave your powers of reasoning and judgment at home just because you are in an unfamiliar situation. When you're appropriately assertive, you become a responsible member of the team. Take responsibility for yourself as well as others.

Mastery, possession of skill, or technique requires time, patience, and experience. Patience is the key as you master your new skills. Remember to be patient with yourself and with others. At first, every thing takes at least twice as long as you think it will. As with other areas in life in which you were once a novice and now enjoy a certain level of mastery, wilderness travel requires you to develop new skills and new perspectives so your experience will be enjoyable and safe.

TRAILHEAD TIPS

Automobiles are by far the most commonly used mode of transportation to and from wilderness trailheads or entry points. Although criminal activity within the wilderness itself is rare, theft and vandalism can be quite common in places where people leave cars unattended for extended periods. Try to park in designated areas and let a ranger know how long your car will be parked. Don't forget to lock your car and consider leaving valuables at home. For further protection, disable your car's ignition or install an anti-theft device on the steering wheel. If you need to use a trailhead that is known to be troublesome, have someone drop you off and return to pick you up.

In some areas you may have to contend with theft and vandalism of a different kind. Bears will force their way into cars, even into trunks, to get at food they can smell. Marmots, porcupines, and other animals may chew on tires or rubber hoses under the hood.

Some of the more remote wilderness areas that don't enjoy a ban on motorized travel have dirt roads and jeep trails penetrating deep into their interiors. It is tempting for those who arrive in four-wheel-drive rigs to maneuver as far as possible into these areas. This can be detrimental to the environment, and it's quite often self-defeating. Trying to save a mile or two of walking can result in getting stuck. You may be faced with no easy way to turn around or hours of tedious digging to free your vehicle from mud, soft sand, or snow.

Not all trailheads have drinking water available, so fill up your water bottles at home. Consider bringing some water in a large container and leaving it in the car to have after you've hiked out.

TRAIL WALKING

People rarely think twice about the act of walking in everyday life. When setting off on a long journey through uneven or hilly terrain, however, carefully consider *pacing, rhythm, rest stops, foot care,* and *maintaining energy.*

Pacing. Finding your own pace or travel style on the trail can minimize fatigue and frustration. On your first few trips, notice whether you prefer a fast, moderate, or slow and steady pace. You will know in the first 15 minutes on the trail. If the pace is too slow for you, you will feel antsy and want to go more quickly. If the pace is too fast, you will find yourself out of breath and struggling to keep up. Whether "piston legs" or ambler, it is important to realize that you can't change the pace that is the most comfortable for you. The faster hiker finds it irritating to slow down and the slower-paced hiker finds it impossible to speed up. Equally important is realizing that once you find your pace and stick to it, you can reach any destination.

Rhythm. Efficient hiking requires a steady, rhythmic pace. Try not to lift your feet higher than you have to, except to swing them around obstacles like rocks and tree roots. It's better to expend your energy evenly throughout a daylong hike, rather than moving too fast in the first hour when you're feeling unbridled and strong.

After about 20 to 40 minutes on the trail, you may want to stop to remove extra clothing and adjust pack straps or shoelaces. Some trip leaders make this first stop a "divided halt," suggesting that men go in one direction and women another, to take care of any unmet needs.

Some hikers, especially those who are physically well trained, experience a second wind—a surge of energy that follows an initial period in which the body accustoms itself to the demands of hard exercise. With a second wind you may feel more comfortable going faster, but, again, resist the temptation to do so if you intend to be walking all day.

When walking up very steep slopes, you won't want to become so winded that you can't continue. One solution is to save energy by using the rest step. In this technique you pause briefly with your weight on your straight leg before you begin a new step: As your weight passes over your leg, move your knee back so that when it straightens, your muscles can relax. This allows full circulation and keeps your legs much happier. The rest step is easier to do on a steep slope than on flat ground, so practice it there to gain a sense of rhythm.

Some hikers swear by a hiking staff or trekking poles, which benefit knees on uphills and downhills. The poles help you to lower yourself (especially with a full pack) down steep trails that would otherwise kill your knees. You can also use your arm and shoulder muscles to help your quads when going uphill. Staffs and poles become part of the rhythm of your hiking pace and can add more stability when crossing water, extending your reach, and testing the steadiness of rocks.

A staff can be advantageous in areas where balance is precarious, but awkward when you need both hands for climbing or where dense vegetation renders it useless. Pick a hiking staff that is not much taller than the level of your hand when your arm is bent at 90 degrees. Trekking poles are like ski poles. Some come with spring-loaded shock absorbers, and most are adjustable. Before you buy, try one on a short hike. If it feels comfortable, it will eventually seem like an extension of your arm. If it seems like an unnecessary nuisance, it is.

Rest stops. Throughout the day, stop at regular intervals of 30 minutes or an hour to rest, relieve the pack weight, stretch, or grab a snack. Make these rests brief—5 minutes is good—so that you don't cool down too much or become stiff. Experiment with taking breaks. Some find that a 10-minute stop every hour works best. Others may decide to stop only when hungry. In unfamiliar areas, you should be keeping track of your position, so rest periods are excellent times to update or confirm your location on a map.

For longer rest stops, put on extra clothing immediately if the

Rest stops are important to adjust gear, hydrate, have a snack, and enjoy the view. (Photo by Arleen Tavernier.)

weather is cool or cold. The sensation of warmth you get from hiking uphill is your body shedding heat while it expends extra energy. Warm, sweaty skin can turn cold within minutes after you stop.

Slower hikers often need as much—or more—time for breaks as faster hikers. It can be most frustrating when a slower hiker catches up to others taking a break, only to have them take off moments later. Feeling pressured to stick with the group, the slower hiker may not have enough time to recover, eat, and drink, thus increasing fatigue even more. In the case of a trip designed on a tight schedule, this may be unavoidable. If there's discretionary time on the hike, though, the slower persons should be assertive and make their needs and desires known. The benefit of a rest stop is not resting (that takes hours), but eating, drinking, taking bathroom breaks, attending to feet and clothing, and applying more sunscreen. If you neglect any of these, you will be sorry. Make sure that everyone in your group has all the time they need before you proceed.

Foot care. Foot blisters simply can't be ignored. Heed the first signs of friction (hot spots): Adjust your socks, put on moleskin, or do whatever it takes to relieve the pain and prevent damage to the skin. (See Chapter 16, Wilderness First Aid, "Blisters.")

Maintaining energy. When extra energy is needed, your body usually tells you so—you get hungry and feel fatigued. Dehydration is more insidious. When you're strenuously exercising, your body usually needs more fluids than thirst dictates. In hot weather, it's difficult for the body to absorb moisture fast enough. While in dry, cold weather, a surprising amount of moisture can be lost from breathing hard and from "insensible perspiration," perspiration evaporating just to keep the air humid near your skin. Your skin tries to maintain humidity even when the air is dry. Sip water or other fluids at frequent intervals, even though you may not feel thirsty. If you don't feel the need to urinate every couple of hours or if your urine is bright yellow, you aren't drinking enough fluids and your body will not be working at its peak performance.

Different people have different lengths of stride. For example, a 5-foot-4-inch-tall person either has to have a naturally faster pace to keep up with the longer strides of a 6-foot-tall person, or they have to agree to not worry about hiking at the same pace. This is also true when there is a difference in physical condition. Realize that sharing your wilderness experience may mean you share lunch breaks and camp time, but not necessarily every step along the way.

If you know you're significantly slower than others on a trip, it's

essential you communicate this. If it's a formal or club-sponsored trip, let the leader know. Slower-paced hikers are most likely only 5–10 minutes behind the fastest hiker, anyway. You can verify this easily by having the lead hiker time how long it takes for you to reach him or her after he or she has stopped. Normally the leader keeps the group together, but that's not always realized in practice. In such instances, consider using two-way radios, which are inexpensive and effective for communication within the group. For safety reasons, it is vital that slower-paced hikers learn to read their trail maps. Before setting out, look at the map with your hiking partner or the trail leader and identify possible points of confusion (e.g., where other trails cross your trail). Agree when or where to meet next, such as when the trail splits off or at the first water crossing. Agree to a trail marker at unexpected points of confusion: a bandana tied on a bush down the correct trail, or an arrow drawn in the dirt or made with pebbles with a word or phrase that identifies it for you alone. Once you have reached your special trail marker, remove it to avoid confusing others using the same trail.

Hikers in groups can get spread apart just as readily when hot shots insist on forging ahead. Courtesy dictates that on organized hikes, anyone wishing to go ahead of the leader asks permission first. Trailblazers, the faster-paced ones in the lead, need to be alert to points where there is unanticipated confusion, such as a missing trail sign or a false trail. Leave clear directional signs or wait until your partner or group reaches you. Always stop at the agreed-upon rendezvous point or time.

Hiking etiquette also requires that you yield the right-of-way to horses and other pack animals. The pack-train leader, who knows his or her animals well, may ask you to move to a position where the animals can pass safely. This can be a tense moment; gather the group to one side of the trail, stand quietly, and don't do anything that may play upon the animals' skittish tendencies. If you are on a hill, the safest side of the trail is uphill. However, this may make you look bigger and hence unfamiliar to the pack animals. Take guidance from the rider or the pack-train leader, who knows the animals' tendencies. Talking in quiet tones to the animals may help put them at ease.

CROSSING STREAMS AND RIVERS

Most trails have bridges of some sort across streams and rivers. Bridges might be elaborate structures or simply large logs with cross-hatches

Opposite: *McGee Creek, in the Sierras. (Photo by Carol Murdock.)*

carved in them for better traction. However, some trails require crossing streams or rivers on foot. This can be accomplished safely, though fording fast-moving streams can be deceptively dangerous.

First you'll need to choose the best spot to cross. Where water flows through a constricted area, as between boulders, you may be able to hop over safely if the gap is narrow enough. However, the water flows fastest there, so these areas are most dangerous if you fall in. Wider stretches may contain either deep pools with slow-moving water or fast-moving, shallow water with riffles.

Take the time to thoroughly investigate well above and below where you want to cross. Make certain there are no waterfalls or swift rapids below your intended crossing spot in case you stumble. If the water is more than knee deep and very swift at the most favorable spots, consider turning back, outflanking the stream via a long detour, or waiting until the water flow decreases. The latter alternative is often practical for streams fed by snowmelt. In the early morning, such streams may be running at far lower levels than during the heat of the afternoon.

When fording fast-moving streams, always wear shoes to protect your feet from sharp rocks. Many people change into a pair of sneakers or river sandals, but wearing your boots—snugly laced to your feet, with or without socks and liners—will protect your feet better. If you're going to be wading through water quite often, consider wearing lightweight boots with uncoated fabric panels and polypropylene socks. The water quickly drains from the boots and socks, preventing a clammy feeling. Applying a lubricant such as petroleum jelly or Bag Balm (a veterinary product for cows) helps prevent prune toes and keeps your feet a little more comfortable. Gaiters help keep sand and gravel out of your boots.

Before wading in, try to estimate the stream's depth and toss a twig in to gauge the speed of the flow. Loosen your pack straps and unhook the hipbelt and sternum strap in case you fall in (your pack is expendable, you're not). Use a hiking staff, trekking poles, or a sturdy branch as a third leg upstream of yourself while crossing. Cross facing upstream and move sideways so your three points of support form a triangle. If the current is swift, choose a path that takes you diagonally across and downstream so that you won't have to fight the force of the water quite as much as you lift each foot.

More sophisticated methods of stream crossing involve rigging a rope across the stream to assist passage. Never tie yourself to the rope—if you fall, the rushing water can hold you under. Cross on the downstream side of the rope, holding on as you walk across.

Be especially careful about waterfalls downstream of your crossing. Every year, people are killed in the mountains by being swept over waterfalls.

CROSS-COUNTRY TRAVEL

Cross-country, or off-trail, travel can be more challenging and more fun, but often more dangerous and environmentally harmful. Cross-country doesn't mean shortcutting switchback trails—a harmful practice that promotes erosion. Cross-country travel can take a hiker or climber to remote peaks and other secluded destinations where there are no trails, but it's usually slower and more difficult than trail travel. Navigational difficulties increase as well. In a few well-traveled wilderness areas, off-trail travel is prohibited because the impact is too harmful, or it is restricted because of wildlife. In some very remote areas, such as parts of Alaska and northern Canada, there are very few trails and hikers routinely travel cross-country.

Make sure your equipment and clothing are up to the task. Wear long pants to protect against rocks, ticks, and low-lying vegetation; wear a long-sleeve top if scratchy vegetation is likely to be at least waist-high. Sturdy boots help protect against ankle twists and stone bruises caused by rolling rocks. Gaiters (normally used in deep snow) fastened around your ankles and boots can keep debris out of your boots.

Cross-country travel is more appropriate for smaller groups than for hordes of people. Groups should stay close together in order to remain within earshot of one another. Single-file travel is usually most efficient, especially in areas choked by dense brush or vegetation. Don't let tree and shrub limbs that you have pushed aside snap back into the face of the person who follows you. Keep a good distance.

In general, it is best to keep to a single-file, low-impact system. However, there are certain times when you need to make your own choices. When crossing rough terrain, hopping streams, or scrambling over boulders, leg length, physical condition, and pace make a difference. Learn to identify routes that work well with your ability, level of comfort, and leg length. It can make the difference between an easy and a difficult experience.

When traversing delicate ground or vegetation, single-file hikers can cut a deep furrow and hasten erosion. To minimize impact, spread out and, when possible, try to skirt delicate areas such as wet meadows.

Plotting a cross-country route, either at home (with maps on the

Cross-country travel can be the most challenging, and most enjoyable part of your trip. (Photo by Carol Murdock.)

table) or in the wilderness itself, is intriguing and challenging. In most cases, you should try to follow the same route that a trail builder would. Trails are often intentionally routed to avoid steep ascents, steep terrain, and obstacles such as rock outcrops—even though hikers using them will have to walk farther to get from point A to point B. When planning or choosing a cross-country route, weigh the advantages of ascending or descending a steep hill against the advantages of a longer but more gradual route around the hill. Take into account the nature of the terrain along each alternate route. Try to avoid crossing steep gullies that could contain drop-offs or harbor snow late into the season. Take into account the types of vegetation—thick brush, open forest, or perhaps a lack of vegetation (as on scree)—that might be present on any of the alternate routes.

Whether it is more efficient to travel along canyon bottoms or streams as opposed to parallel ridges depends on the nature of the local geography. Does the canyon bottom or stream meander excessively? Will frequent stream crossings slow you down? Are the ridgelines spiked by rock outcrops, or are they smooth and relatively free of impeding vegetation?

In practice, routefinding over rough terrain is an exercise in improvisation. Despite your initial planning, you will find it necessary to change your intended course many times. Just keep your eyes open and your mind focused on the important milestones or destinations ahead on your intended route.

When traveling cross-country, keep safety uppermost in your mind at all times. Shortcuts over difficult terrain may be tempting, but often they're a waste of time and effort if not outright dangerous. Cross-country travel is a mind game involving elements of intuition as well as standard navigational skills. Improvements in skill only come through experience.

TRAVELING AT NIGHT—A SPECIAL SKILL

Generally, wilderness travelers should always try to arrive at camp or at the car before nightfall. If lost at night, it is almost always better to stay put and resume hiking in daylight. For a properly equipped hiker with the Ten Essentials (see Chapter 5, Outfitting), an overnight bivouac should present no problems.

Under certain circumstances, it may be preferable to press on at night, assuming you're not lost. Experienced outdoorspeople may elect to travel over familiar trails or terrain at night in order to gain a unique nocturnal perspective of nature.

Travel at night requires that you see as well as possible. If there's a full or nearly full moon in the sky, you're in luck. When traveling by moonlight, try to preserve your night vision. Generally a trail is more visible to a dark-adapted eye than to one dazzled by a glaring flashlight beam. If you do use a flashlight, hold it low to pick out the shadows of obstacles on the route ahead. Headlamps are of limited value for hiking because shadows cast by the light are in the same direction as the hiker's line of sight and therefore can't be seen. Two flashlights—one a broad-beam lamp on the head, the other a regular flashlight in the hand—work best.

You'll discover that if you can retain your adaptation to darkness, your peripheral vision is quite good because the periphery of your retina is rich in the rod cells that come into play under low light levels. In order to preserve this advantage while also using some artificial light, some hikers use a red filter over their flashlight (a single or double layer of red cellophane over the flashlight lens or around the bulb works well). This eliminates other colors present in white light that tend to spoil a person's night vision.

WILDERNESS CAMPING
Selecting a Campsite

When you choose a campsite, do so not only with your comfort in mind but also the care of the environment. Strive to observe Leave No Trace principles and to clean up or restore camping areas that have been abused by others. If not done properly, camping can affect the wilderness far more seriously than any kind of travel through it. (See Chapter 2, Outdoor Ethics, "Leave No Trace Skills and Ethics")

Even when not required, try to use designated or previously used campsites. Your site should be a minimum of 200 feet from lakes, streams, and trails. Avoid camping in areas subject to runoff or rockfall, or below rotten trees. Never camp in delicate areas such as alpine meadows. Sandy areas or forest duff are preferred over those covered by vegetation. Since cold air often flows downward at night and collects in low-lying spots, a higher campsite may be warmer. Flying insects are often much less abundant in the higher and drier areas as well. Consider also the effects of wind and the position of the sun as it rises the next morning. Camping on an east-facing slope sheltered from a west wind will make it easier for you to get up the next morning.

When camping in popular areas, be a considerate neighbor. Don't crowd other campers. Leave sound equipment, pets, and other reminders of the civilized world at home. Peace and quiet are two of the earth's most valuable resources. Listen to the soft music of the wilderness: wind, water, and birdsong.

When selecting a site for your tent or sleeping bag, remove small rocks and twigs, but avoid wholesale grading. (And when leaving a campsite, be sure to return the rocks and twigs to where you found them.) The century-old practice of cutting branches for bedding is environmentally harmful and unnecessary. Lightweight sleeping pads provide you with all the cushioning you need. During mild weather, sleeping under the stars can be carefree and enjoyable. Cold, rain, or mosquitoes, however, may require more shelter and dictate the need for a tent or shelter such as a bivouac sack, a tube tent, or a tarp rigged overhead. You can eliminate the annoyance of mosquitoes and other biting insects by applying insect repellent, using netting in a tent, wearing a head net, or moving to a breezy spot where the insects can be blown away.

Sanitation

Another challenge at the campsite is sanitation. The techniques of eliminating body wastes and maintaining privacy—especially when part of a group—can be problematic.

Urination is not a complicated issue, since urine is normally biologically sterile, although it can cause odor problems too close to camp (try to keep your toilet downwind from camp). If nature calls in the middle of the night, clearly elimination is simplest outside the tent, but you might use a tent bottle. This is common on mountaineering expeditions, when weather conditions may not allow you to go outside.

Women can use a tent bottle along with a special funnel designed for their anatomy. Some backpacking shops and mail-order companies carry funnels. At home, set aside a one-liter plastic bottle with a narrow top. Spray-paint the bottle, except for an area masked from top to bottom to provide a clear space to view its contents.

A one-liter bottle handles about two to four average "pees." Set up your private indoor bathroom before you go to sleep: have your pee bottle and funnel, a small pack of tissues, a couple of premoistened towelettes, a self-sealing plastic bag, and your flashlight (a headlamp works best) nearby. Stay off your sleeping bag when first practicing the technique. After filling the tent bottle, screw the top back on immediately. Let the tissues catch any drips from the funnel, leave the funnel out to dry, and stash the tissues and towelettes in the plastic bag. Next day, empty the bottle (scatter the urine and try to avoid hitting plants), rinse if possible, and let it air out.

To deposit solid body waste when a pit toilet or latrine is not available, travel 200 feet or more from camp and any water source. Dig a cat hole 6–8 inches deep, squat down, and when finished, fill in the hole with soil and tamp it down. Pack out all toilet paper to the trailhead.

The squat position may be difficult and can become unbearable if maintained for a long time, but there are a number of options: If there's a tree with low, strong branches nearby, hold on and balance yourself over the hole. If you can find a small log or a rock in a private spot with soft soil beside it, use it as a kind of a toilet seat while extending your buttocks over the hole. Or dig the cat hole near something you can lean back into, although this is tricky and it is better to put something soft between your lower back and the log or rock to prevent scrapes. Try balancing with your hands behind you and your feet in front of the hole. Or rest your hiking stick on your shoulder and hold it in the middle for balance.

Many people report that half of their internal plumbing system refuses to function smoothly while on wilderness trips. Of course, no one ever dies from a few days of constipation. In some cases, it is due to a change of diet. Some people are susceptible to "inhibition constipation," which is probably triggered by being uncomfortable about toileting in the outdoors. Inhibition constipation can be overcome by first understanding that you are not the only one who has experienced it. Try drinking something warm shortly after waking up. Take the time to find a pleasant spot far enough away from camp that affords absolute privacy. Allow yourself plenty of time to relax and let nature take its course. If you're on a trip with a tight schedule, then plan to wake up earlier so you'll have enough time. You can even prepare your latrine the evening before. Be careful where you dig a hole, though. You won't want some unsuspecting member of your party tripping in the night.

For women, the decision of whether or not to travel in the wilderness during menstruation depends on experiences at home. If cramping and flow are normally no problem, you'll find your menstrual periods in the wilderness are only slightly inconvenient. Bring along zipper-locked plastic bags for used sanitary products, extra tissues, and moistened towelettes.

Always pack in a full supply of sanitary products. Even women with menstrual cycles like clockwork may find that altitude, heavy exercise, or excitement can alter the normal pattern. Even if you don't end up using most of your supplies, there may be a less-prepared woman in the group who might be very grateful for your foresight.

In the event you are caught short of supplies, extra panties, socks, tee shirts, bandanas, or handkerchiefs can be used. Fold the piece of cloth to fit, and secure to underclothes with safety pins, if available. When your improvised items are used up, wash them out at least 200 feet away from any water source, or bag them up in a zipper-locked plastic bag and pack them out as you would with used sanitary products. Don't burn used sanitary products or toilet paper. Some products don't burn completely anyway, since they're made of other substances in addition to paper.

While there used to be many options for getting rid of garbage, now there are only two: Use trash cans where available, or pack out all garbage from areas where garbage cans are not available.

Washing Up

How to live without the conveniences of a bathroom is a major concern for beginners, but life without a shower is simple to master. Generally on shorter trips you won't need to wash your whole body, your hair, or your clothes, but on longer trips bathing can be a welcome refresher. Often you can find a good swimming hole to wash off the day's dust, but don't use soap or shampoo because they degrade slowly and leave a lot of suds. For freshening up, use moist towelettes or baby wipes, but remember, for this type of convenience, you will be carrying in extra weight that you have to carry out.

The simplest bathing facility is the largest cooking pot you already have along. (There are plastic fold-up basins that can serve as a mini-bathtub for washing feet and clothes, but this extra weight is probably only necessary on longer trips.) Bathe a minimum of 200 feet from the main water source. With a sunny site, you can wash with cold water. If you have enough fuel, heat some wash water or use any clean hot water left after washing dishes. Use only biodegradable soap, and use it sparingly.

For full luxury, bring a portable, plastic minishower bag, which, when filled with water and left on a sunny rock for a few hours, gives you an adequately warm shower. (The bag is also useful for bringing water to camp.) Or fill the shower bag with water you've heated—this is quicker and ensures the water is warm enough, but it does use fuel. The 1.5-gallon shower bag is fine for a two-person shower, including hair washing, if you are each conservative in your water use. Remember to put your shower setup in a place where the runoff does not go into a water source. If possible, stand on a rock to keep your feet clean.

Arrange your after-shower clothes for easy access. Pick a sunny and draft-free site to rig a shower enclosure with your poncho, some rope, and a couple of trees.

Campfires

Many hikers look forward to the pleasure of a crackling campfire. Remember, though, that in many wilderness areas they're prohibited or regulated by fire permit. Actually you rarely need a fire. Cooking needs can be easily met with a camping stove (see Chapter 5, Outfitting, "Stoves and Cooking Equipment"). A candle lantern, used instead of a fire, can add a nice warm touch, and your high-tech clothing should keep you reasonably warm.

If you do have a fire, make it small. Bonfires waste large amounts of wood and are difficult to extinguish. Besides, you'll enjoy the closer companionship of your friends as you crowd around the glowing embers of a small fire. Whenever possible, use the stove units found at some designated campsites, or use existing rock rings at other sites where fires are permitted. Make sure your fire is completely out when you turn in. Empty your water bag on it, and stir the coals to make sure you've found all the hidden hot spots.

With or without a fire, being cold at night is a common complaint. For a list of tips to keep you warm, see Chapter 15, Winter Mountaineering, "Tips for Staying Warm at Night."

SAFETY CONCERNS

In wilderness areas, there are often hazards that you may encounter and should be prepared for, though most travelers do not experience these misfortunes.

Poison Oak, Poison Ivy, and Poison Sumac

Poison oak, poison ivy, and poison sumac thrive in moist ravines and canyons, as well as on hillsides and even hilltops (if protected from intense sunshine), below about 5000 feet elevation. The maxim "leaves of three, let it be" is a good one. Learn to recognize these plants and to distinguish them from other three-leaved plants (wild blackberries, for example) that are harmless.

By wearing long pants and a long-sleeved shirt, you can keep skin contact to a minimum. In winter, and sometimes in very dry conditions, poison oak loses its leaves but still retains its irritating oil. Learn to recognize the stem color and structure of the plant before you do any cross-country hiking among the leafless plants. For treatment options if you've been exposed to poison oak, sumac, or ivy, see Chapter 16, Wilderness First Aid, "Rashes."

Ticks

When hiking along overgrown trails or bushwhacking (traveling cross-country in brushy terrain), check yourself frequently for ticks. These small, blood-sucking parasites feed on wild animals such as deer and domestic animals such as horses, dogs, and cattle. They lie in wait on the tips of shrub branches along hiking or game trails, lodging on warm-blooded creatures that come along.

If you're in tick country, wear long plants and a long-sleeved shirt. Tuck the hems of your pants into your socks for further protection. Wear a scarf around your neck and a hat. Scan your clothing—and your hiking partners—for ticks, and brush them off before they crawl out of sight.

If a tick successfully hitches a ride on a human host, it usually crawls to some protected spot underneath clothing before choosing a spot to attach itself. By visually checking yourself often, and by being aware of the slightest irritations on your body, you can intercept the tick before it digs in. If it does bite, you will almost certainly be aware of an itchy irritation.

Ticks can be difficult to remove when attached. For instructions on removing ticks and treating their bites, see Chapter 16, Wilderness First Aid, "Bites." Lyme disease is carried by ticks. A red ring spreading outward from the bite may indicate Lyme disease, which can produce arthritis-like joint problems. See your doctor for tests and treatment.

MOUNTAIN RUNNING

Another form of nonmotorized travel in wilderness areas, in addition to hiking and backpacking, is mountain running, or adventure running, which is becoming popular among hard-core athletes. A trained runner carrying minimal gear can easily cover two or three times as much distance over trails as a lightly burdened day hiker can. A good technique used by some is to mix running and walking. The easier stretches of trail (the smoother, flatter, or slightly downhill parts) are run, while the rougher, steeper stretches are walked.

Running a trail allows you to get to and from remote areas quickly, but it also exposes you to danger if you are not aware of your limitations or are careless about preparation. As on any wilderness outing, you need to carry enough survival gear to cover emergencies. Small backpacks that strap on tightly and hip-hugging fanny packs that don't bounce can be used to stow minimal gear such as extra clothes and food. Carry water bottles in your hands or in a special carrier secured to the back of a belt. Or use a water delivery system that stores water in a pack and has a plastic tube so you can drink while on the run.

Traveling with companions is especially important when on running excursions. Usually the amount of survival gear you carry is quite meager, and you may need to send for help if you run into a serious problem.

chapter
10

ANIMAL ENCOUNTERS

Bob Feuge

Encountering wild animals in their natural habitat can enhance your enjoyment of the wilderness. If you're quiet and observant, you'll increase your chances of spotting wildlife and observing their behavior. But unexpected encounters can be surprising and exhilarating, causing you to forget that the wilderness is really their home and that you are the intruder. As a considerate intruder, do not disturb wild animals or their habitats; do not feed, harass, or handle wild animals (even if they're injured); and do not disturb the nest or den of a wild animal.

No matter how cute or how tame a wild animal appears, never feed it. When animals develop a taste for human food, such as the goodies in your pack, they can easily come to depend on it. Reliance on unnatural and unpredictable food sources may reduce the animal's chances for survival in the wild. By accepting food handouts, wild animals quickly lose their fear of man, their natural predator. This process, called habituation, can become destructive. A classic example of habituated animals is the black bears of Yosemite National Park, which raid trash cans and campgrounds for food, undeterred by human presence. These animals became pests and a danger to humans. When animals become dangerous, they are evacuated to remote areas or destroyed. "A fed bear is a

Though a marmot may look tame and friendly, you should never feed it or any other wild animal. (Photo by Blake Cournyer.)

dead bear," states Stephen Herrero, a leading authority on bear ecology, behavior, and attacks. The very act of feeding a wild animal can also be dangerous. Some animals do "bite the hand that feeds." If bitten, you risk rabies, serious injury, and even death.

Never harass wild animals, even if it seems the animal would suffer no harm. Harassment includes throwing rocks, chasing, and invading their habitat, unless such actions are necessary for self-defense. Photographers are often guilty of unwittingly harassing animals to get better shots. In doing so, they risk retaliation. A harassed mother bear can charge and even kill a person if she feels her young are under attack. It's better to remain quiet and simply observe or photograph animals from afar.

The practice of handling wild animals, even if they appear tame and friendly, carries risk as well. Wild animals carry fleas and ticks that spread plague, Lyme disease, and Rocky Mountain spotted fever. Handling can promote harmful habituation of the animal and increases your risk of being bitten. It may lead to injuring the animal as well. Handling young animals (especially birds and eggs in nests) can result in parental abandonment.

In the wild, you'll occasionally come upon an injured or abandoned animal. Being compassionate, you'll want to intervene and assist the animal. According to many naturalists, however, human intervention is not the best course of action. Animals have natural defensive abilities that may be thwarted by human actions, leaving them even more defenseless later on. A doe, for instance, deliberately abandons a young fawn to lure a would-be attacker toward her and away from the fawn. In such situations, the fawn (which has no odor) simply lies down and waits motionless for the doe to return. Human intervention can destroy this natural defense strategy and cause the doe to forsake the fawn. Injured animals in the wilderness should be left alone to nature's course. This can be a heartrending decision, but it's best in the long run.

BEARS

A sudden encounter with a bear in the wilderness is both exciting and potentially dangerous. Grizzly bears and black bears live in the temperate regions of the western United States and Canada. Encounters with each type must be handled differently to minimize the chance of injury.

Within the North American continent, the modern range of bears has shrunk to encompass the larger mountain ranges of the West and a few areas in the East (see fig. 10-1). The black bear is found in almost

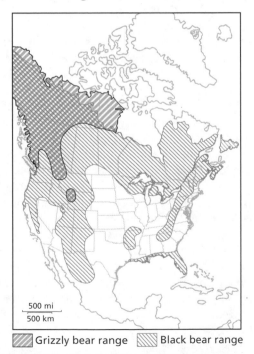

500 mi
500 km

░ Grizzly bear range   ░ Black bear range

Figure 10-1: *Comparative ranges of black and grizzly bears.*

all mountainous regions of the western United States and beyond. The grizzly is mostly limited to regions in and around Yellowstone and Glacier National Parks in the United States—though there have been sporadic sightings of grizzlies in the Cascades, some as far south as the Mount St. Helens area—and in many provincial and national parks in western Canada. Alaska is prime habitat for black bears and grizzlies, as well as for the coastal variety of grizzly known as the Kodiak or the Alaskan brown bear.

Bears are omnivores—they'll eat almost anything, including nuts, berries, bark, insects, fish, and small animals. A bear's diet changes with the seasons and the climate. Bears spend much of their waking hours foraging far and wide for food, moving mainly along established trails or stream banks, or through wildlife tunnels in dense vegetation. In dry seasons, bears readily invade populated areas to look for food.

Much of the conflict that occurs between humans and bears stems from an underestimation of a bear's mental and physical prowess. Bears are not far behind primates in order of intelligence. They're extremely curious animals that tend to investigate whatever piques their curiosity. While humans rely primarily on visual sense, bears rely on a very keen sense of smell. Bears readily investigate unusual smells, not necessarily those related to food. They'll check out sunscreen lotion, toothpaste, and lipstick, to name a few. Relative to humans, bears are superior in strength, probably poorer in vision, and probably equally endowed in hearing. Despite their ponderous appearance, they're quite capable of outrunning humans, climbing trees, and swimming.

Is it foolish for women to go into areas frequented by bears menstruating? Experiences vary. Plenty of women have visited bear country while menstruating with no incident. Female bear-keepers at zoos report that no additional precautions are taken, or recommended, during their menstruation. There has been only one report of a menstruating woman being fatally mauled. A basic precaution is suggested in the book *Bear Attacks: Their Causes and Avoidance* (Stephen Herrero, Nick Lyons Books, 1985): Wear unscented tampons, not pads.

Black bear or grizzly? Figure 10-2 shows some anatomical differences between black bears and grizzly bears. The black bear is shy, preferring to avoid humans unless it is habituated, protecting its young, or desperate for food.

A grizzly bear must always be regarded as a potential threat. Grizzlies may interpret a sudden encounter with a human as a threat and

Figure 10-2: *Comparative physical characteristics of black and grizzly bears. Black bears, despite their name, range in color from black to brown to cinnamon. Grizzlies are generally brown in color and larger than black bears.*

will charge, maul, and even kill with little warning. What seems threatening to a grizzly may not coincide with your idea of a threat.

The best way of preventing an attack by a bear is to avoid surprising or threatening the bear. Do not do *anything* to threaten cubs, since the mother is certainly nearby and will defend her cubs aggressively. If you somehow provoke a mother bear with cubs, do not defend yourself, and do not run, but retreat as quickly and unthreateningly as possible.

In grizzly country, it's wise to make noise (sing, talk loudly, ring bells) on the trail. Look for signs of grizzly presence, such as claw marks on trees, scat (feces), and prints. If you do spot a grizzly, it's best to circle about widely (staying downwind of the bear), or simply abort the hike. With grizzlies, you have little control of the situation, so aborting the hike may be the wisest course of action.

If a grizzly attacks, however, it is usually responding to what it considers a territorial dispute. You have only one alternative: play dead (see fig. 10-3). Playing dead removes the perception that you are a threat. Never charge a grizzly or run from it. The passive response may result in some mauling, but generally the bear will not continue the attack once it has asserted its dominance. If the bear continues to be aggressive, then change tactics and do whatever is possible to save your life. If a tall tree is immediately available, you might try to outclimb a grizzly. Since grizzlies are fast and also climb well for a large animal, this strategy may not work. Your best strategy, of course, is early detection and avoidance.

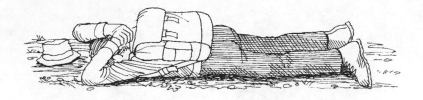

Figure 10-3: *Positions for "playing dead" during a grizzly bear attack: Top, hands behind neck, with arms protecting the face and side of the head; Bottom, fetal position, lying on one's side.*

Black bears are not prone to attack. Their occasional attacks on humans are most likely to be predatory—a child or small adult may be viewed as prey to a large, hungry black bear. If that happens, don't be passive! Defend yourself—kick, yell, throw rocks, swat it with a branch. The bear will usually back down. Don't climb a tree, since black bears can probably climb a tree as high as—and much faster than—you.

Camping techniques in bear country. When selecting a campsite in bear country, it's best not to camp immediately alongside a trail or a stream, because bears travel in these areas searching for food.

Bears also like to investigate regularly used campsites, usually at night. If you detect tracks, scat, or other signs of a bear (e.g., claw marks on trees) in the vicinity of your selected campsite, keep moving. By understanding bear behavior, you can ensure that the only bear victories will be in Chicago!

At the campsite itself, try to eliminate food odors that may attract bears (fig. 10-4). Cook downwind and away from the main campsite. Pack out food residue. Bury fish remains as deep as the soil allows and well away from camp. Wash fish odors from hands and clothing. Strain dishwater, pack out any food particles with trash, and scatter water 200 feet from camp and from water sources.

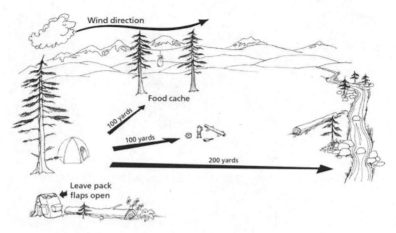

Figure 10-4: *An ideal campsite in grizzly bear country.*

Food Storage in Bear Country

All food and odorous items (e.g., cosmetics, toothpaste, lotion) should be placed in stuff sacks and stored downwind at least 300 feet from the campsite. In certain campgrounds, you can store your food supplies in bear-proof boxes (fig. 10-5), on cables (fig. 10-6), or on poles (fig. 10-7). If these are not available (in most designated wilderness areas, they are not), use the counterbalance method of hanging food from trees, recommended by the National Park Service (fig. 10-8), or the loop-and-stick method (fig. 10-9). You may also store food in a bear-resistant canister.

Counterbalance method. Find a tree with a sturdy limb that is not dead nor close to other limbs, stands about 20 feet high, and extends at least 10 feet from the trunk (see fig. 10-8). Next, divide your food into two equal bags of no more than 10 pounds each, and attach to the first sack a ½ inch or larger nylon rope that is at least 50 feet long. To the opposite end of the rope, tie a rock that is light enough to toss over the limb but heavy enough to fall to the ground after it has crossed

Figure 10-5: *Bear-proof box with double latch and chain.*

Figure 10-6: *Cable for hanging food.*   Figure 10-7: *Pole for hanging food.*

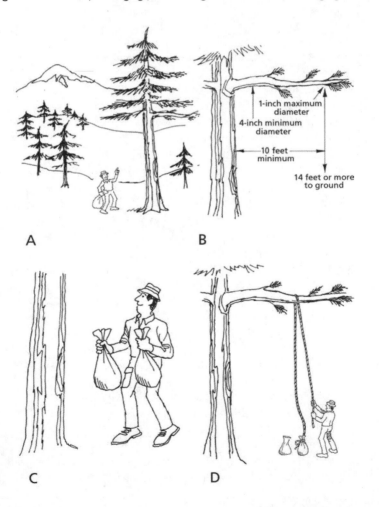

A

B

1-inch maximum
diameter

4-inch minimum
diameter

10 feet
minimum

14 feet or more
to ground

C

D

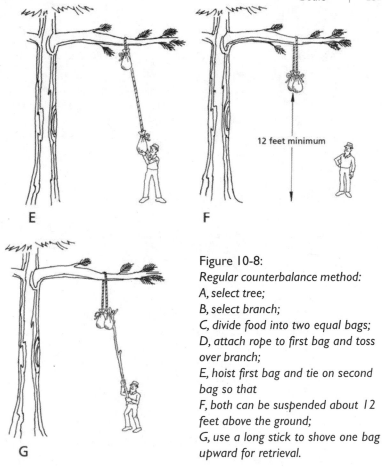

12 feet minimum

E

F

G

Figure 10-8:
Regular counterbalance method:
A, select tree;
B, select branch;
C, divide food into two equal bags;
D, attach rope to first bag and toss over branch;
E, hoist first bag and tie on second bag so that
F, both can be suspended about 12 feet above the ground;
G, use a long stick to shove one bag upward for retrieval.

the limb. Before tossing, ensure that the rope isn't snarled. Toss the rock over the end of the limb at least 4 feet away from the trunk of the tree. Pull the rope to elevate the stuff sack, remove the rock from the other end of the rope, and replace it with another food sack or a rock that weighs the same as the food in the first stuff sack. The sack or rock should be tied at a point on the rope that allows both weighted ends to be suspended about 12 feet from the ground. Stuff excess rope into either or both stuff sacks. Find a long stick (or use a ski pole or hiking staff) to shove the second sack upward and also to retrieve the stuff sack later.

Alternate counterbalance method. An alternative to the stick is a second rope, looped through the strings of the first stuff sack before it is hoisted. The second rope can be used to pull the first bag down to a counterbalanced position with the second bag. To prevent a bear from using this rope to pull the food bag down, separate the two ends of the rope by several feet. When you want to retrieve the food, simply pull the two ends of the second rope together and pull them both downward. This action lowers the first stuff sack while raising the rock or second stuff sack. Once the stuff sack is released, the counterbalanced rock or second stuff sack should come down easily. But watch your head!

Loop-and-stick method. An alternative to the counterbalance method is the loop-and-stick method shown in Figure 10-9. First, select a tree limb of the same dimensions as in the counterbalance method. Throw a rope over that limb and tie one end of the rope securely to the stuff sack. Just above the stuff sack, tie a 4- to 6-inch loop (using the simple loop knot shown in fig. 10-9). Thread the other end of the rope through this loop and pull on it until the stuff sack reaches the limb. Reach as high as you can on the rope and tie a stick onto the rope using a clove hitch knot (also shown in fig. 10-9). If possible, stand on a rock or log in order to reach higher on the rope. **The higher you tie the stick, the more secure your bag will be.** Lower the bag until the stick lodges in the loop and let the remainder of the rope dangle. Bears will play with the rope, but the loop and stick keeps the bag securely hung until you wish to retrieve it.

If there are no trees in the area, wrap all odorous materials in two or more plastic bags, taking care to seal them tightly. Stuff the bags into a deep crevice in rocks, if possible, or leave on the ground at least 300 feet from camp. This may or may not work, but it may be your only option. Never simply give up and sleep with the food—this practice may invite a midnight bear encounter!

Bear-proof boxes. Many state and national parks now provide bear-proof boxes at campsites to prevent bears from stealing food from campers. Bear boxes are heavy metal boxes that are firmly anchored to the ground (see fig. 10-5). If you are fortunate enough to camp at such a site, using bear boxes is much easier and more convenient than hanging your food. The boxes have dual latches on a heavy, front-facing door. This system operates on the assumption that bears lack the manual dexterity, patience, or intelligence to open two separate latches and drop the door. Where bear boxes exist, all campers in the area store their food in the same box. It is best to keep your food well organized and marked in some manner (e.g., stuff sack with your name on it). All bear box users are expected to keep the box fully locked except when depositing or extracting food. Upon leaving camp, be sure to

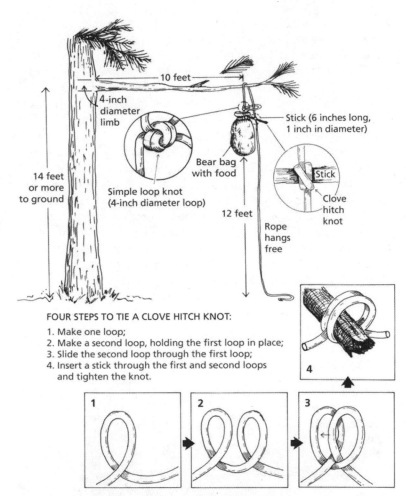

FOUR STEPS TO TIE A CLOVE HITCH KNOT:

1. Make one loop;
2. Make a second loop, holding the first loop in place;
3. Slide the second loop through the first loop;
4. Insert a stick through the first and second loops and tighten the knot.

Figure 10-9: *Loop-and-stick method: tie loop knot next to food bag before tossing rope over; thread rope through loop; tie a stick high up on the other end of rope; allow stick to lodge in loop; let rope dangle.*

check the bear box to ensure that you have actually removed all of your food and be certain you are taking only *your* food.

Bear-proof food canisters. If you are hiking outside of state or national parks, you may not find bear boxes or other bear-proof food storage methods at your campsites. If you intend to camp in an area with few suitable trees from which to hang your food, or if you don't want the hassle of hanging food every night, other options are available. One technique that is gaining popularity among hikers is the use of bear-proof food canisters. From the outset of your hike, you store food in the canister and transport the canister inside or outside of your backpack. Cylindrical in form, the canisters fit readily within most backpacks. They are strong enough to withstand the onslaught of bears yet light enough to pack. Once in camp, you need not hang the canister. Made of rugged ABS plastic, the canisters are virtually indestructible. Most importantly, they maintain their structural integrity in the grasp of bears so that food inside is not harmed. Bears may fumble with the canisters for a while but eventually they abandon them for easier pickings.

For the technically minded, the canisters weigh less than 3 pounds. They measure approximately 12 inches in length and 8.5 inches in diameter. Depending on the type of food, a bear canister can carry at least 3–4 day's worth. Pack them inside of either internal-frame or external-frame backpacks, or lash them to the outside of a pack. In addition to their ruggedness, the canisters include a bear-proof latching system, which has two internal bar locks that can only be opened or closed with a slotted tool or coin. The latch system contains a lever button that pops the top up once the locks have been opened. Bears

Grizzly attacking a canister. (Photo by Garcia Machine.)

lack the manual dexterity to operate this small latch system (especially with their claws).

The National Park Service has done extensive testing with food canisters in bear country (e.g., Yosemite, Glacier, and Yellowstone National Parks) and has established that they are effective at keeping food from bears. As a result, bear-proof food canisters are now recommended, and in some parks required, as a means of preventing bears from stealing human food.

Bear-proof sacks. Another way of storing food in the backcountry involves the use of bear-proof sacks. A bear-proof sack is basically a stuff sack made of a rugged fabric somewhat like the material used to make bulletproof vests. Bear-proof sacks measure about 8 inches by 12 inches and have sturdy draw cords used to close the sacks. Unlike canisters, the sacks should be hung in trees where possible (much as you would use a bear bag) or cached in rock crevices or on the ground, at least 300 feet from camp. While the sacks offer some security, they do not eliminate food odors, and bears will still be attracted to them. If a bear does succeed in getting to the sack, it should not be able to penetrate the bag and take food. In the process, however, the bear may crush some of the food within the sack or leave saliva on it, making some of the foods inside unusable. Bear-proof sacks do have some advantages over canisters in that they are lighter, more easily stored in packs, and cost less than canisters, but they do not have the structural integrity necessary to prevent bears from ruining some of the food inside. You might consider using a bear-proof sack to protect food that can withstand being crushed (e.g., granola) and putting the rest in a canister or hanging it in a tree.

Protection against Bears

If a bear decides to take your food or attack you, pepper spray may be effective with both black bears and grizzly bears but less effective on a sow protecting her young. According to research by Stephen Herrero and Andrew Higgins, pepper sprays that contain capsaicin, or extracts from the variety of tropical plants of the genus *Capsicum,* drive away bears if sprayed from a short distance directly into their faces and eyes. Pepper spray seems to be effective with both black bears and grizzly bears, but less effective when a mother bear is protecting her young. The spray, however, does not prevent bears from returning later. While sprays may repel bears, pepper spray is *not* a bear deterrent. You cannot keep bears away by spraying your clothing or camp equipment ahead of time. Pepper spray is only effective when it is sprayed directly into a bear's face. The odor of pepper spray around camp not only does not repel bears but may actually *attract* them. Research has found that bears seem to be attracted to red pepper sprayed on an object. You should not, therefore, spray your tent or sleeping bag.

Before you leave home be certain that your spray canister actually works. When in bear country, keep the spray canister handy, in a holster or clipped to your shoulder strap. As you hike, be alert for signs of bears. If you see a bear, assess the situation. Is the bear after your food, or is it protecting its young or its territory? Is it a grizzly or a black bear? Take note of the wind direction. Reroute your hike to avoid an encounter. If the bear behaves aggressively, ready your spray canister and position yourself so you don't spray into the wind, which may cause the spray to blow back into your face, disabling you instead of the bear. When the bear is within 10–20 feet, fire the spray continuously and directly into its eyes, nose, and mouth. This action will probably halt the bear's progress but may not drive it away, particularly if the bear is protecting its young. Spray again and again until it leaves. If the bear is after your food, it will probably be back later. Research has shown that pepper spray does not enrage bears or lead to an escalation of the encounter. Thus, it is a good idea to use spray when necessary. If you are with a group of hikers, everyone should have a spray canister and know how to use it.

MOUNTAIN LIONS

Also known as cougars or pumas, mountain lions are stealthy, elusive creatures. Hikers who encounter the relatively scarce big cats are impressed with their sleek beauty and graceful movement. Behind that calm façade is a dangerous animal. Tawny in color, these cats are distinguished from other cats in the wild by their size, color, and unusually large tails. As pretty as they are, they should always be regarded as very dangerous.

Lions are carnivores and are constantly on the hunt for deer, elk, mountain goats, and other animals that compose its natural diet. They stalk their prey and attack when the advantage is in their favor. For this reason, they are classified as ambush predators. Mountain lions usually attack from the rear or overhead, dispatching their victim with a vicious bite to the neck. A mountain lion that approaches you frontally and acts in a menacing manner is not behaving normally. Mountain lions generally regard humans as a threat, not a food source. Only in extreme cases (e.g., dire hunger, defense, disease) will mountain lions attack and kill humans. To prevent further attacks the offending cat is

Mountain lions are ambush predators.

then hunted down and killed by federal game wardens.

The likelihood of encountering a mountain lion on a hike is very small. Nonetheless, encounters do happen. According to the U.S. Fish and Wildlife Agency, there have been fewer than a hundred dangerous encounters between mountain lions and humans in the past 100 years. Of those 100 or so encounters, there have been only a dozen or so fatalities, but the trend is upward due in part to governmental protection of mountain lions. At one time, mountain lions were almost an endangered species. Limits on hunting have allowed their populations to increase dramatically. At the same time, the human population has increased and new homesites have pushed into the backcountry, further reducing the lion's habitat. Expansion and overlap of the domains of both mountain lions and humans have created more and more opportunity for encounters and conflicts.

Overpopulation of the mountain lion's domain has also triggered territorial disputes among the big cats. Each mountain lion needs about 100 square miles of territory. When one cat invades another's territory, one will be displaced. Often, the offending lion in an encounter with a human is a young hungry cat that has been pushed out of its territory by other lions. These displaced lions then enter human-populated areas looking for food. Pets and livestock become targets in these circumstances, increasing the risks for their owners who try to protect them.

How to behave in lion country. When hiking in lion country, it is best not to hike alone. The presence of other hikers poses a greater threat to a mountain lion and therefore decreases the chances of a dangerous encounter. As you hike, look around and be aware of what is going on around you. Take the time to look over your shoulder occasionally. Look down the path that lies ahead, particularly noting overhanging limbs and boulders where a lion might lie in ambush. While they are difficult to spot, that big tail may tip off the presence of a lion. Learn to recognize mountain lion tracks (see fig. 10-10) and distinguish them from dog tracks. Cats move with their claws retracted, so you will see no claw marks at the ends of their toes as you would with a dog's paw print. If you do see fresh mountain lion tracks, increase your vigilance and plan your next move carefully. It may be prudent to abort the hike.

Managing an encounter with a mountain lion. If you do cross paths with a mountain lion, you should immediately assess the situation and take action. You must convince the lion that you are a threat to it and not its prey: Stare intently at it and shout as loud as you can, and do not break eye contact. Raise your arms and make yourself appear as large and as menacing as possible. Do not appear meek—meekness here only brings you trouble. Unlike a grizzly attack, do not play dead.

Figure 10-10: *Mountain lion vs. dog tracks—note the claws on dog prints.*

Arm yourself with a limb or some other weapon, if possible. If the lion attacks, use the weapon and swing it with authority to defend yourself. During the encounter, however, try not to corner the animal. Cornered and threatened, it may attack! Give the lion a chance to break off the encounter and flee. To do so, edge away but maintain firm eye contact. Continue to face it, and **never** turn your back on it, even if it appears to be disengaging. If you are hiking with a partner, slowly move away back to back, so you can keep eye contact with the lion while your partner makes sure you don't trip while walking backward. Resist the temptation to turn and run! Running reverts you from a threat to prey. Remember that the lion is an ambush predator, and it is just waiting for an opening to attack. Given the opportunity, normal lions will seek to get away from you once the attack has failed. Allow it to do so but keep sight of it as long as possible. Once the cat has left, slowly move away yourself, keeping a wary eye out for its return.

If the big cat does not choose to disengage, then keep it at bay and edge away from it in the direction of help. Use pepper spray if you have it. If you have a cell phone, try using it to get help. Be certain to provide your approximate location. Keep your guard up, abort the hike, and retreat toward your car or toward a populated area, if you can. Once safely back in civilization, report such encounters to authorities and provide as much information about the encounter as possible.

Keep in mind that such encounters with mountain lions are extremely rare and should not deter you from hiking in the wilderness.

POISONOUS SNAKES

Poisonous snakes thrive in a broad range of environments. Water moccasins and coral snakes can be found in the South, and copperheads in the East. Perhaps the best known of poisonous snakes, however, are rattlesnakes. Different types of rattlesnakes are found all over the country. You'll find them in rocky terrain or near canyon bottoms where the small creatures they prey upon are abundant. You're most likely to see them out and about when temperatures are in the 75–90°F range. Remember that snakes may enjoy sunning themselves or relaxing where you might also choose to be.

Normally not aggressive, rattlesnakes usually buzz unmistakably if you approach too closely. A rattlesnake can strike only about a third to a half of its length but you will be wise to give it more space than this. When in snake country scan the path ahead, and never put your feet or hands in places where you cannot see. Probe ahead with a stick, if

Coiled rattlesnake.

possible. Wear long pants and ankle-high boots, since a snake's strike would likely occur on the lower leg.

Learn to identify the types of poisonous snakes that inhabit the areas in which you plan to hike. Remember that, like most other wild animals, a startled snake prefers to leave the area quickly if an escape route is available. Step rapidly away from the snake, and it will probably slither away in the opposite direction as fast as it can. Rarely are hikers bitten by poisonous snakes. If you are bitten, and the snake injects venom (you will know!), get to a hospital and begin antivenom treatment as soon as possible. Some snakebite kits have effective suction devices that extract some—but only some— venom. Do not cut or freeze the bite area (see Chapter 16, Wilderness First Aid, "Environmental Hazards in the Wilderness").

CONCLUSION

One of the greatest joys of hiking in the wilderness comes with encountering wild animals in their natural habitats. Before venturing into the wilderness, learn how to recognize dangerous situations and how to respond appropriately. Learn to recognize threats ahead of time and either avoid them or counter them effectively. Such knowledge will give you the confidence to venture into the wilderness and wander more freely.

chapter
11

Children in the Wilderness

Marianne Ringhoff, Ellen Feeney, Liz Gabrych, Paul Kater, Denise McClellan, and Heather Tatton

Hiking and camping with children can be most enjoyable. Filled with enthusiasm and curiosity, kids are natural explorers. When accompanied by little ones, your world seems a bigger and more wonderful place. By sharing in their experiences, you become like a child yourself, liberated from the cares of adulthood, at least temporarily.

Children learn quickly by observing, and they readily imitate your behavior. Be a positive role model. Also be receptive to your children's moods. Whenever possible, tailor your activities to their interests. A successful outing is both enjoyable and educational. It is one that your children may remember for the rest of their lives.

PREPARATION
Conditioning
Children may be physically more resilient than adults, but they still need plenty of conditioning prior to a big trip. It's important to prepare a child's mind as well.

Walking is the easiest form of conditioning. Walk to the park, walk around the neighborhood, walk on the beach, climb some hills. Stick to a routine—walk in bad weather as well as good. But always make it fun.

Curious children find the wilderness an exciting place. (Photo by Marge and Ted Mueller.)

Let them catch raindrops and look for a rainbow. Sneak in a natural history or science lesson while you're at it. In addition, try practicing some of the routines you'll follow when on the trail, for example, shedding and adding clothing as the weather changes.

Children have short attention spans, so vary your routines to keep things lively. March to a song, count trees or fence posts, or spy on birds. This is a good opportunity to give children some freedom—let them choose the direction of travel, or let them play tag on the beach or in the park. Pique their curiosity and follow through in answering their questions.

Destination and Route

The trip destination should be appropriate for both your children's and your own interests and not beyond the scope of your experience and training. Include your children in the process of planning. Ask them what they would like to see and do. Plant the seeds of anticipation by gathering information about the places you'd like to visit. Aside from queries to tourist bureaus and parks, try your local library. Consult or borrow guidebooks as well as books on geography and natural history. Some libraries now have video departments with tapes offering previews of popular parks. Kids can get bored with just hiking but get highly motivated for activities such as climbing, skiing, and snowshoeing. Let your children participate in the decision-making process.

. When planning for a day trip, allow for some exploratory time. On an extended trip, be sure to allow for one or more layover days. The immediate area around a campsite can seem like a whole universe to a

Varying activities keeps children interested in the outdoors. (Photo by Jerry Schad.)

little one. Let the child gain some familiarity with the surroundings; allow him to bond with nature. Be sure to modify the ratio of adults to children when hiking with a group. Older children are more independent than younger children, and having the right number of adults can be critical.

Safety Training

The most important aspect of pretrip planning is teaching your children how to avoid getting lost, and what they should do if they do get lost or separated. In a larger group of kids, the buddy system works well. By having children pair up, each buddy always knows the whereabouts of the other. If someone leaves for any reason, he must tell the buddy and also the parent or leader.

On the trip, be sure each child carries at least one item of bright-colored clothing, a whistle, and a plastic trash-can liner in addition to other items that might be in her pack. The first two items are quite effective for signaling to rescuers, while the third serves as emergency shelter.

If they get lost, children should be taught to STOP—Sit, Think, Observe, and Plan (fig. 11-1). They should be secure in the knowledge that their parents, and possibly others, are out looking for them. They must realize that the farther they wander, the more lost they become.

Some basic survival techniques to teach your child include hugging a tree, which helps a lost child avoid panic and not wander aimlessly. Train your child to blow a whistle, rather than using his voice, and to listen for any response. If an aircraft passes overhead, teach your child to make himself big by wearing brightly colored clothing and lying flat in a clearing. Train your child to use a plastic trash-can liner as a sunshade and, with a hole cut in it, as an impromptu shelter from rain and cold.

Prepare a tracing and imprint of your child's boot or hiking shoe to be used for a search in case he becomes lost: Place a piece of paper on soft ground. With your child wearing his hiking shoes, spread ink on the lugs or sole pattern of either the left or the right shoe. Have him carefully step on the paper with the inked shoe and leave it in place while you make a pencil tracing of the sole rim. To clean the sole afterward, blot it with a rag and then let him scuff through some sand or dirt.

A Lost Child

What should you do if your child is missing? First, don't panic! Second, use a whistle to call to your child. If there's no response, retrace your

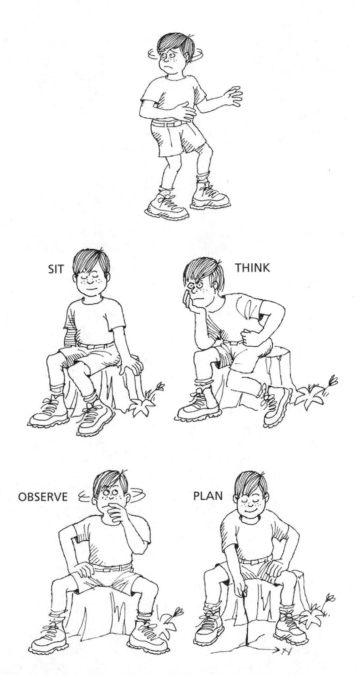

Figure 11-1: *The STOP method: Sit, Think, Observe, Plan.*

steps and mark the spot you last saw him. If there's no response, send for help. Include information such as his physical description, his clothing and footwear, and the time and point where he was last seen (see Chapter 17, Search and Rescue, "Dealing with a Missing Hiker").

EQUIPMENT
Footwear

When choosing footwear, remember that kids don't just walk. They invariably spend much of their time running, jumping, and climbing. Don't hobble them with boots that are too heavy and uncomfortable. On the other hand, you'll want shoes with enough support to handle rocky or uneven ground.

Running shoes or sneakers with good tread often work fine, especially for the younger child starting out on short, easy day hikes. Once the child is ready to hike longer distances or over rough terrain, though, the proper choice of footwear becomes important.

Today you can choose among a wide variety of lightweight hiking boots in children's sizes. These boots break in quickly, offer good foot support and traction, and sell for a moderate price. They're comfortable and stylish enough to be worn at home or school. Don't forget to allow a break-in period—your child should wear them on at least a couple of shorter walks or hikes before the main event.

When choosing a boot size, consider your child's rapidly growing feet. Have him try on boots using two socks on each foot—medium and heavy-weight. There should be enough room to wiggle toes but not enough room to allow the heels to slip when the boots are snugly laced. Have your child squat down to check for heel slippage, and walk down an incline to check for cramped toes in front. Check that neither the big toe nor the little toe gets pinched on the side (boots with square toe-boxes usually prevent this problem).

Before the trip, make sure that toenails are clipped. On the trip, carry foot fleece (soft wool) for placing between the toes if needed, and moleskin for hot spots and blisters. Check your child's feet during rest stops and be receptive to any complaints. Don't allow a hot spot to develop into a blister—apply moleskin at the first hint of redness and discomfort.

Clothing

Temperatures can change quickly in the wilderness. Dry, sunny conditions on a south-facing slope can instantly turn into damp, chilly conditions on a north-facing slope. A single thundercloud blotting out the sun's rays produces an instant nip in the air. Taking off extra clothing in warm weather is a minor inconvenience, but not having enough clothing in cold conditions can precipitate an emergency situation.

As with adults, a three-layer clothing system works well with children. Generally, the first layer is for comfort, sun protection, and a small amount of insulation. The second layer insulates and retains body heat, while the third layer protects by shedding rain and wind. Pile on or remove the layers as appropriate. Remember that a child's body has a larger surface-area-to-mass ratio than an adult's, therefore a child loses body heat more rapidly. Warm headgear (a knitted cap or balaclava) and mittens are essential items for cold conditions.

For sunny conditions, don't forget to protect your child's delicate skin from the sun's ultraviolet radiation. That means long-sleeved tops, a wide-brimmed hat or a cap with a bill, and sunscreen on all exposed parts of the body such as the back of the hands.

Collecting all this specialized clothing may be quite costly. But kids' clothing seldom wears out before being outgrown, so your child can be the recipient or the donor of hand-me-downs. Consider sewing identification labels into your child's outdoor clothing; this could be helpful for searchers if your child ever becomes lost.

Diapers

This essential item for very young ones merits considerable creative thought. For an extended trip, cloth diapers are less bulky to carry than disposables. They can be used with diaper liners, which usually contain most of the waste. Bury or pack out waste from both disposable and cloth diapers. Bury the waste in a cat hole 6–8 inches deep, at least 200 feet from water, camp, and trails. If using cloth, wash them in the cat hole, cover the contents, and pack out the diapers. Disposables must also be packed out. Neither diapers nor diaper liners should be burned. Burning may start a wildfire and also requires a very hot fire to completely burn, potentially leaving unsightly and unsanitary remains.

Biodegradable diapers are appearing on the market. However, in the harsh climate of many wilderness areas, it takes many years for them to disintegrate. Even if you bury them deeply, animals may locate and dig them up. Consider how you would feel if you discovered the remains of diapers at a prospective campsite.

Sleeping Bags

Children sleep colder than adults, so the choice of a sleeping bag should reflect that fact. Usually a child sleeps warmer in a lighter, more compact mummy bag than in a roomier, rectangular-style bag; however, some children cannot tolerate the confinement of a mummy bag. Most junior-size bags fit children up to about 5 feet in height. The leftover length, if any, can be tied off or tucked under as a mattress. When choosing between down or synthetic fill (see Chapter 5, Outfitting, "Sleeping Bags"), take into account the issue of bed-wetting as well. Down sleeping bags lose their insulating qualities when wet and are difficult to launder.

Packs

Any child old enough to walk can wear a pack. Start out with a small "play" day pack for your toddler. Put special toys and snacks in it for trips to the park or to the babysitter. The child gets used to carrying things on his back and feels helpful to boot.

Most children old enough to use day packs for school can easily graduate to a pack with a rigid frame. Junior-size, external-frame packs often have adjustments that accommodate a fair range of growth. When checking for fit, load up the pack and adjust the straps so that the hipbelt lies on the hip bones. The weight of the pack should be borne by hips as well as shoulders. A well-padded hipbelt may be needed for a thin child; a broad frame will be necessary for a heavy child. Make sure there are no buttons, zippers, or extra folds on the pressure areas of the hips that may cause chafing. See how easily the pack's closures (zippers, cinch cords, Velcro) allow your child to get to items stored inside.

Shoulder straps should attach to the frame about 1 or 2 inches below the top of the shoulders. While you are on the trail, check from time to time to see if the pack is riding comfortably. Sometimes the hipbelt slips down and results in too much weight on the shoulders.

Child Carriers

One of the best ways to get children interested in the outdoors is to start early. Newborns who lack the ability to hold their heads up should be transported in a sling-type carrier worn on the front of the parent's body. From roughly four months and up, most children are comfortable in a standard backpack-type carrier. The better models have a capacity of up to 40 pounds. In addition to providing the child a good view of the surroundings. A carrier's rocking motion can soothe even the crankiest baby.

When shopping for a carrier, make sure you try it on with the child in it. Have someone check for pinching on the child's arms and legs.

A good backpack-type carrier can soothe even the crankiest baby. (Photo by Bob and Ira Spring.)

Look for any stray belts, buckles, or snaps that can get into little mouths. Some kind of head support is desirable if the child is very young. Make sure the pack is comfortable and does not throw you off balance when you walk.

The child in a backpack-type carrier should face forward with his or her head high enough to see over your shoulder, but not higher than your head. When on the trail, avoid the possibility of the child climbing out by making sure all belts are securely fastened and snug. Some carriers feature a kickstand that supports the pack upright on the ground. In that position, the pack can serve as a high chair in camp.

HEALTH AND FIRST AID

Forethought is necessary to ensure children's safety on wilderness trips. With sufficient preparation, wilderness travel can be safe and fun for all ages. Knowing basic first aid is essential. Adults taking children into the wilderness should be comfortable taking care of minor injuries and illnesses and know the basics of caring for more severe problems.

You should know the route and the potential dangers of a particular trail. Are there cliffs, rattlesnakes, poison ivy, mountain lions? Every trail has unique and inherent dangers, which should be considered prior to taking the first step. (For more information on dealing with animals in the wilderness, see Chapter 10, Animal Encounters.) If appropriate, let the kids know what to watch out for and how to deal with potential problems. Bring equipment and a first-aid kit stocked with items designed to handle the most likely problems. Children get scrapes, strains, and sunburns most anytime, so know how to deal with them, take steps to prevent them when possible, and bring appropriate equipment. Be sure your first-aid kit complements the needs of your children with such items as child-strength aspirin or antihistamines, as well as specific medications your child may need.

With some instruction beforehand, your children will know that if they see "leaves of three," they should "let it be." But if they do blunder into poison oak (or ivy or sumac), wash the affected area with a mild cleanser and apply an analgesic to relieve the itching (see Chapter 16, Wilderness First Aid, "Environmental Hazards in the Wilderness"). Don't allow your kids to use sticks for cooking; they may be from poison oak or contain toxins.

Know how to get help in a particular area. Know where the nearest emergency room, fire department, or ranger station is located. Find out beforehand if cell phones will work, and if so, keep one handy. And never be afraid to ask for help from others in your group, others on the trail, or rangers and emergency personnel.

Familiarity with an area certainly increases safety, as does familiarity with the children. If taking youth groups other than your own children, know the kids you are taking. Know their unique health issues such as allergies, asthma, food intolerances, and hiking abilities.

Unfortunately, despite preparation, accidents and illnesses occur. If you are prepared you can remain calm and deal with the problem—and staying calm helps children stay calm. Compassion helps you stay in touch with children's feelings and wins you their trust. Remain outwardly confident, and you alleviate children's fears. Then use common sense to deal with the problem as best you can with the tools you have.

FOOD AND WATER

Get the kids involved in the fun of pretrip menu planning. Consider their likes and dislikes, and try out the meals before the trip. Kids build up an amazing amount of energy during a trip, and therefore always seem to be hungry. Plenty of snacks should be available. Chocolate-covered raisins, peanuts, candy, granola bars, and fruit rolls are tasty, nutritious in varying degrees, and rich in the calories that kids need on the trail. Have the kids mix their own GORP at home before you leave. You may be surprised by what they put in it!

Weight and packaging of foodstuffs is especially important on family trips. Younger children won't be able to carry the weight they use and consume, and that adds to your burden.

For the main meals at camp, quick and easy preparation is an important consideration, particularly if you run into bad weather. Finger foods keep the little ones busy while you are preparing the main course. Encourage the older ones to get involved in the kitchen chores. It's amazing how kids do things willingly in the backcountry that you can't get them to do at home.

Don't forget that proper hydration is important for kids. On hot days or strenuous trails, stop often for water breaks. Water is heavy (16 ounces equal 1 pound), so have kids carry smaller water bottles and periodically replenish from larger bottles carried by adults. Don't forget to remind kids not to drink from lakes and streams.

ON THE TRIP

As long as your child has had adequate preparation, the real trip will be just another adventure, though a bigger one. Remember that having shorter legs means more steps must be taken, so your child will probably tire more quickly than you do. Start out slow, then gradually increase the pace to match the ability of the least able child in your party. Don't let the more energetic ones run ahead of the group—you'll never be able to keep track of everyone that way.

Remember to incorporate some environmental education into your outings. Discuss the kid-friendly motto, "Take only photographs, leave only footprints." Model good nature-attuned behavior by stopping often to smell the wild roses.

Inner City Outings (ICO) is a community outreach program of the Sierra Club and is devoted to providing youth with outdoor experiences. Use a few of their tips to help kids develop their appreciation of wild places:

- Employ the senses.
- Build respect for the dignity of living things.
- Emphasize interrelationships rather than classifications.
- Foster a sense of wonder.

- Ask "Why?" (Don't feel obligated to provide the answer.)
- Keep it simple and make it fun.

Suggested Children's Games

Sames and differents. This game involves things of various shapes and sizes, including leaves, rocks, trees, and clouds, that bear some resemblance to each other. Have the child look at one object, then have her discover another object that is similar in some way.

Nature's shapes. From heavy paper, cut out different shapes, such as circles, squares, rectangles, and triangles. Have the child match the shapes to natural features, small and large.

What am I? Blindfold the child in a safe area. Have him use all the senses except sight to discover the world around himself. Ask questions like: What do you hear? How does that feel? Soft, rough, sticky, wet, smooth, warm, cold? What does that taste like? (Use edible foods, of course.)

Next stop. Count steps to the next rest stop or destination. Identify a point ahead on the trail, and allow the child to hike on his own to reach it. Let your child measure the time taken during a rest stop—a great way for him to learn how to tell time and get a sense of the passage of time.

Night walks. Visit a place at night that you saw earlier in daylight. What is different about it? This may be a little scary for some kids, but most love it.

chapter
12

Coastal Travel

Emily B. Troxell

Coastal travel provides opportunities to explore unique parts of the world. Here nature reigns supreme, but it's possible to find a lulling sense of serenity that supports your inner being. Often beaches are overcrowded, but there are still areas in the public trust where you can find spots for rest and relaxation along with a place to watch local wildlife. However, exploring the coastal habitat requires different travel techniques in order to minimize the impact to the area.

THE DYNAMIC COAST

Much of the coast is composed of sedimentary rock commonly known as sandstone. Sandstone is inherently weak and erodes quickly when exposed to waves, wind, and rain. River silt and sand deposited in low-lying areas along the coast created rock formations. The succession of deposits and erosion created the cliffs towering above the narrow coast.

The tides cause rapid and repetitive changes to the coastal environment. The gravitational pull of the sun and moon as well as a variety of additional factors result in two watery "bulges"; one on the side facing the moon, the other on the side facing away from the moon. As the earth turns on its axis each 24-hour period, it passes through the bulge cycle

Coastal travel requires special preparation, but spectacular scenery makes it worthwhile. (Photo by Bob and Ira Spring.)

twice daily. Consequently during new and full moons, the solar influence becomes aligned with that of the moon, resulting in higher high and lower low tides. Tides can be accurately calculated and are found in printed form as tide tables.

Where the edge of the land meets the sea, and when adequate rocks are part of this environment, a unique set of circumstances provides an area more densely inhabited than any other. This area is neither land nor sea, but a bit of both and is called the intertidal zone (see fig. 12-1).

Biologists find this ecosystem, a place where diverse habitats converge, to be a wild and mysterious study site. During the past ten years, a tremendous amount of research has been conducted in the intertidal zone. It has been firmly established that the physical act of walking over the algal turf controls the amount of life found in the area. Algae are food, homes, and hiding places for many intertidal species. If an area has received heavy foot traffic, limiting human access goes a long way to restoring intertidal health. It is also clear that pollutants play a part in the health of the intertidal zone. Runoff brings a wide variety of substances to coastal waters. Some of this runoff may be harmful to people. But even that which is not harmful to people does change the availability of food and water conditions for the species living here. Water temperature plays a part in reproduction of species as well.

People frequently feel that taking just one little rock or shell for a souvenir is OK. After all, the absence of the one shell or rock makes no detectable difference in the environment. If the coastal and intertidal areas had only one visitor per year, very little harm would be done by taking the occasional souvenir. But this area is visited by thousands of people every year. If every visitor becomes a souvenir collector, the area is soon changed so drastically that it no longer promotes life. It is easy to understand that people are a major destructive force for the intertidal zone.

TRAVELING THE COAST

The coast almost always has a cooler, windier, and more humid environment than areas even a short distance inland. The sun's rays are more intense due to reflection from sand and water. Hikers are quite likely to get wet feet, and the salt-laden water or spray may damage gear. It is important to keep this in mind when planning a coastal trip.

Leave the mountaineering boots at home. Light hiking shoes (properly treated to repel water), sneakers, sandals, and even bare feet work fine on the easier terrain. Of course, negotiating rocky shorelines may require more substantial footgear. For very wet areas, mud boots with rubber lug soles are ideal. Be sure to wear thick socks with these boots for extra cushioning.

In terms of clothing, remember that it is important to protect against both wind and ultraviolet radiation. Keep as much of the body covered as possible, wear a hat and sunglasses, and apply sunscreen to exposed skin. Remember that even the most innocent of overcast days can pack a bad burn (especially in spring and summer). Choose clothing that offers many temperature-regulating possibilities. Wear shorts on warm days, and the rest of the time, comfortable, loose slacks that dry quickly work well. Top-quality raingear is essential for wet or misty conditions. Storms on the coastline often bring wind-driven torrents of rain, and there is no easy way to dry wet inner clothing. Being well prepared for rain allows visits to coasts during their most savagely beautiful times. Within these brief periods, the power of the breakers can become an awesome spectacle.

Be sure to include an ace bandage in your first-aid kit. A twisted knee or sprained ankle is a very real possibility when traveling over slippery or jagged rocks.

Hiking on the beach requires you to be doubly aware of where you

place your next step. When water from a breaking wave runs up onto the shoreline, it must return to sea. Frequently it does so as a narrow, outgoing stream called a rip current, undertow, or riptide (actually, this type of water action has nothing to do with the tides). This flow of water extends into shallow waters, creating dangerous situations for swimmers unfamiliar with these characteristics. Swimmers caught in rip currents may find that they are unable to swim to the safety of the shore. The best course of action is to swim parallel to the shore until the rip current subsides.

It is vitally important to stay on established trails, especially when hiking through the semiarid sandy soils of coastal sandstone and siltstone bluffs. Such soil holds very few nutrients, and root systems frequently extend far past the top growth of the plants. Where no trails exist, spread a group of people over a wide area in order to minimize impact.

Topographic maps are a must for unfamiliar coastlines. They indicate the precise shape of coastlines and the height of bluffs as well as identifying sandy beaches and shoals. It is important to know where rocky outcroppings occur that can block safe passage along the shoreline. Plot escape routes in such areas in case emergencies occur.

While it is possible to backpack for miles along parts of the Pacific coast, there are many places where it is necessary to leave the beach and walk on forest trails to get around headlands. Tide tables are very important for routes that involve tight passages between cliffs and surf. By using maps and tide tables, it is possible to safely backpack wild coastal areas and avoid having a route rendered impassable by a high tide.

Water is everywhere, but there is not a drop to drink so remember to take plenty of drinking water or a means of treating available freshwater. Many freshwater streams near the ocean are slightly brackish due to their low elevation and proximity to salt water. Some coastal areas have streams with high levels of tannin from the redwood or cedar forests. Neither tannin-laden nor brackish water are harmful to drink if properly treated, but they may have an unsettling brown color and/or have a slightly unpleasant taste. It is possible to use powdered drink crystals to mask these problems.

Finally, consider the potential effects of exposure to salt water or salt spray. Whether the excursion is a day hike or backpacking, choose a pack that has tough, waterproof material, padded shoulder and hip

Opposite: *Narrow, rocky, heavily forested coastlines can become impassable at high tide. (Photo by Marge and Ted Mueller.)*

belts, and nonmetallic zippers, buckles, and closures. (Electrical storms are common in this area.) Carry items such as cameras and binoculars in sealed plastic bags so that they avoid contact with salt water and sand.

Some coastlines (such as those in Olympic National Park in Washington) are true wilderness areas. There and in other areas where remote camping is allowed, it is possible to have a whole beach or cove as a campsite.

Observe the following common sense practices:

- Consider the prevailing direction of the wind when seeking a sheltered spot.
- Use heavy rocks to secure tent stakes in the sand.
- Camp well above the highest high tide. Consult your tide table.
- Be sure to shelter all fires from coastal winds.

The hazards of coastal travel are many and varied, and sometimes unexpected. For example, poison oak and rattlesnakes may be found in the ravines or on the bluffs just behind the beach. The coastal bluffs themselves are often very unstable; never camp or spend much time beneath or at the edge of steep cliffs. The seemingly solid brink of a cliff can crumble in the blink of an eye if a person steps too close to the edge.

The intertidal zone—a narrow strip of coastline between the highest reach of the waves during the highest and lowest tides—contains one of the world's most fascinating environments. It is a bit subtle though. You will not notice the churning life underfoot unless you pause and take a very close look.

The animals living here have had to adapt to many different environmental forces. Most live both in and out of the water. Food is usually brought to them. Each animal's territory is quite small and most of them do not move around very much. There are four basic intertidal zones.

The **splash zone** lies above the reach of high tide but not beyond the surges or splashes of breakers. Some parts are never covered by water; other parts can be inundated for short periods of time. Animals living here must move about and hunt for food without the aid or cover of water. Certain kinds of limpets, crabs, and lice are found here.

The next lower zone is the **high intertidal zone.** This area experiences the pounding of waves almost every day. Animals here must withstand the great crush of water as well as alternating wet-dry conditions. Limpets, chitons, certain crabs, and periwinkles are found here.

The most diverse of the four zones is the **middle intertidal zone** where creatures spend about as much time in the water as out. Mussels, barnacles, sandcastle worms, turban snails, green anemones, aggregate anemones, and sea hares make their homes here. Sea hares are giant sluglike creatures that live on algae. They are slimy and so unpalatable

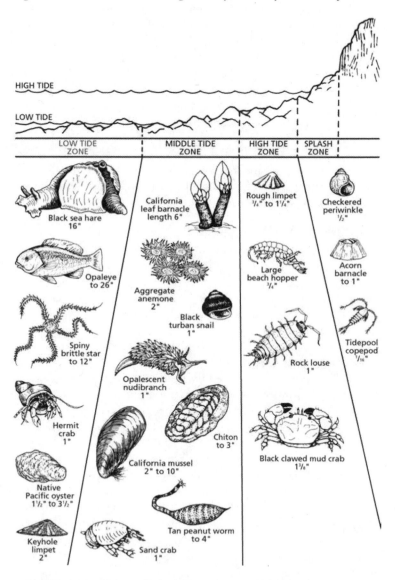

HIGH TIDE

LOW TIDE

| LOW TIDE ZONE | MIDDLE TIDE ZONE | HIGH TIDE ZONE | SPLASH ZONE |

Black sea hare
16"

California leaf barnacle length 6"

Rough limpet
¾" to 1¼"

Checkered periwinkle
½"

Opaleye to 26"

Aggregate anemone
2"

Large beach hopper
¾"

Acorn barnacle to 1"

Spiny brittle star to 12"

Black turban snail
1"

Opalescent nudibranch
1"

Rock louse
1"

Tidepool copepod
¹⁄₁₆"

Hermit crab
1"

California mussel
2" to 10"

Chiton to 3"

Black clawed mud crab
1¾"

Native Pacific oyster
1½" to 3½"

Keyhole limpet
2"

Sand crab
1"

Tan peanut worm to 4"

Figure 12-1: *Some typical life-forms of the intertidal zone.*

that no other creature will eat them. Most interesting are the aggregate anemones. These beautiful flower-appearing mollusks are far from beautiful in their behavior. Their tentacles shoot poison barbs at invading creatures and at prey (interestingly, humans are not affected by the barbs). When the tide is low, aggregate anemones look like masses of broken shells and sea trash in the cracks of rocks found in the tidal pools.

Some of the most mobile intertidal creatures are found in the **low intertidal zone.** This area is seldom free from water and seldom accessible to beach walkers. Sea hare, sea stars, urchins, keyhole limpets, and sea cucumbers are found here.

The name of the game when visiting the intertidal zone is carefully planning the time of the visit. Scan the tide tables and find the lowest tide possible. Plan to arrive about an hour before low tide and stay until after the tide turns. On the Pacific coast, tides of lower than minus 1.5 feet (tides are measured relative to a reference level of mean low tide) are needed for you to gain access to the lowest of the four intertidal zones without getting soaked.

WATCHING SEA LIFE

A wide variety of sea life is visible from shore. At some locations Pacific gray whales swim close enough for their spouts to be seen during their migration, from November through April. Elephant seals are found in the northern areas. Sea otters often play in the kelp forests as well as in other coastal areas. California sea lions and harbor seals may also provide good entertainment.

Shore and sea birds are found in abundance along coasts. These birds are easy to observe because there are few bushes where they can hide. Gulls are particularly friendly, especially for handouts. As with all wildlife, remember that providing human food does not enhance the lives of these species. When planning for coastal trips, include binoculars and bird-watching guides suitable for the areas that are on the itinerary.

Estuaries are always a part of coastal travel. The most important thing to remember in these areas is that foot traffic does make a difference. Keep to trails if possible. There can be an abundance of birds as well as sea life to observe in estuaries. These areas are also influenced by tides, so it is vitally important to plan any trip so that the incoming tide will not make it difficult to leave the area.

Minimize the chances of encountering unfriendly marine life. Stingrays, bat rays, and jellyfish like to hang around in the surf and shallows, especially when the water is warm. Sea urchins, found in the rocky intertidal zones, are equipped with brittle purple spines that can break off if stepped on. If severe pain results from any of these encounters, seek medical attention.

THE FRAGILE COAST

Because much of the life found along the coast is fragile and inconspicuous, exercise great care during all visits. Footprints left on the beach wash away but not the effects of a heavy-footed traveler. Here are some basic guidelines:

- Large groups of people should spread out when crossing fragile beach areas. Each person should try to step on the ledges and rocks that do not have creatures attached to them.
- Cliffs are unstable. Always stay far back from the top edge. Never stay close to the bottom.
- Camp well back from the high tide line but not in fragile dunes or sand areas.
- Look at the creatures, but let them live their lives undisturbed.
- Take nothing from the seacoast and bring nothing (permanently) into these environments. Each natural object plays a role in the healthy functioning of the ecosystem. Even small shells and shell fragments have uses. For example, hermit crabs use shells as homes, and anemones use shell fragments to coat their bodies when exposed to air.

Special rules apply when visiting intertidal areas:

- Safety should always come first.
- Do not throw rocks.
- Use shoes that have soles adequate to protect feet from sharp rocks.
- Walk on rocks that contain as little life as possible.
- A sturdy walking stick is very useful.
- Walk with care as many of the algae species are quite slippery.
- Trample as little as possible. Algae is a primary food of the intertidal inhabitants.
- Do not pry, jab, or relocate any of the intertidal inhabitants.
- Never remove animals from pools in the intertidal zone. Even short exposure to wind and sun can put their lives in jeopardy.
- Do not overturn rocks in the intertidal zone to look for creatures. Many are nocturnal and hide under rocks during the day. It is now understood that overturning rocks disturbs the lives of these creatures. It is very difficult to return a rock to the exact location where it was found, and it is easy to

understand that turning over a rock changes the habitat in ways that are hard to determine.

There's a sense of peace and serenity on the shore. Perhaps you've had the experience of sitting on the beach, sand between your toes, sun-warmed rock against your back, watching and feeling the ocean ebb and flow with every wave. There's a sense of comfort and a sense of coming home. At day's end, the sun bathes the bluffs and dunes in a golden radiance and then disappears under a glistening horizon. The world, at least for the moment, is at peace.

The intertidal zones host fragile, miniature ecosystems—particular care should be taken when exploring these delicate areas. (Photo by Jerry Schad.)

Mountain Travel

Mike Fry and Bob Feuge

Most backpackers visit the mountains from late spring through early fall. In the alpine and timberline zones, these warm seasons may be compressed into a period of just a few weeks, so you may have to time your visit carefully. A severe winter may have left high passes blocked by snow into August, and swollen streams at lower elevations may have knocked out bridges or rendered certain streams impassable. Be sure to inquire with the local agency (national park or forest service) before your visit.

In the Sierra Nevada, which is fairly typical of the big mountain ranges of North America, early summer is the best time for flowers, as well as for rain and mosquitoes. August and September usually have fine weather, and the occasional thunderstorm. Sunny weather usually prevails in the morning, but clouds building over the higher peaks signal that all prudent hikers should seek refuge from the rain, wind, and lightning by early afternoon.

Early autumn—anytime from mid-September through October—is the best time to enjoy the fall colors of trees such as aspens, cottonwoods, and maples. Mountain weather in the early fall is usually calm and stable, but this is also when the season's first heavy snowstorms are likely to arrive.

Overlooking the Pacific Crest Trail, Inyo National Forest. (Photo by Skip Forsht.)

Deer-hunting season in the national forests and other public lands usually runs from mid-September into October. Check with your state fish and wildlife agency or local sporting good stores for schedules and maps, and to see where most deer tags are sold. In the drier and higher alpine areas, the deer and hunters have moved to lower elevations. You should be extra careful: wear bright colors and make your presence known. Better yet, visit state and national parks, where hunting is prohibited.

PERMITS

Most alpine areas are now within official wilderness areas. Each agency has its own management plan and permit system. Generally, national forests and national parks only require a permit for overnight use. Day hiking is usually permit-free except in the very popular areas, such as Mount Whitney from the east side. Most trailheads have daily quotas in the popular seasons, and some have quotas all year. Some remote trailheads have self-issue permits, while some ranger stations supply self-issue permits when they are closed. Rangers always check permits in the backcountry, so you better have one!

Most wilderness areas offer advanced permit reservations for a fee, about $5 for each person on the trip. Agencies may start taking reservations on a certain date each year, or five to six months in advance of your planned hike. Read the fine print on your reservation: You may lose your permit if you are late picking it up. If you don't make reservations you can take your chances on the unreserved numbers or the no-shows when you arrive at the ranger station, but you may not be able to hike the trail you desired. Once you have your permit make sure you know where to park and whether you can camp near the trailhead.

ALTITUDE EFFECTS

Air at higher altitudes is both thinner and drier. Both of these characteristics affect the local climate. Temperatures tend to be much cooler than in the lowlands, and they can swing from warm daytime highs to bone-chilling nighttime lows.

While trying to keep cool in the midday sunshine, you may be tempted to shed as much clothing as possible. Think twice, since ultraviolet radiation is intense at altitude. Bombardment comes from all directions as UV reflects off of snow, rocks, and water. Even cloud cover will not protect you.

Unprotected skin at high altitude burns quickly. Your face, arms, and the backs of your hands are affected the most. Apply sunscreen frequently and liberally with an SPF of 45 or greater. Cover up with a long-sleeved shirt and a wide-brimmed hat; wear a bandana under your hat or visor to cover your ears and the back of your neck. Some hats have skirts for the same purpose. To protect your hands, wear lightweight cotton gloves during the day.

In the mountains especially, wear sunglasses or goggles with side shields (glacier glasses) and a 100 percent UV absorption rating. Exposure to high-intensity sunshine and excess UV causes snow (or sun) blindness. Repeated episodes of UV overexposure may trigger serious vision problems later in life.

Thin mountain air is refreshing once you get used to it, but that can take some time. If you live at sea level and have little experience at high altitude, you should plan a series of trips at increasing altitude to acclimate yourself. Don't expect to accomplish too much in the first days of your trip, and restrict your camp changes to 2000 feet of altitude per day. You will be more comfortable sleeping low and climbing higher during the day. Your body is making changes that require you to drink a lot of water and learn to take much larger breaths (even while you're sleeping). Your appetite may suffer, and mild headaches can be treated with aspirin or ibuprofen. You should acclimate faster on subsequent trips.

Some people cannot acclimate properly to high altitudes (sometimes as little as 8000 feet) and develop a dangerous and life-threatening malady known as acute mountain sickness or AMS (see Chapter 16, Wilderness First Aid, "Altitude Illness"). During altitude acclimation, while at rest or asleep, many people tend to fall into an alternating cycle of rapid breathing and very slow breathing known as apnea. This is normal and should lessen with time.

MOUNTAIN TRAVEL CONCERNS
Snowfields and Ice

In the mountains, the north sides of high passes may be choked with snow year-round. In the morning, and again late in the day, these slopes may be too icy to cross. A slip and a fall on such a slope could result in a long and fatal slide. An ice ax and crampons (see Chapter 15, Winter Mountaineering, "Winter Travel Techniques) may be essential for safe passage. Otherwise, bide your time and wait for the snow to soften in the afternoon.

Sometimes snow can be helpful for travel on cross-country routes. Consolidated snow can cover brush, boulders, and downed logs on the less steep terrain. Watch out for the holes around rocks and bushes that will capture your leg. Be especially careful when you cross snow bridges over streams. These eventually collapse when the temperature warms.

Backpacking below Muir Pass. (Photo by Skip Forsht.)

Ice-covered lakes pose another obvious hazard. It can be all too tempting for an inexperienced person to venture out on what may appear to be thick ice. If the ice breaks, it's almost impossible to haul yourself out. Without a rope to toss or special equipment, a would-be rescuer can easily fall into the same trap. By simply staying on the shore, you won't have to worry about these possibilities.

Glacier travel is an integral part of wilderness travel in the northwestern United States, western Canada, and Alaska. Because it is dangerous, considerable planning and training is required for a safe outing. Ropes should always be used, regardless of how simple the crossing appears. All members of the team should have ice axes, crampons, helmets, climbing harnesses, and crevasse rescue gear. If you're a novice, get training on glacier travel and then travel with experienced mountaineers on your first attempts at negotiating a glacier field. Additional information on glacier travel is available in *Mountaineering: The Freedom of the Hills* (The Mountaineers Books, 2003).

When trails are obscured by snow, you may have to follow blazes (ax marks in the trees) or other markers. Shallow trail depressions are often visible on the surface of the snow, and the cut ends of fallen logs mark the way. Where snow is present, a trail hike can often turn into a cross-country ramble, so keep your map handy and be prepared to use your navigational skills.

Lightning

In many mountain areas, the pattern of crystal-clear mornings, afternoon thunderstorms, and evening clearings repeats like clockwork for days on end. If you're planning to cross a high pass or climb a peak in a thunderstorm-prone area, the obvious thing to do is get an early start, and get off the peak well before the storm moves in.

To determine the distance between yourself and a bolt of lightning, count the seconds between the visible streak of lightning and the audible thunder: 5 seconds equals a mile.

Sometimes there's not much advance warning. First there's a billowing cloud above, then hail, then the first lightning strike somewhere nearby. Your hair may stand on end, and sparks (corona discharge) may jump from eyeglasses, pack frames, or other metallic objects. If this happens, you're clearly in trouble—a lightning strike is imminent. Immediately assume a position as low as you can. To avoid ground currents sit or crouch low on your pack, sleeping pad, or other nonmetallic, insulating object. After the strike, move quickly downhill. When you feel the charge building again, get into a low position

A quiet hike along the Pacific Crest Trail. (Photo by Arleen Tavernier.)

as before. Ice axes, tent poles, and metal hiking sticks should be carried horizontally or abandoned if lightning is a threat.

Any tall object, reaching above its surroundings, is a highly probable target for a lightning strike. Obviously, you do not want to be that object. Sharp-edged objects also have a tendency to attract lightning discharges. A good strategy, then, is to find a safe haven in a low spot close to but not directly under an object such as a tree that would bear the brunt of a strike.

A 30-foot-tall tree offers some protection if you're 20 or 25 feet away from it. When seeking a low spot, don't position yourself in a soggy basin, along a creek, along the base of a cliff, close to cracks in the rock, or at the entrance of a cave (the center of a spacious dry cave is okay). These places are likely to conduct ground currents and are not safe.

FRAGILE ECOSYSTEMS

The short growing season of the alpine and timberline zones poses severe challenges to the survival of the unique plants and animals existing there. Campfires are rightfully prohibited in these areas. Leave dead wood to build soil or for someone to use in an emergency.

When below timberline, restrict your campsites to forest duff (pine needles, dead leaves, but no shrubs or grasses), bare soil, or sandy areas free of vegetation. Never build a campfire on duff, however, since duff burns and smolders for a long time, possibly triggering a wildfire. Mountain meadows, especially just below timberline, are attractive as campsites but are not appropriate. Meadows are fragile and too wet and bumpy for a good camp; however, if you must make camp in a mountain meadow environment, do so on the outermost edge.

chapter
14

Desert Travel

David M. Gottfredson and Hal Brody

A certain spiritual quality can be found in the desert that is not found on the seashore, in the mountains, or along the rivers. There's an overwhelming sense of stillness, solitude, and space that is awe inspiring. The isolation and quiet is restful and you seldom encounter the hordes of people you often meet on mountain trails. With its meager vegetation and clear, dry air, the desert is full of mind-expanding perspectives. When was the last time you sat down on a hillside overlooking dozens, if not hundreds of square miles of open land with no sign of human activities?

There are no established trails in most parts of the desert, so hiking is considered cross-country. Going cross-country in the desert is relatively easy. Pick a direction and start walking. Just be aware of that occasional dry "waterfall" you have to scale or the patches of heavy vegetation that occur in the bottoms of washes and stream courses. These could involve some tricky maneuvering. Actually, some preplanning avoids most heavy bushwhacking. There's often not much to screen the view so even a slight elevation gain yields tremendously broad vistas. When camping, you needn't be concerned about bears getting into possessions and food, though rodents can be a minor problem.

When you travel through the desert, its geologic structure is laid

bare, revealing a kaleidoscope of shapes and colors. But the desert is full of other surprises as well. It's a real thrill to come upon a rare cactus, a trickling spring, a hidden palm oasis, or an ancient Native American artifact.

NORTH AMERICAN DESERTS

The desert regions of North America have little (about 10 inches or less) and irregular rainfall. Often the rain comes suddenly in the form of violent summer thunderstorms. Other common features are high daytime temperatures in the summer; low humidity; wide swings in temperature from day to night; frequent sunshine and clear, blue skies; soil that is low in humus and high in minerals; and a ground surface that gets easily eroded by wind and water. Under these severe conditions, plants and animals have had to employ unique—and sometimes bizarre—strategies in order to survive.

In addition to true deserts, there are semiarid areas that have many similarities to deserts. The Four Corners area of southeastern Utah, southwestern Colorado, northwestern New Mexico, and northeastern Arizona is perhaps the best-known example. The true North American desert can be divided into four regions based on distinct kinds of vegetation: the Great Basin, the Chihuahuan, the Sonoran, and the Mojave.

In general, the most interesting places to explore in any of these regions are the mountains that rise from the desert floor, the storm-carved canyons and dry river courses (washes) that infrequently carry runoff from these mountains, and the enigmatic, salt-encrusted sinks that collect the runoff. Wherever water has forced its way through soft earth (often old seabed sediment), fascinating "badlands" are formed.

DESERT TRAVEL

As in all wilderness travel, water is critical for travel in the desert. Water availability and abundance are subject to the whims of nature. Although many natural water sources exist in the desert, you cannot necessarily trust maps that show springs and permanent streams. Springs dry up, seasonally or permanently, and cartographers have a tough time keeping up with such changes. Check with rangers or people at other agencies such as the Bureau of Land Management (BLM) regarding water availability in the area you plan to visit.

More often than not you'll be traveling to areas of the desert that have no reliable sources of water. If you are unsure of the availability of

Opposite: *Hiking along a ridge in the desert. (Photo by David Gottfredson.)*

Many hikers are drawn to the stark, remote regions of the Southwest.

water, carry all the water you'll need for both drinking and cooking. A rough rule of thumb is 1 gallon per person per day, but this actually refers to sunny, mild weather conditions. Actual requirements could range from as little as 2 quarts per person per day on an overcast winter day in the high desert to more than 2 gallons per person per day on a 100°F day in the low desert. Since water weighs 8.3 pounds per gallon, your mobility may be severely limited if you're forced to carry your entire water supply. Remember that the heavier your pack, the more energy you exert and the more water you need.

Carry your water in several sturdy, leak-proof containers. If you divide up your water into several containers and one of them is punctured, you still have water in the others. Outdoor recreation stores sell a variety of plastic water bottles, but soda pop bottles from the grocery store are a great, lightweight way to carry water. From time to time you may encounter someone carrying a gallon water jug on a desert trail. Not only is this cumbersome and leaves you with one fewer free hand, but all those spiny plants found in the desert are great at poking holes in things and you may lose all your water before you know it. All water should be safely stowed in your pack. Keep a small bottle of water close at hand or use a water bladder to facilitate drinking often while walking.

If you're planning a trip where you hike in and out the same way, consider stashing some of your water on the way in. However, you must be able to find your stashed water on the way out. Unless you trust your memory absolutely, make a written note or a GPS reading on your map so you can find your water on the way out. And remember to take a look at where you stashed your water from the perspective of coming out on the trail. The trail often looks much different when traveling from the opposite direction.

Because it's possible to hike in almost any direction in the desert, it's very tempting to do so. If you're accustomed to staying on marked and maintained trails in the mountains you may not realize how easy it is to become lost or disoriented out in the open. Navigational skills are of paramount importance in the desert as is a constant awareness of major landmarks around you. When traveling cross-country be sure to bring all appropriate maps and your compass, and use them! Don't rely solely on GPS receivers as they often don't work well in deep, narrow canyons (no clear view of the sky to acquire satellites) and batteries do die. Check your location often; landmarks have a way of changing appearance as you move along. Don't allow yourself or others to become separated from the group. The desert's corrugated surface, just like a dense forest, can conceal a separated person in very little time.

The desert harbors a wonderful variety of beautiful yet potentially troublesome cacti and shrubs. These plants survive heat, drought, and hungry and thirsty animals through various strategies. Being sharp and thorny is one. If you're not watchful and careful of their sharp defenses, then you deserve what you get! Ocotillo branches contain long, sharp spikes. Look up often if you are hiking through an area that contains these plants; the branches have a tendency to bend over the trail just at head height.

Another fun plant is the cat claw acacia. A close look at the branches of this plant reveals sharp, curved thorns that resemble a cat's claw. These claws are great at ripping flesh and clothing, so it's best to steer clear whenever possible. If you become entangled in cat claw, usually the easiest thing to do is back out the way you came in so that the curved spines will slip out.

The cholla cactus is one of the prickliest plants in the desert. One variety is even nicknamed the teddy bear cholla because from a distance the light through its needles gives it a soft, fuzzy appearance. This plant is anything but soft and fuzzy. Each stem is covered with thousands of barbed needles that catch on anything, and the barbs make the needles hard to pull out. Adding to the threat this plant presents is its unique strategy for propagation: from the end of its branches it drops spine-laden balls that sprout to form new plants.

Because of the barbed spines, these balls can easily attach themselves to animals (including humans) to further their propagation. Another common name given to the plant is the "jumping cholla" because of the proclivity of the balls for attaching themselves to everything. If you aren't watching where you step you can pick up a ball on your boot and then jam it into your other leg. Or you could launch the ball from your foot to the person in front of you. In either case the effect is unpleasant.

If you do end up with a cholla ball attached to you, don't grab it. The easiest way to get the ball off is to slide a comb with wide teeth between your skin and the ball and then pull it off quickly. Make sure that no one is standing in your line of fire or you will just expand the agony. In a pinch, a rock or stick in each hand usually does the trick. Small pliers or hefty tweezers are useful for removing any remaining spines.

Another hazard in the desert is climbing steep, rocky slopes. When traveling up or down in this terrain, have the party spread out so that everyone is climbing or descending in a diagonal to the fall line rather

Cholla cactus, nemesis of desert hikers. (Photo by James Glenn Pearson.)

than straight up or down. If any rocks are kicked loose they will then pass to the side of your companions. If a rock is set in motion, yell out "Rock!" to warn those below.

Some people are quite anxious about rattlesnakes in the desert, although there tend to be more of them in the mountains. Between late fall and early winter, most desert-dwelling snakes are in hibernation. When they're out and about at other times, they're usually not aggressive unless provoked. Most retreat if given the opportunity. Still, always avoid placing your hands and feet in places you can't see clearly (see Chapter 10, Animal Encounters, "Poisonous Snakes"). Never harass or provoke a snake.

Desert washes are particularly prone to flash flooding, especially during the summer months when thunderstorms occur. Remember that runoff can be funneled into places far from where the rain falls, resulting in a wall of water packing enormous momentum. People have been killed on hot, sunny days because of heavy rains 30 or more miles from where they were hiking. If a flash flood is coming, there's usually some forewarning in the form of a low roar but often not enough time to get to higher ground, assuming there is high ground nearby that you can climb. Before your trip, keep a close check on the weather report for the region where you will be hiking. During the hike keep a watchful eye on the clouds, wind, and sky for signs of rain. Don't sleep in a wash even if you're sure no rain will fall either locally or upstream.

In all seasons except summer the weather in the desert is often quite mild. Expect daytime highs in the 60s to 80s. Winter nights, however, can get downright frigid—low 30s in the lower deserts, 20s in the Mojave, and even colder in the higher elevations of the Great Basin. Even the driest parts of the desert can get occasional heavy rainfall, while snow dusts the upper-elevation Mojave and Great Basin Deserts regularly. Hypothermia can be an unexpected threat.

Springtime weather in the desert can be quite fickle, ranging from high winds with mild temperatures to ovenlike heat. If the weather service says a warming trend is building with predicted temperatures in the 90s or higher, you should consider either canceling your trip or scaling back the miles you expect to cover.

Late May through September is usually too hot for strenuous activity in the desert. You should also be wary of early May, when the daylight hours are long and the sun's high angle at midday steals away the shade. Early October can also bring high temperatures. Again, check the weather before you depart on your trip and plan accordingly.

Clothing and Equipment

The desert can be extremely tough on the feet. The stiff and spiny vegetation, rocky terrain, and soft sand present unusual challenges. Boots with leather uppers provide excellent protection from cacti and rocks as well as providing good support. When walking over rocks of all shapes and sizes your feet and ankles need as much support as possible, especially if you're carrying the weight of a full backpack. Before wearing boots made of flimsier material, consider that a cactus spine can penetrate nylon boot material with almost the same ease as a sewing needle passes through nylon fabric.

In desert areas, shade may exist only in caves. (Photo by Al Hofstatter.)

Wear loose-fitting (not baggy) or stretchy long pants to avoid bruises and scrapes from climbing over rocks and brushing against cactus. The pants won't hinder your stride and will protect your legs from the ravages of the sun and plants.

Shade can be very hard to come by in the desert. A sun hat with a large brim is a necessity to keep from frying your brain. Gray matter is very sensitive to heat. It will be the first part of your body to malfunction when overheated. Without a hat you risk sunburn, headache, nausea, dizziness, or worse.

When the sun's up wear sunglasses that block ultraviolet rays, and wear long-sleeved and long-legged garments—especially if you're fair-skinned. Don't forget sunscreen with an SPF of at least 30 (or an SPF that is appropriate for you) on the exposed parts of your body.

Depending on what part of the desert you are traveling to you may need to be prepared for cold temperatures, rain, and even snow, so travel with the appropriate clothing and sleeping bag (see Chapter 5, Outfitting). Carry lightweight raingear and a tent if you'll be camping away from the car.

One word of caution regarding raingear in the desert: Those ponchos that are so popular in the mountains may become a worthless liability in the desert. Any clothing that is baggy or subject to billowing will snag on the many thorny plants in the desert. In no time those plants have shredded the raingear. This goes for garbage bags and other forms of makeshift raingear. A rainsuit is the superior option for desert travel.

Desert Survival

There are several techniques for locating water in the desert in an emergency. As you survey the desert landscape for possible water sources look for a line of trees or bushes that may indicate water at or near the surface. Palm trees are an indicator of surface or near-surface water, as are clumps of grass or sedges. Another likely place is the base of a steep canyon wall. Flocks of birds can sometimes be seen circling over waterholes, especially during mornings and evenings. Take note of the types of vegetation around a source of water. If perennial grasses or cat-tails aren't present, then the source probably dries up during the summer. When you find water, mark it on your map with the date, so you can build a valuable history of water sources in your favorite areas.

Tanks, or *tinajas* (naturally formed, water-filled depressions in rock), often serve the needs of desert animals. If the water supply is especially low, don't draw water from them unless you have to, as they should be left for the native animals. Large tanks holding thousands of gallons are good sources, though the water probably needs filtration or chemical purification. Spring-fed pools should be used only for drinking. Never do any washing (clothing, dishes, self) in a natural water source; always carry the water at least 200 feet from the stream, and wash with a small amount of biodegradable soap. Swimming in pools of the larger streams is a real treat in hot weather!

A few areas of the desert contain springs with unpalatable (salty or alkaline) or even poisonous water. Beware of water sources close to mine tailings (spoils). If the water has a normal amount of algae and crawling or wiggling critters, it's probably not poisonous. Beware of stagnant water with nothing alive in it. Tracks of animals are another positive sign—unless there are a lot of skeletal remains in the area. If in doubt about the water quality, check first with local authorities or rangers or avoid it.

If you find yourself in the grip of a heatwave and low on water, start thinking and planning immediately. Rest in the shade during the hottest part of the day, and make haste to get back to your car (or other point of safety) in the cool of the evening and early morning. Drink your remaining water as your thirst dictates. Saving your water is not the best solution if you're slipping into dehydration. Water left in your bottle does you no good. Don't waste time on schemes to extract water from cactus. Contrary to some popular (Hollywood-inspired) myths, lopping off the top of a barrel cactus does not reveal a reservoir of water. Instead you find a bitter, pulpy mass and you'll sweat out more water than you extract from the plant. Avoid eating also, as digestion uses water.

High-Temperature Strategies

For most people it makes good sense to stay out of the desert during the summer months, yet it can be frustrating to be "locked out" of your favorite desert areas for three or four months each year. Below are some strategies that make summer desert backpacking not only feasible but actually enjoyable. These strategies are quite applicable to the hot and dry conditions often found elsewhere in the arid West. Remember, however, that the hazards of summer desert travel are severe and should never be taken lightly or without proper training and preparation.

If you'd like to try high-temperature hiking or camping, then work up to it slowly. Start in the spring with short trips in the 90°F range. Try camping near your car and experiment with hikes that take you only a short distance away. Never let yourself become isolated from a source of water. You should stay close to a stream or spring or carry a supply that is adequate for any emergency, as discussed earlier.

Conditioning. Good aerobic conditioning is a prerequisite for any kind of high-temperature exercise. Always consult with your doctor before beginning a new exercise regimen, particularly one that involves high-temperature training. For three weeks before a trip practice heat conditioning in conjunction with normal exercise. Evidence of proper heat conditioning is profuse sweating. If the weather won't cooperate, then wear sweat clothes or other heat-retaining clothing while exercising to induce heavy perspiration. This practice trains the body's sweat glands to dilate quickly in response to overheating and the blood to circulate near the skin so as to liberate the body's internal heat. Psychological acclimation to heat is another benefit of heat conditioning. You become more comfortable with the feeling of simply being very warm. Forty-five minutes per session, 3 or 4 days per week seems to be adequate. Never withhold fluids while exercising or afterward; ignoring thirst is a dangerous practice. If you begin to feel dizzy or nauseous, stop immediately and cool down. Watch for signs of heat exhaustion or heat stroke (see Chapter 16, Wilderness First Aid, "Overheating").

Clothing. In a high-temperature environment, head-to-foot clothing offers protection from the radiant heat of the sun and from high winds that might evaporate perspiration too quickly. For the same reasons that cotton clothing is discouraged for most hiking situations

White clothing helps keep desert hikers cooler. (Photo by Hal Brody.)

(e.g., doesn't dry, doesn't retain heat, etc.), white, loose-fitting cotton clothing and a white, broad-brimmed hat can perform well for hot, dry days in the desert. In the absence of wind, some air circulation is needed to evaporate moisture from the skin, and thereby cool it. Cut slits or holes in your clothing where the sun doesn't shine—from armpits to elbows, from crotch to knees. Holes in the hat also help. Shirts that can be easily opened in the front when walking with the sun at your back are a real advantage. Skirts solve the air-circulation problem too, though they're awkward when climbing or scrambling and can get caught on all of the spiny bushes. Modern fabrics, such as silkweight polyester, are also acceptable options.

Although not a part of clothing, carry a small misting bottle full of water. A few sprays now and then on the face, neck, wrists, and other body parts can go along way in helping keep the body cool.

Electrolyte maintenance. The body must have a proper balance of electrolytes to function at peak efficiency. The electrolytes to be most concerned with are potassium, sodium, magnesium, and calcium. These, of course, are lost in part through perspiration. Normally you replace any losses by eating a normal diet. High-temperature activity causes per-spiration fluid loss of up to 2 gallons per day and consequently a very rapid loss of electrolytes. Fatigue and muscle cramps are the typical signs of electrolyte depletion.

Replenish electrolytes with commercial sport drinks or "thirst quenchers." Products such as Gookinaid ERG (Electrolyte Replacement with Glucose) and Cytomax are sold in ready-to-mix powder with ex-tra glucose (sugar) that gives a boost of energy and an "isotonic" mix that ensures quick absorption by the body. Other sport drinks may be overly sweet or too concentrated, so experiment with dilutions.

Emergencies. Even if you do everything right, you can still overheat. Watch each other closely for signs of heat exhaustion. A victim is often the last to notice the adverse effects of an overheated body and brain. Early signs are fuzzy thinking (slurred or incoherent speech), loss of balance, and stumbling. Nausea is also a sign of overheating.

Act quickly if this happens: Steer the victim to a shady spot. Every-one should be carrying a lightweight emergency blanket or space blan-ket, which can be used to create shade. If possible, insulate the victim from the hot ground by placing him on insulating sleeping or sitting pads. Other sitting pads or items of clothing can be used as fans if the air isn't moving fast enough. Remove excess clothing to ensure the maximum cooling effect of evaporation. If a water source is nearby, immerse the victim or shuttle water from the source to pour over his body (see Chapter 16, Wilderness First Aid, "Overheating"). If there's no water source nearby then at least mist the victim using two or three spray bottles that the group should carry. Meanwhile, assuming the victim is conscious, coax him every few minutes to take a few sips of water laced with electrolytes. Do not have him drink large amounts all at once, as that can be dangerous. And never try to give fluids to an unconscious person.

On the Road

Automobiles are essential tools for reaching the edge of the desert wilderness, but when broken down they can leave you miserably stranded. Keep in mind that the farther you drive into the backcountry, the farther you potentially drive from help. Unpaved desert roads can be in very poor condition, especially after severe weather. Never push your vehicle beyond its limits. It's better to turn back when in doubt than to find yourself stranded far from help. The following suggestions are meant to help you with the reliability of your transportation.

When traveling the back roads of the desert it's better to travel in two or more vehicles rather than one. If one breaks down someone can go for help.

Any vehicle used in the desert must be in good mechanical condition. Before going make sure your cooling system is in good working order. Get it pressure-tested. Your radiator should be filled with a mixture consisting of water and a coolant designed to withstand higher-than-normal temperatures. Check the condition and tightness of the hoses and fan belts, but also carry spares and the necessary tools to install and tighten them. If it's been a while since your car's last tune up, it may be a good idea to have your mechanic inspect it. It's also wise to carry an extra 5 gallons of water in case you lose your radiator water through a ruptured hose. Carry clean water in case you need to drink some of it.

Monitor your temperature gauge or warning light as you're driving. If overheating is indicated, stop your vehicle and engine as soon as it's safe to do so. Check the fan belt; if too loose it slips and reduces the effectiveness of your fan and/or water pump. Check the coolant level at the overflow tank—determine if and where you are losing coolant. Do repairs if necessary and, once the engine has cooled down, add water back into the system if needed. (Note: Never remove the radiator cap while the engine is hot. You will get a face full of dangerously hot steam.)

If the problem is due to a ruptured hose and you don't have the right hose to replace it, radiator-hose repair tape (duct tape may work) can get you moving again. Wrap, as tightly as possible, the ruptured section of hose and don't forget to loosen or remove the radiator cap to reduce pressure in the system and the rate of any leaks. The tape prevents the coolant from escaping. However, without the radiator cap the coolant slowly boils away. Be sure to check the coolant level often and once you're on the road again check and refill the coolant level at least every half hour. The repair tape is, of course, a very temporary fix.

A less likely cause of overheating is a stuck thermostat preventing coolant from reaching the radiator. This can be cured by removing the thermostat once the engine has cooled (learn how to do this ahead of time). You will lose coolant while removing the thermostat so again be sure to carry extra water.

If, after stopping with a hot engine, everything looks OK, then proceed at a slower speed as soon as the engine has cooled. Slower speeds mean less power output and less heat production. Don't turn on the air conditioner since it requires the engine to work harder, thus generating more heat. By turning on the heater (uncomfortable as it may be) you can draw off additional heat from your engine to help cool it. Watch your temperature gauge and take it easy, especially on the uphills.

If you need to carry extra gasoline, do so in an approved container. Legally these containers must be carried securely attached to the outside of the vehicle rather than packed inside. This is for obvious safety reasons.

Extra motor oil, jumper cables, and a gas-tank patch kit should be carried. It's easy to puncture your gas tank while bouncing over rocky roads, especially if you yield to the temptation to cover those endless desert miles too quickly. Use caution even if you are driving an SUV that has a gas tank skid plate. Often the stock skid plates are thin and only offer limited protection. However, they are better than nothing. If you will be driving off-road often, consider installing upgraded skid plates.

When driving through rocky areas be particularly aware of components that hang down under your vehicle. Typically the minimum clearance under the vehicle is at the differential (both front and rear if driving a four-wheel-drive vehicle). Steer around rocks to avoid hitting the differential(s), oil pan, or transmission. If you hit one of these components you could crack the case causing it to loose all of its lubricant. There is no repair in the field for a cracked oil pan, and you may find yourself stranded. Sometimes it's better to drive the tires over rocks rather than trying to straddle them. However, be sure that rocks are not taller than the clearance between the vehicle frame and the ground or you may become high centered. The potential for high-centering becomes greater the longer the wheel base of the vehicle.

Stash a tow rope and shovel in the vehicle and know how to use them. Getting stuck in the sand happens to almost every desert adventurer sooner or later. A 1-foot-square piece of plywood acting as a base for a jack allows it to lift more efficiently in soft sand. Strips of old carpet or hardware cloth placed under the tires can help you escape problem spots. When you start to drive out of the soft spot, keep the front wheels straight and apply power slowly. Don't spin the wheels, as this digs the tires in deeper. Soft, sandy roads can be more easily negotiated by deflating the tires to about 15 pounds per square inch (psi) of pressure, but the process of pumping them back up to recommended pressure can be time consuming, even with a battery-operated tire pump.

However, if you get stuck in sand in the middle of nowhere, let some air out of the tires even if you don't have a tire pump. Reducing the air pressure increases the footprint of the tire, giving you better traction. Once you're out of the sand, even at 15 psi you can drive short distances on the highway at slow speeds (less than 35 miles per hour; slower on winding roads). Keep in mind, however, that driving on the highway with reduced tire pressures can be dangerous, should only be done in an emergency, and should never be done at high speeds. Repressurize the tires to the appropriate level at the first opportunity. Don't wait until you get home.

Hone your tire-changing skills and make sure the jack is operational and the spare tire is pressurized. The jack is a powerful tool for getting your vehicle off a big rock or anything else that might keep the weight off the wheels. However, the jack that came with your vehicle was made for lifting on smooth, level surfaces, and it may not work in the soft, uneven terrain of the backcountry. Become familiar with its operation and limitations. If you travel the back roads frequently, consider purchasing an off-highway jack appropriate for your vehicle.

If your vehicle breaks down irreparably, stay with it unless it's obvious you can walk for help. Consider both your capabilities and the weather conditions. There are many stories of people stuck in the desert in which one person goes for help leaving the other with the vehicle; the rescuers find the person with the vehicle safe and sound while their partner is found dead just a short distance away.

Use your head. It is much easier to spot a big vehicle than it is to spot a person. In an emergency, call attention to yourself by using the vehicle's horn, lights, and mirrors. For instance, remove the spare tire and drag it away from the vehicle. Deflate it, douse it with gasoline, ignite it, and let it burn with copious black smoke for a long time (be careful not to set the desert on fire and only consider burning a tire as a last resort). If you spot a rescue plane flying overhead, lie flat on the ground and make yourself big by spreading your arms and legs; don't jump around. Use a mirror to signal the plane by reflecting the sun. If you need shelter from the sun, dig out enough room under your vehicle to comfortably lie on your insulated sleeping pad. Store water in your body, not in your water bottles. Don't drink radiator water unless it contains only water, and filter it if you do. (See Chapter 17, Search and Rescue, "Being Lost and Dealing with It," for more information.)

PRESERVING THE DESERT

More so in the desert than almost any other place, it's important to pack out all trash, including paper items like toilet tissue and sanitary supplies. Everything decomposes very slowly in the absence of water. If buried around a campsite, paper can be unearthed by the winds, by animals, or by an unfortunate hiker, thereby announcing the earlier presence of careless humans. Don't burn your toilet paper. As strange as it may sound, numerous fires have been started in the desert through this simple act. The simple rule is: If you pack it in, pack it out.

When you break camp in the desert, return the site to its natural appearance. Scatter or remove campfire rings or blackened rocks and sand. Never build a fire under or next to a rock overhang, as the smoke will blacken the rocks. Many state and national parks allow ground fires only if they are contained in a metal pan and the ashes packed out. Consider doing this even if it isn't required to reduce the impact on the land.

A "buddy burner" is often all you really need at night. To make one, cut a strip of cardboard as wide as the height of a small can such as a tuna-fish can, spiral the cardboard inside the can, and then fill the can to the top with melted paraffin. When ready to use, light the cardboard, which acts as a wick. Ideally, use a can with a (metal) lid. Replace the lid to extinguish the burner and it's ready to go the next evening. A buddy burner of this size burns for about 2 hours, even in a strong wind, and has a flame sufficient for a group of fifteen. It does not create much heat but enough warm light to chat by. A larger-diameter can yields a larger flame, and a deeper one burns longer. Bigger, however, means heavier— an important consideration when backpacking.

The toughness of the desert is, in a way, just a façade. The desert ecosystem is actually quite fragile. Desert plants grow very slowly and are always struggling for survival. Any damage inflicted can scar the land for decades. In some areas of the desert you can still see tank tracks left by U.S. military training efforts during World War II. In other areas, grazing cattle have displaced the native wildlife and pulverized the vegetation. One insensitive person with an off-road vehicle can do a tremendous amount of destruction in only a few minutes. Even hikers can do damage.

One little-known life-form that needs protection is cryptobiotic crust, a brittle layer made up of lichens, mosses, algae, and fungi. It appears as a lumpy ground cover about 1 inch thick, and black, green, or white, depending on the organisms it contains.

Cryptobiotic crust is an important link in the desert ecosystem because it stabilizes and builds fertile soil by preventing erosion and fixing nitrogen. Spongy and resilient when wet, it becomes vulnerable

A buddy burner provides a surprising amount of heat and light. (Photo by Carol Brody.)

when dry, which is most of the time. Crunched to a powder when stepped on, it can blow away with the next breeze. Research has shown that it can take from 50 to 200 years for cryptobiotic crust to regenerate. Hikers needing to cross areas covered by cryptobiotic crust can minimize impact by using a single set of footprints while walking single file. Please avoid cryptobiotic areas whenever possible, particularly when selecting a campsite. Whenever possible, restrict your route of travel to durable surfaces such as washes or over rocks to avoid crushing this delicate desert resource.

If you find something of interest in the desert, your grandchildren and their grandchildren will probably find it fascinating too. Leave it there for others to see and enjoy. Artifacts of past human habitation, such as pottery shards, are still found in relative abundance. In the desert they provide an almost magical reminder of past civilizations and spiritual heritage. In many desert areas it's illegal to remove anything at all. So should it be for all wilderness areas. Native American pictographs and petroglyphs (rock art) are particularly vulnerable. Do not touch them or build a campfire too close to the rocks. Please do your part to protect the land's cultural heritage. Take your souvenirs home in your camera, not in your backpack. See Chapter 2, Outdoor Ethics, for more information.

In *Desert Solitaire,* Edward Abbey offers us a powerful insight into the nature of the desert wilderness: "Despite its clarity and simplicity . . . the desert wears at the same time, paradoxically, a veil of mystery. Motionless and silent it evokes in us an elusive hint of something unknown, unknowable, about to be revealed. Since the desert does not act it seems to be waiting—but waiting for what?"

Searching for that "unknowable" is what keeps us going back to the desert again and again.

Winter Mountaineering

Dave Ussell and Bob Feuge

The mantle of white enshrouding the winter landscape is simultaneously an invitation to experience one of nature's most beautiful spec-
tacles and a warning to be more wary and respectful than usual of the
dangers that await the unprepared. Fortunately, preparations are not
as difficult as they may first appear. An outing in the snow is enhanced
by breathtaking scenery, a virtually unspoiled wilderness, and a dearth
of insects and dangerous creatures. The stillness and tranquility of the
winter landscape is seldom spoiled by hordes of fellow travelers, and
the winter traveler is not restricted to staying on trails, if, indeed, trails
can be found at all.

CLOTHING AND EQUIPMENT

Winter travel places stringent demands on clothing and equipment.
Certain advantages claimed for equipment used during the warmer
three seasons can be more pronounced when the same equipment is
tested during the fourth season. A case in point is the performance of
internal- versus external-frame packs. An internal-frame pack's stream-
lined design sheds snow, hail, and wind more easily than an external-
frame pack does. Its body-hugging shape does not impair the wearer's
balance as much as an external-frame pack. With no exposed metal,

internal-frame packs are easier and safer to handle with bare skin under extremely cold conditions.

Winter Clothing

Clothes retain body heat in cold conditions, but less clothing allows for evaporative cooling in warmer conditions or when generating a lot of heat through exercise. The winter traveler must be prepared for both and must do so with a limited wardrobe that is multipurpose and efficient. Thus, the layering system discussed in Chapter 5, Outfitting, becomes critically important.

The winter traveler should be prepared to put on any combination of layers that accomplish the following:

- Trap warm air
- Hold in body moisture (when not exercising heavily)
- Keep winds from removing body heat
- Resist the passage of water from outside to inside
- Allow ventilation and encourage the passage of moisture from inside to outside (when exercising)
- Allow freedom of movement
- Provide some protection from abrasion and penetration

These layers, ideally, are light in weight, low in cost, and easily repaired. Several synthetics—such as polypropylene, Capilene, pile, bunting, Synchilla, and fleece—do a good job of letting body moisture escape from the skin. Wool is the only common natural fiber that can provide significant warmth when wet. Most kinds of wool are too scratchy to be considered an acceptable choice for underwear. For this reason, Capilene and polypropylene are some of the most popular choices, but some synthetic underwear may have a tendency to retain body odors, even after laundering.

For warmth, almost any material that traps air and minimizes its motion can be potentially useful. Wool, duck or goose down, and synthetic materials such as Quallofil, Polarguard, and Hollofil work well, with various advantages and disadvantages. The synthetics have the advantage of providing some warmth when wet, whereas down provides more warmth for the same weight but is ineffective when wet.

To block the wind, a nonporous synthetic shell (outer garment) is best. There are many materials suited to this task, including nylon

Opposite: Hiking poles can be indispensable when climbing steep areas. (Photo by Skip Forsht.)

(Taslan) and Gore-Tex. The design of the shell should include adequate provision for ventilation. Jackets or parkas lined with an outer shell are fine for urban use, but they don't offer enough versatility for use under changeable winter conditions. Consider as an alternative a pile jacket and a separate shell garment. This affords comfort in moderately cold conditions (using just the jacket) and/or in windy conditions.

The use of vapor-barrier materials, such as plastic, urethane-coated nylon, or rubber, can be advantageous in certain situations. When the temperature is extremely low, a vapor-barrier layer under a jacket can add as much as 15°F of apparent warmth, although effective ventilation must be assured by such features as underarm zippers for use while exercising. Vapor-barrier mittens and socks are usable over a much wider range of temperature and activity. A simple way to test the effectiveness of vapor barriers is to wear plastic bread bags between inner and outer socks. As a result, your feet may feel slightly clammy but will most likely stay warmer while out in the snow.

With the right combination of long underwear, a layer or layers of insulating garments, and a wind- and rain-resistant shell, comfort can be achieved under almost any conditions. Of course, it must be remembered that heat losses also occur from the extremities and from the head—more than 30 percent from the head alone. Polypropylene liner gloves and a ski mask, or balaclava, are good first layers. On top of those should be insulating layers consisting of gloves or mittens and a wool/polypropylene hat. Nonporous overmitts and a hood can be used for extreme conditions. Hoods work best when they are attached to a jacket or parka. Outer gloves should have a nonslip surface on the palm and a large gauntlet with a tightening arrangement to minimize drafts. It is common practice on winter expeditions to keep gloves on lengths of cord attached to the wearer in some way to avoid loss if they are removed for any reason.

It's worth mentioning that sometimes winter conditions can be more dangerous on warmer days. Sunshine or higher temperatures may cause snow to melt on contact with your clothing. If seams are not sealed properly or the outer material is porous, your clothing may absorb a lot of water, which then greatly reduces the effectiveness of the insulation when the sun sets and the temperature begins to fall.

It is very important on any winter outing to have at least two sets of clothing, particularly those garments that stay close to your body, such as long underwear. At all times, at least one set of clothing should be dry or at least in the process of being dried. Few things can ruin a winter trip faster than wet, cold clothing.

Wrap your extra dry clothes in plastic bags and seek opportunities to dry moist or wet clothing when your travel itinerary, or sunshine, permits. Many tents have loops inside to accommodate stringing up clotheslines. A candle lantern can do a remarkable job of drying clothes under adverse conditions.

Packs

Proper gear and clothing is often neglected by novices who, by not taking extra clothing and other items, foolishly count on near-perfect weather and no delays. It's better to take along a larger day pack or backpack than needed. This reduces the temptation to leave important things behind and makes carrying the extra load more comfortable. For cross-country ski touring in particular, a pack must allow the arms to move freely past the body while poling. When loading a backpack for overnight use, put the heavy items close to the back, not near the top. Pack medium-weight items at the bottom, and afterward stuff the lighter items anywhere they'll fit. Use plastic bags or coated nylon sacks to protect all items from snow and to group items by use.

Boots

Boots used for winter mountaineering should keep feet dry and warm. Don't try to keep feet warm by putting on more socks to the extent that circulation is reduced; it only makes feet colder. Waterproof conventional leather boots with a sealer specifically designed for that purpose. Gaiters (the knee-high size is best) are helpful not only for keeping boots dry from the outside, but also for keeping snow from spilling in from the top. Certain expensive gaiters have such features as full boot-upper coverage, Gore-Tex material, and insulation.

Even properly sealed boots can become soaked on long trips. A neophyte might handle the problem by merely setting the boots aside in camp and putting on some warm booties. By morning, the boots are frozen solid. A better choice is to slowly dry the boots near a campfire. Another alternative is to put on a dry pair of inner socks and then vapor-barrier socks (plastic bags will do). On top of that, put on the outer socks (ideally dry ones) and then the wet boots. To further the drying process, either place the boots in a plastic bag and sleep with them, or put a trash bag in the bottom of your sleeping bag (to protect the bag) and sleep with your boots on. This approach may not produce the most comfortable of nights, but life will be easier in the morning.

Plastic mountaineering boots with removable inner boots are an excellent choice for the fourth season. They're rugged, warm, and waterproof, and easily accept crampons, gaiters, and snowshoes. The inner boots alone can be worn in the tent. On the negative side, they're fairly stiff, heavy, and expensive. Stiffness in a boot can be an asset in many climbing situations, however. Even when walking on flat terrain, the snow gives a little, which compensates for the lack of flexing in the boot.

Walking in deep, soft snow with a pack is an exhausting process. With each step you can sink up to the crotch, and forward progress is excruciatingly slow. This is called postholing. The solution: Wear either snowshoes or skis, which lower your pressure on the ground by spreading your body weight over a larger area. It's also possible to lighten or eliminate any load on your back by placing your gear in a lightweight sled specially designed to be towed by a skier or snowshoer.

Cross-country skis, unlike snowshoes, require special boots. When shopping for skis, you're really looking for a system of skis, bindings, boots, and poles. Ski boots are designed for use with particular types of bindings, which are attached to the skis by special tools. An outfitter can help sort through the many options and help you choose the right system.

Ski boots for day tours or ski backpacks should be durable and warm, have good torsional rigidity yet some forward flex, and extend just above the ankle bone to provide lateral support and ankle protection. Boots with uppers made of Gore-Tex or other synthetic fabrics are OK for light uses; leather boots are much better, as long as they're waterproofed with the appropriate silicone or beeswax sealant.

Snowshoes

Snowshoe selection is based on the user's weight (with gear) and the type of terrain to be covered. Snowshoes with an upturned lip are best for powdery snow. Flat and open terrain allows larger snowshoes to be used. Smaller snowshoes with various lip curvatures are better for steep, rough, or brushy terrain. Your local outfitter can offer advice about appropriate sizes and types of bindings. Older snowshoes consisted of little more than a wooden frame with a rawhide weave. Many newer snowshoes have lightweight aluminum frames, reinforced neoprene pad areas, easily disconnected bindings, and fixed or movable toothed grips for climbing slopes.

Cross-Country Skis

Cross-country skis are designed to grip the snow when your full weight is applied and to slide smoothly on the snow when less weight is applied. This allows you to "kick and glide" forward on the snow. Proper ski length and stiffness is important since the middle, or kick zone, of the ski bottom must be in contact with the snow during the kick, and should be off the snow during the glide.

Generally, the length of a properly fitted ski should reach from the floor to the wrist of your raised arm. When you stand on the skis during the fitting, a piece of paper should easily slide under the kick zone (middle) when both skis are equally weighted, but each ski should touch the floor when weighted singly.

Cross-country skiing opens new worlds to the outdoor enthusiast. (Photo by Jerry Schad.)

For ski travel in mountainous terrain, off-track touring skis are needed. These have a narrow waist, a wider tail, and an even wider tip. Skis without these characteristics are suited for use on groomed tracks or race courses, but not for true cross-country travel. For general ski touring, skis should have enough camber (flex) so that they can be pressed together, bottom-to-bottom, with one hand.

Unless you're willing to spend the time required to gain enough experience in waxing, start out with no-wax skis, which have a relief pattern on the bottom to grip the snow when kicking. "No-wax" is a bit of a misnomer, since even they can benefit from the application of a glide wax (paraffin candle wax will do) on the tip and tail portions. Waxable skis, with a smooth bottom, require the application of wax on the kick zone to provide the needed grip.

Metal-edged skis are best for technical demands of steep, icy slopes, but they are normally not required for skiing in softer snow. Metal-edged skis are heavier and less flexible, and wet snow tends to freeze and stick to the metal edges.

When wearing a heavy pack, you may need to have skis that are either wider (to provide additional flotation) or metal-edged (for stability).

Skins are an optional but very useful aid in ski touring. Today they're made with mohair (goat hair), nylon, or polypropylene fibers. One side has short hairs facing one direction, and the other side has a reusable adhesive. When the sticky side is applied to the bottom of the skis, the hairs grip the snow (but not ice) and keep the ski from back-sliding when climbing steep hills. Skins, of course, prevent efficient gliding, but this can be an advantage when it's necessary to keep your speed down on steep downhills.

Ski poles are essential to maintain balance and to assist with forward propulsion. Aluminum alloy poles, preferably a high-grade aircraft type, are best. If bent, they can usually be straightened in the field. Fiberglass poles, while cheaper, can shatter. Generally, the poles should just fit under your underarms when the tips are touching the floor.

Ice Ax

For winter mountaineering, there are not many pieces of equipment as useful as an ice ax (fig. 15-1). For a person falling on a steep slope, the ice ax is the only piece of equipment that can arrest the slide in a rapid and controlled manner.

Select a longer ax if your travels are mostly on gentle inclines and a shorter one if you're climbing a lot. Lightweight, metal ice axes are very

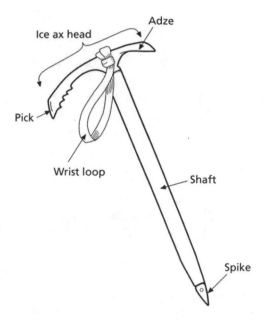

Figure 15-1: *Parts of an ice ax.*

strong, moderately priced, and require little maintenance. But they're always cold to the touch under winter conditions. Carbon-fiber axes are strong and absorb shock well but are very expensive and not so forgiving if a boulder should bounce off the shaft. Ice axes with wooden shafts are weaker and less expensive than the others. Hickory shafts are usually preferred to ash. Gouges in wooden or synthetic axes are greater cause for concern than in metal. Holes should never be drilled in axes for any kind of attachment. Most ice axes already have a hole in the head for utility use. The ax should be kept free of rust and deposits and sharpened with a file when needed. Sharpening with a grinder can cause excessive heat that could affect the temper of the metal.

Crampons

For icy conditions there's no substitute for crampons, boot attachments with sharp metal points designed to penetrate and grip hard snow and ice (fig. 15-2). Crampons are designed with either a full strap binding or a step-in attachment that slips over the toe-end welt of the boot and attaches with a strap around the ankle.

Crampons typically have ten primary, downward-pointing points and two forward-pointing points for climbing. Like the ice ax, the

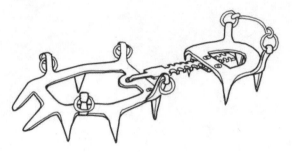

Figure 15-2: *Crampons (strap binding not shown).*

points should be kept sharp at all times. Protective sheaths for the points are commercially available but can be improvised with tape and old inner tubes, or something similar.

Sleds

There are a few decisions to make in selecting a sled for toting gear. All of the standard considerations of weight, material, cost, and ease of operation and maintenance apply. In addition, some ridges or runners, which function like a keel on a sailboat, must be on the bottom to allow easy forward motion and tracking but to limit lateral motions. A special, semirigid harness is used to maintain the separation of traveler and sled when descending.

Special Climbing Gear

Winter climbing involves most of the usual rock-climbing gear discussed in books on technical climbing. Somewhat unique to winter climbing are the ice ax, ice screws, and "deadmen." Ice screws take the place of pitons, nuts, and chocks for use as anchors on ice. A deadman anchor (fig. 15-3) is simply a big, flat object that resists movement

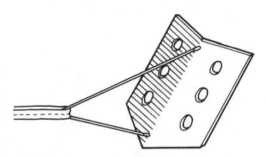

Figure 15-3: *Deadman anchor.*

perpendicular to its plane. If driven into consolidated snow at a slight angle, like a tent stake, it becomes a very good anchor. The angle should be such that increased pull drives it deeper into the snow, anchoring it more firmly.

Sleeping Equipment

Sleeping equipment for winter mountaineering should be maximized for warmth. It may be worth 5–15°F of extra warmth if an optional vapor-barrier or flannel liner is used. An obvious and easy way to increase insulation is to wear some or all of your insulating layers of clothing inside your bag—assuming there's enough room.

A weight-conscious backpacker who takes a lightweight, three-quarter-length sleeping pad for the other three seasons shouldn't skimp on a full-length pad for winter use. Much of a sleeping person's body heat escapes downward into snow if there isn't a sufficient insulating barrier.

Many people like to zip together two sleeping bags, which provides extra warmth and space for the pair. During cold-weather campouts, however, this arrangement may be less practical for restless sleepers, since warm air easily escapes and cold air rushes in. Attaching sleeping bags in the winter should be used for emergencies involving hypothermia, where it may be necessary to help warm a victim by body-to-body contact. It's a good idea for a group of winter wilderness travelers to have at least one pair of mating sleeping bags.

Special Items

Certain items not normally needed on most three-season trips may be of special use on winter trips. A lightweight snow shovel can help speed up tasks such as digging trenches or snow caves for shelter. An aluminum snow saw is indispensable for cutting blocks used for igloos.

Altimeters can be critical if it's necessary to navigate in white-out or poor-visibility conditions. They can also be used to keep track of barometric pressure and changes in the weather.

Weather radios can be a good tool, but remember that batteries must be in top condition to perform at reduced temperatures. In remote areas, the signal strength of the nearest station may not be adequate for good reception.

Most sunglasses are not adequate for snow travel in bright sunlight. In addition to a pair of sunglasses for use in shady conditions or on overcast days, you should carry glacier glasses, which feature extra-dark lenses and opaque panels on the sides to keep out glare.

If you're bringing equipment to cover an expedition's special needs, include repair items to keep that equipment in working order. Consider taking extra fasteners and lightweight tools for equipment such as snowshoes, rope to lash things together and for making splints, and possibly hose clamps, duct tape, and wire for general repair of a variety of equipment.

WINTER TRAVEL TECHNIQUES
Over Snow and Ice

When traveling on a hard crust of snow or ice, an ice ax and, in more extreme cases, crampons become necessary tools.

When carrying an ice ax that isn't needed for emergency use, tie it to your pack, or carry it in either of two ways (fig. 15-4): Grasp the shaft at the balance point with the tip forward and the pick to the rear and down. Or use the ice ax as a hiking stick with your palm resting on the head of the ax directly over the shaft with the pick forward (see fig. 15-1 for ice-ax terminology).

In the ready position (fig. 15-5), hold the ax diagonal across your chest, with the pick to the rear, and grasp the lower part of the shaft with the opposite hand. Normally the ax head is in the uphill hand. In the ready position, the wrist strap is used to retrieve a lost ax if necessary. The ready position allows you to immediately go into a self-arrest maneuver (fig. 15-6) that minimizes sliding after a fall.

During a slide or fall on snow or ice, the pick must be driven hard and quick into the surface to stop the slide. This must be done while

Figure 15-4: *Carrying an ice ax, left to right: carrying at balance point with pick down; using as cane; tied to pack.*

simultaneously keeping the spike off of the surface. If the spike snags, it has a tendency to pull out the pick. If wearing crampons, it is important that they don't become snagged either.

During most falls, speed builds rapidly, so quick reflexes are mandatory. Personal instruction and considerable practice is necessary for learning the various ways of self-arrest for the various types of falls. An ice ax does little good, and may even do harm, to an unskilled user.

When ascending steeper slopes with consolidated snow that is not too icy, use your ice ax as an anchor, planting its spike in a new spot ahead of yourself after every step or two. If you're

Figure 15-5: *Top, the ready grip; Bottom, the ready position.*

Figure 15-6: *Self-arrest.*

wearing boots, kick-step by driving the toe of the boot far enough into the snow to form a level platform to step up on.

On steep, hard-packed snow or ice, either resort to wearing crampons or chop-stepping. Chop-stepping uses the adze of the ice ax to cut a small platform for weight transfer. In either case, rope up with others or belay (protected by rope). Detailed information on these techniques can be found in *Mountaineering: The Freedom of the Hills* (The Mountaineers Books, 2003).

When descending a steep slope, all of the same conditions for ascending must be considered, with some additions. Descending is less exhausting, but the tradeoff

Figure 15-7: *Plunge step.*

Figure 15-8: *Sitting glissade.*

is that it can be much harder to locate secure footings. If the slope is not too steep, use a plunge-step technique (fig. 15-7) to walk downhill, or glissade. A glissade (fig. 15-8) is nothing more than sliding on your feet or backside to the bottom of a slope and using an ice ax (in a ready position with spike dragging) as a kind of brake and rudder. In the plunge step, compaction of snow does the braking. The descent becomes a bouncy and somewhat animated jaunt down the slope with the ice ax ever ready to handle a fall.

Glaciers present different problems such as crevasses (cracks) that develop when a glacier flows over a convex surface. Some crevasses are visible, while others may lie under a thin veneer of snow, ready to swallow the incautious traveler. Even when on level terrain, all members of a climbing party must be tied into a rope so that if someone drops into a crevasse, the others can use their ice axes to arrest the fall. The rescue of that climber is an advanced but necessary technique that must be mastered by prospective glacier travelers.

Cross-Country Skiing

Cross-country skiing, also known as Nordic skiing, is becoming a popular means of gaining access to the wilderness in the winter. It may require you to traverse both flat and mountainous areas during a wilderness trek, sometimes on groomed tracks and other times on virgin snow. The latter conditions particularly attract those who cherish the solitude and unblemished natural beauty of winter scenery as well as a good physical workout.

There are many ways for the cross-country skier to move through the backcountry. The diagonal stride is a good way to get around on the flats or on gently rolling terrain. This technique resembles walking, except that the feet slide instead of being lifted. At the same time extra propulsion is gained by planting one pole at a time in the snow and pushing back and down on it.

Proper position is important to avoid fatigue and falls. Keep the knees slightly bent and the body's center of gravity above the ski bindings. Bent knees serve as shock absorbers that cushion the effects of moving over uneven snow.

On level or near-level terrain, the step turn is the basic technique for changing direction. The step turn is carried out as though you are walking and turning at the same time, using poles for balance. However, each step can provide only a small amount of turn because you cannot cross skis without risking a fall. Another basic technique for changing direction is the kick turn. The kick turn is accomplished by first lifting one ski and thrusting it forward and upward, finally placing it in a vertical position with the heel of the ski resting on the snow at a point approximately even with the shovel of the other ski. Now lower and pivot that ski so that it ends up on the snow parallel to the first ski but facing in the opposite direction. Use your poles to maintain balance while lifting and swinging the second ski into place beside the first ski, both now facing in the same direction. The kick turn is an excellent means to make quick reversals of direction or turns in tight spaces.

When going downhill, it is frequently necessary to change direction while on the move. Such turns can be accomplished by a simple snowplow (wedge) technique or by the more sophisticated telemark technique. Such turning techniques also allow you to control your speed on the slope. To make a snowplow turn, push outward from your heels to force the backs of the skis apart and bring the shovels (tips) of the skis together. This action produces the $\wedge$ pattern of the snowplow. By pinching the knees together, the skis are rolled onto their inside edges, increasing the friction of the skis against the snow. To turn with the snowplow, simply shift your weight onto the ski that is opposite the direction you want to go. Thus, a right turn is accomplished by shifting your weight onto the left ski and holding it there until the turn is accomplished. To stop completely, hold the snowplow wedge through the turn until you are heading slightly uphill. Gravity and friction combine to bring you to a stop.

The telemark turn is an advanced technique requiring considerable athletic ability and practice. The telemark technique is well described in *Cross Country Skiing* by Ned Gillette and John Dostal (The Mountaineers Books, 1988). It is used in conditions that do not let you use the snowplow (wedge) or kick turn.

When skiing downhill, don't bend forward from the hips, which puts your head in a vulnerable position during a fall. Instead, bend your knees deeper, especially when going faster. The bent position lowers your center of gravity and makes it easier to recover from being off balance. If a fall is inevitable, then try to relax and fall to either side, with both legs together and bent. Don't try (which is instinctive) to catch the fall and land on a hand or elbow. This response invites injury.

Another instinctive problem for beginning skiers is fear of the fall line. This fear is triggered when a turn is initiated and as the skis turn toward the downhill direction, you sense that you are leaning downhill. Instinctively, you recoil from danger, lean back on the skis, and the skis zoom downward, now out of control. What the beginner skier must remember is to keep composure and maintain center of gravity over the turning ski, even when pointed downhill. By keeping the knees bent, **center of gravity slightly forward,** and weight on the turn ski, the skis will turn smoothly. And best of all, you won't lose control.

If you do fall, recover by getting the skis below you and perpendicular to the slope. Roll your body forward so that your knees are over the front of the skis. By pushing off your poles, you should be able to resume standing on your skis with some effort. This technique also requires practice.

When choosing a route on skis, look for areas where the snow has been softened slightly by the sun. Try to stay away from shaded spots where an ice crust can occur. Avoid embedded rocks and trees—holes may lie next to them. Also try to pick routes away from windblown or icy patches (these often have a sheen), and always be aware of avalanche hazards. With experience, you'll be able to read the snow and pick the most efficient and safest routes.

A host of advanced techniques (best left to personal instruction or references listed in the Appendix) can be used for both ascending and descending on skis.

SHELTER

Shelters in the winter wilderness can range from easily moveable four-season tents to semipermanent igloos and emergency snow caves. Any shelter—even a cozy cabin—may require frequent attention if snow is falling thick and fast. It may be necessary to go outside often and dig out entrances or doors, clear ventilation holes, or brush off accumulated snow from tent walls.

Tents

Four-season tents are generally heavier to carry, but their safety and comfort in the winter environment are well worth the extra weight. Compared to ordinary tents, they usually have the following:

- Weather-resistant tunnel for entering and exiting the tent (more than one entrance is desirable)
- Vestibule for cooking and storing gear
- Structural design that withstands severe winds and resists collapse when weighed down by an accumulation of snow
- Adequate separation maintained between the tent's inner walls and an outer, waterproof shell, or fly, which improves

ventilation, reduces condensation on the inner walls, and improves the tent's insulating ability
- Enhanced water resistance

Regarding the last point, some tents designed for use in the snow lack a sewn-in floor. This allows ski poles to be used as tent poles, and it also reduces the likelihood of a fire in the tent due to a cooking mishap. The lower edges of this type of tent should be buried in the snow to eliminate drafts.

Flimsy tent stakes normally used for summer camping are practically useless in the snow. Use wide, strong, lightweight aluminum stakes or improvise in the field and make your own deadman tent stakes: Tie a 2-foot section of $1/8$-inch or thicker rope to each staking grommet on the tent, and tie 6-inch or longer pieces of rigid material (thick tree or shrub branches will do) to the other ends of the ropes. Never break off live branches for this, always use fallen wood. Dig a shallow pit in the snow for each deadman and bury it with rope attached. By compacting the snow above and around each deadman, you can create anchors almost as rigid as blocks of ice. If the snow is powdery and compaction is inadequate, try pouring water into the snow above the deadmen to freeze them in. Very secure deadman anchors can be difficult to remove; either use an ice ax or snow shovel or chip away at the snow by kicking it with a boot.

When choosing a tent site, avoid spots beneath trees that collect large amounts of snow. High winds or a rising temperature could dump that snow on the tent. Never pitch a tent with an entrance facing the prevailing wind, where falling or drifting snow will pile up.

Once the tent is pitched, set up some kind of comfortable quarters outside for cooking and eating—if the weather is good. Use a snow shovel or improvise using pots and pans to scoop out a two-tier trench to be used as a kind of picnic table. In a larger group, it's fun to construct a circular trench with an island in the middle.

Igloos

There's no doubt that igloos are the most luxurious accommodations a traveler can fashion in the winter wilderness. A well-built igloo with warm bodies inside can maintain a temperature well above freezing, regardless of the weather outside. An igloo can make a wonderful base camp for longer trips, but it should not be the shelter of choice when time, energy, or daylight are in short supply. A group may require up to 4 hours to build one, assuming at least one experienced person directs the operation.

First, a flat site with a thick base of consolidated snow is selected as a quarry. Then members of the party stomp on the quarry site to compress the snow as much as possible. It may be helpful to wait an hour or two to let the snow consolidate further after compaction.

Blocks of snow are cut from the quarry using a snow saw, carried to the igloo site, and placed in an ascending spiral pattern. The first level, or "race," should be about 6–8 feet in inside diameter—or larger if the builders are experienced. The blocks must lean inward, slightly on the first race, and more severely on successive races. Begin the curve in the walls almost immediately or else the top becomes too high to install the final wedge-shaped ceiling blocks. Chink the gaps between the blocks with loose snow. With a little foresight, blocks can be cut from the quarry so as to sculpt outside dining quarters.

When the igloo dome is completed, dig (opposite the prevailing wind) a short tunnel under the wall with the exterior opening below the floor level of the igloo. This helps prevent warm air from escaping. Punch a hole in the top of the roof for ventilation. A single candle can provide all the necessary light, even on the darkest nights. If you must cook inside, make absolutely certain there's plenty of ventilation.

Emergency Shelters

If caught unexpectedly in the winter wilderness without a tent, you can fairly quickly create an emergency shelter. In a real pinch, a large trash bag can be used as a kind of emergency bivy sack. Compact emergency bags made of technologically advanced material can be purchased and carried with your first-aid kit for such possibilities.

Other solutions may exist in the form of caves or crevices in rocks for short-term shelter. While bivouacking, it's helpful to assume a fetal position to minimize the body's surface area that comes in contact with the cold environment. Snow trenches can be quite easy and quick to construct, especially if you have a shovel or items to scoop snow. A snow trench is little more than a rectangular pit dug into compacted snow. Dig to a sufficient depth and length to accommodate your body and whatever gear you want inside, but don't make the trench so wide that it can't be covered easily. Snow blocks can be cut to form an inverted V for the roof. Gaps should be chinked and a ventilation hole must be installed if the shelter is sealed. Ideally, you would dig a tunnel with an entrance lower than the sleeping enclosure to keep out cold-air drafts. If that isn't possible, a horizontal entry with a wind block can be fashioned.

Snow caves can be described as igloos built from the inside out. Select a place where a thick blanket of consolidated snow lies against a slope—except where an avalanche might occur. Start by digging straight in and then up, where a sleeping platform can be hollowed out. When finished, poke a hole in the roof for ventilation. Snow caves are easier to construct than igloos and are used in normal situations as well as for emergencies. (See the Appendix for further reading about emergency shelters.)

COOKING

There are some significant differences between cooking and nutrition during summer and winter camping. If the weather forces you to cook inside a tent, make sure there is enough ventilation, especially if a blanket of snow surrounds you. Also be aware that all tent materials are flammable. Be extremely careful to control the size of the flame, and keep the stove in a location near the doorway or inside the vestibule if your tent has one. If your stove tends to become warm or hot underneath, don't place it on the tent floor, as it will melt the snow underneath and possibly tip over. Instead, place it on a small insulating pad, a piece of wood, or another stable platform.

Besides adding more fat to your diet for calories and warmth, heated foods and hot drinks should be an integral part of every meal. As mentioned in Chapter 6, Foods and Cooking, "Nutrition Basics," alcohol is a depressant that causes body heat loss faster under cold conditions, so avoid excessive use.

Refueling liquid-fuel stoves can be dangerous under subfreezing temperatures, because stove fuel remains in a liquid state down to about -40°F. It evaporates very rapidly, causing a pronounced chilling effect even at room temperature, and it can cause instant frostbite if spilled on bare skin at very cold temperatures. Always wear nonporous gloves when pouring fuel under these conditions.

In the winter, it may be impossible to locate a source of flowing water, so you will have to collect and melt snow—a tedious process. On clear days fill water bottles (dark-colored bottles work best) with snow and let the sun melt it. Melting snow with a stove is much faster but uses considerable fuel. When planning fuel needs, consider both the extra demands of cooking in the winter environment and the need to melt snow for water.

On subfreezing nights, your water will freeze unless you take precautions. Consider keeping a full water bottle inside your sleeping bag and using body heat to keep it warm. Or bury bottles in the snow, where ambient temperatures, which are probably much warmer than the winter air, often stay close to the freezing point. Make sure you can find the bottles in the morning.

TIPS FOR STAYING WARM AT NIGHT

It is crucial to stay warm at night after a day on the snow. Follow these tips to help ensure you will stay warm:

1. After your return to camp, put on your warmest clothing. Use your rain gear as a vapor barrier.
2. Don't allow yourself to even begin to get cold! If you shiver, that is a sign that your body is cooling down. If you feel cold, add more clothing and move around a bit. If that is not enough, get into your sleeping bag until you feel warm and then re-emerge into camp life.
3. Eat a big, warm dinner with plenty of carbohydrates and fats.
4. After dinner, snack on fatty foods, such as peanuts. The process of digesting fatty foods increases body heat. Keep snacks in the tent for the same reason—no need to worry about bears in the winter!
5. Exercise. When feeling cold, get up and stretch or go for a brisk walk. The exercise will increase body heat. Dress so that you capture that extra body heat. When in your sleeping bag, do isometric exercises if you begin to chill.
6. Drink warm fluids. Through the night, continue to drink warm fluids. This will increase the likelihood that you will have to urinate during the night, so be sure to urinate just before crawling into the tent.
7. While in camp, sit on pads, not on snow. Find a wind-sheltered spot or orient yourself so that your head is downwind. Wear dry gloves and stocking caps to offset heat loss from your extremities.
8. Create a tent bottle (clearly marked!) that you can use to urinate into while in your tent. This bottle will save you from getting up at 2 A.M., getting dressed, and going out in the cold during the night.
9. Just before you turn in for the night, make an extra bottle of hot water, ensure that the bottle does not leak, and then put the bottle into your sleeping bag. This will be something you can snuggle with during the night to keep you warm and provide "warm" water to start morning coffee.
10. Share your tent or shelter with others to add body heat.

These tips will help you spend winter nights more comfortably and enjoyably.

HAZARDS AND INJURY AVOIDANCE

During winter travel, be aware of special hazards and the possibility of injury.

Hypothermia

Hypothermia (once called exposure) is the decrease of core body temperature to a level at which normal muscular and cerebral functions are impaired. Hypothermia occurs most rapidly in cold and windy environments, especially if wetness is a factor. In the winter environment, hypothermia is brought on by immersion in cold water, thin clothing, physical activity or struggle to the point of exhaustion, slim body mass, or a combination of these.

Mere temperature readings are not always a reliable indicator of the severity of the cold environment. The windchill index (tabulated in fig. 15-9) provides a better guide for cold, windy conditions. When wetness is a factor, the effective temperatures are even lower.

It's important to recognize the signs of hypothermia, both in yourself and in companions, so that remedial actions may be taken immediately. The symptoms and treatment for hypothermia are discussed in Chapter 16, Wilderness First Aid, "Chilling."

WINDCHILL TABLE								
Wind Speed (in mph)	Actual Temperature in °F							
Calm	40	30	20	10	0	-10	-20	-30
	Equivalent Windchill Temperature in °F							
5	35	25	15	5	-5	-15	-25	-35
10	30	15	5	-10	-20	-35	-45	-60
15	25	10	-5	-20	-30	-45	-60	-70
20	20	5	-10	-25	-35	-50	-65	-80
25	15	0	-15	-30	-45	-60	-75	-90
30	10	0	-20	-30	-50	-65	-80	-95
35	20	-5	-20	-35	-50	-65	-80	-100
40	10	-5	-20	-35	-55	-70	-85	-100

Figure 15-9: *Windchill table.*

Frostbite

Unlike hypothermia, frostbite is a local effect, readily affecting extremities such as fingers and toes, or the tips of the nose and the ears. When exposed to cold temperatures (or windchills), blood vessels in these areas tend to shrink, reducing or cutting off circulation, and subsequently lowering the skin temperature in those areas. With continued cooling, the tissue freezes and the frozen area enlarges and extends deeper. The tissue is injured by ice crystals in the frozen area, by dehydration, and by disruption of osmotic and chemical balances in the cells.

Frostbite can occur in any cold, winter environment but it is usually associated with inadequate clothing, reduced food consumption, exhaustion, injury, or a combination of factors. A good preventative measure is vigorous physical activity (if that's possible). When the body tries to cool itself, blood flows to the extremities where it circulates and sheds its heat. For more about frostbite signs and treatment, see Chapter 16, Wilderness First Aid, "Chilling."

Dehydration

Though it may seem unlikely, you can easily become dehydrated during winter conditions, particularly at higher altitudes, because cold air and thin air contain little water vapor. Every time you inhale and warm the air inside your lungs, moisture is absorbed by that dry air. With each exhalation, moisture is lost to the outside environment.

Since the sensation of thirst may not be strong in a winter environment, you need to make a conscious effort to consume enough fluid during winter travels. Hot liquids, of course, are best, but cold water is fine as well. Don't eat snow unless you become overheated from exertion. In that case, only small quantities are of any use, as it requires a great deal of energy (body heat) to transform snow into water.

If you are consuming enough fluid, the need to urinate at least every few hours (preferably more often) should be felt. If you're not properly hydrated, you'll experience the symptoms of dehydration: fatigue, dizziness, and a feeling of faintness.

Sunburn

The winter environment presents some unique challenges pertaining to excessive ultraviolet radiation. Clean, dry, thin air allows ultraviolet energy to pass more easily than thick, warm, humid air does. Snow and ice act like a mirror that directs the UV rays upward to such uncovered areas as the cheeks, ears, nose, lips, and chin. Even the inside of the nostrils can burn. Keep this in mind when applying sunblock.

Avalanche

Depending on the season and location, avalanches can consist of just snow, or snow mixed with rock, mud, and dirt. Avalanches represent one of the most serious hazards for the winter wilderness traveler. They can occur without warning, carry a hapless victim down a steep slope at high velocity and bury him beneath tons of icy material. An avalanche can only occur where snow has collected on an inclined surface and where the snow cover, built up in layers, lacks the necessary cohesion to stick together. Cohesion depends on the following:

- Steepness of the slope
- Crystalline nature of the snow of adjoining layers
- Temperature change over time
- Depth of the snow mass

As temperatures rise and fall and as snow falls or melts, the snow cover can become either more or less stable. When unstable conditions exist, the slightest mechanical force—even the sound pressure of a sonic boom, thunder, or gunfire—can set off an avalanche. A traveler walking or skiing across such an unstable slope can also easily trigger them.

There are basically two types of avalanches: loose-snow (sluff) avalanches and slab avalanches. Loose-snow avalanches (fig. 15-10) occur when snow accumulates on a slope that is steeper than the maximum "angle of repose." Loose snow can become unstable when light, fluffy snow falls onto the slope, by loss of cohesion between new snow and old, and from lubrication between layers produced by percolating meltwater, popcorn snow, or rain. These conditions cause a chain reaction, starting with a small amount of moving snow that snowballs into a much larger, ominous mass of sliding snow and debris. In spring and summer, loose-snow avalanches are often caused by wet snow falling on top of cold, dry snow. The wet snow, which fails to stick to the layer underneath, can be destructive, even at low velocity, because it is heavy. In fall and winter, loose-snow avalanches consist of powdery snow that packs less punch because of its lighter weight.

Slab avalanches (fig. 15-11) are the most destructive. They consist of a layer or layers of snow that break off and slide as a large block, pushing other snow in front. The slab breaks loose suddenly, often accompanied by a loud crack like that of a gunshot. Tons of icy debris

Figure 15-10: *Loose-snow avalanche.*

then accelerate downslope. The larger slab avalanches are capable of flattening forests and buildings.

Avalanches of both kinds tend to recur periodically in the same steep gullies or chutes, called avalanche paths. Each path has three segments: a release zone at the top where the avalanche begins and the snow accelerates; a middle section, or track, where the snow maintains a steady velocity; and a run-out zone, where the snow decelerates. The top two zones are the most hazardous.

Large avalanches originate in release zones with slopes between 30 and 55 degrees, although small avalanches, or sluffs, start tumbling from slopes as steep as 80 degrees. Open, smooth slopes are more dangerous than those covered with rocks, trees, or brush, because there's little in them to anchor the snow cover.

In avalanche-prone terrain, stick to ridgelines wherever possible. Especially avoid mountainsides with broad release zones and funnel-like chutes underneath that concentrate sliding snow. Always be on

Figure 15-11: *Slab avalanche.*

the lookout for evidence of past avalanche activity, such as icy debris or smashed trees.

Avalanches can start on both concave and convex slopes, although more avalanches originate on convex slopes where the slow creeping of icy snow produces tension. On or near a ridgeline, always avoid the lee side of a cornice (a wavelike feature in the snow caused by prevailing winds; see fig. 15-12). Stay on the windward side of a cornice to avoid dislodging it and starting an avalanche.

When crossing a slope watch for cracks radiating from your tracks or listen for a "whoomping" sound that indicates instability. Either turn back or head quickly to a safer position. More than 80 percent of avalanches occur during or immediately after a major snowstorm. If a recent storm has brought 3–6 feet of new snow in a short time, then a strong possibility of avalanches exists. Aside from that, rapid changes in temperatures (particularly warming) destabilizes layers in the snow cover and increases the chances for avalanches.

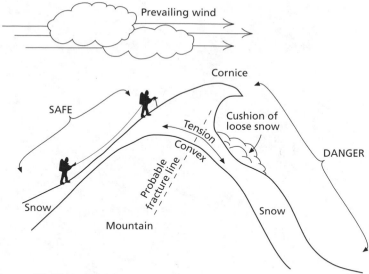

Figure 15-12: *Approaching the windward side of a cornice.*

If you are forced to travel across the paths of potential avalanches, increase safety by doing as much of the following as possible:

- Space the group so that each person can be seen by as many people as possible.
- Loosen belts and straps that could encumber any attempt to dig out of an avalanche.
- Cross hazardous areas one at a time.
- Walk across, rather than ski, hazardous areas if the snow is not too soft. Ski tracks tend to release slab avalanches.
- Wear warm clothing and carry emergency items in accessible pockets.
- Carry shovels and probes or ski pole probes.
- Set avalanche beacons to transmit and use avalanche cords, securely tied to all members of the party.

If you do get involved in an avalanche, heed the following:

- If on skis, try to steer out of the avalanche area. If this is not possible, then get rid of poles, skis, and pack.
- If you are caught in sliding snow, try to "swim" to stay on the surface. Some experts believe the backstroke is the best technique (see fig. 15-13).
- When the sliding snow begins to slow, lunge forward. Reach up with one hand and also keep legs spread. An arm or leg

Figure 15-13: *"Swimming" to stay on the surface when caught in an avalanche.*

sticking out of the snow will be visible to rescuers and speed the rescue. Use the other hand to create an air pocket in front of your face for breathing.

- Once halted, the snow settles and hardens, restricting movement or voice communication. Relax to conserve oxygen, and await rescue.

Self-rescue from an avalanche. Avalanches often occur in remote, sparsely populated areas requiring winter travelers to handle their own rescue efforts until trained search-and-rescue (SAR) teams can take over. Rescue for avalanche victims must be fast and efficient, because the probability of survival drops below 50 percent after 30 minutes. Survivors must act promptly to save any victims.

If an avalanche occurs, fight the instinct to panic. Rather, take a few seconds and formulate a strategy that encompasses the whole group and the whole situation. If anyone can be spared, the leader should send a member of the party (with good navigation skills) to summon a trained SAR team and lead them to the site. Next, someone should be assigned to help the injured get to a safe position. Then, a search party can be organized. If the avalanche area is not overly hazardous, establish a systematic search pattern and assign members to search specific areas. Searchers should use probe ski poles or avalanche probes to prod several feet down into the debris. During the search, look for clues such as clothing, skis, or limbs protruding from the snow. When a victim is found, dig rapidly to uncover him. Assess for life signs, and look for indications of frostbite, hypothermia, or injury. Treat as necessary, but do not reheat victims too quickly.

Continue the SAR efforts until all victims have been accounted for or until rescue becomes futile. In at least one case, a victim encased in avalanche debris for 29 hours survived, so don't give up prematurely. Only after hours of intensive searching should someone go for help. Use all available resources immediately after the avalanche. It may take hours for help to arrive, and by that time a rescue effort may become a body recovery.

Avalanche transceivers/beacons. Each member of a group traveling in avalanche country should carry an avalanche transceiver and a strong, lightweight snow shovel. The transceiver is really nothing more than a low-power transmitter and receiver that operates on a 457 kHz frequency. The three-position switch can easily be switched to off, transmit, or receive. When purchasing an avalanche beacon or transceiver, look for reliability, an impact-resistant case, ease of use with gloves, controls that are unlikely to be adjusted accidentally, and a built-in battery test capability. Use long-life alkaline batteries with your unit, not rechargeable or inexpensive carbon-zinc batteries. Carry spare batteries and test them regularly.

A party entering an avalanche area should switch all units to *receive* and test each member's transmit capability. When all transceivers are verified, turn all units to *transmit* and traverse the dangerous area. When the avalanche area is successfully traversed, units should be turned off to conserve batteries.

In case of an avalanche, everyone should switch their transceivers to *receive*. The area where the victim was last seen should be traversed systematically until the strongest signal is located. The area of strongest signal should rapidly narrow to a small area where digging begins immediately. Victims rarely survive longer than 1 hour, so rescuers must act quickly. Avalanche debris often becomes solid, so digging with your hands is futile. The value of one shovel per party member will never become more obvious than now. If trained, well-equipped help is very close and if someone can be spared, send for help immediately.

Lives can be saved only if transceivers are worn and used properly. A transceiver in the pack or on the belt may be ripped from the victim by the force of the avalanche, and another transceiver will find the buried transceiver whether or not it's with a victim. Strap on the transceiver under clothing. Ownership of a transceiver neither lessens the danger nor certifies that its bearer is competent in its use. Like many things, there is no substitute for training and experience. It cannot be emphasized enough that these techniques must be practiced long before they are needed.

Wilderness First Aid

Carol P. Murdock and Carl W. Trygstad

Once you pass the threshold of wilderness, you trade the conveniences of swift medical attention for the uncertainties of adventure. It is essential, then, to be familiar with the elements of basic first aid, as well as the particular problems and medical complications that may occur in outdoor situations. It is highly recommended that anyone venturing into the wilderness take an American Red Cross standard first-aid course, along with either the American Red Cross or American Heart Association CPR course. And on trips to remote areas, at least one person in the group should have advanced training in wilderness first aid such as a course designed for outdoor enthusiasts.

BEFORE YOU GO

Before you hit the trail, make sure your vaccinations, especially tetanus, are current. Tetanus spores are found everywhere and can be introduced into the body through minor wounds. With prior immunization, tetanus is preventable. Adults should have a tetanus booster at least every ten years. If you sustain a puncture wound or laceration in the wilderness and are not sure of your immunization status, seek medical advice when you return home. Lyme vaccination is recommended for wilderness travel to some areas of the United States, mainly the Northeast and

Midwest. Some physicians recommend it for those who spend prolonged periods outdoors in areas of lower risk, such as northern California. A variety of other immunizations are recommended for trips to foreign countries, but these are not normally needed for wilderness travel in North America.

Awareness of your state of health and any preexisting conditions enables you to anticipate particular problems that you might develop in the wilderness. Add items to your basic medical or first-aid kit to allow treatment of these problems as they arise. If you are on any medication, take it as prescribed, unless advised otherwise by your physician.

WHAT TO TAKE

First-aid kits range from sophisticated to very simple, but the essential contents vary with the length of the trip and how far you'll be from medical help. A minimal kit—suitable for day hikes or short overnight trips—could include only Band-Aids, gauze wrap, some 1-inch cloth tape, a needle for removing slivers and thorns, moleskin, aspirin, and a pencil and notepad. An important item for the first-aid kit is a pair of disposable gloves to protect both the injured person and care provider from fluid-borne disease. Wash your hands before and after rendering aid. Latex or vinyl gloves should be protected in a plastic zipper-lock bag and stored away from heat (such as that in a glove compartment).

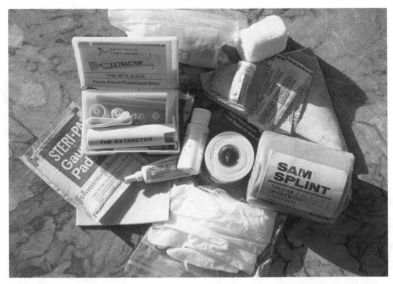

First-aid kit supplies. (Photo by Carol Murdock.)

WILDERNESS FIRST AID KIT

RECOMMENDED ITEMS	QUANTITY	USE
Adhesive bandages, ½" or ¾"	10–15	Treat cuts & abrasions
Cloth tape, 1" roll	1 roll	Secure splints
Gauze wrap, 2" roll & 4" roll	1 each	Secure dressings
Gauze pads, 4" size	6–10	Cover abrasions
Moleskin or molefoam, 6" square	1	Prevent & treat blisters
Triangular bandage, 36"	1	Multiple uses
Elastic wrap, 4"	1	Support sprains & secure dressings
Aspirin, 5 gr (325 mg) tablets	10–15	For pain & fever, also good for someone having a heart attack
Antibiotic ointment, 15 mg tube	1	Treat skin infections
Antihistamine,		For allergic reactions
2.68 mg clemastine fumarate (**Tavist***) or	6–10	& runny nose
25 mg diphenhydramine (**Benadryl**) tablets or		
30 mg Pseudoephedrine (**Sudafed**) tablets	12–24	Decongestant
Rx Vicodin* tablets	6–10	Treat pain
Iodine solution, 2% or 10% Betadyne	1 oz	Clean wounds
Thermometer	1	Measure temperature
Lip balm with sunscreen	1 tube	Prevent sun damage to lips
Insect repellent	1 oz tube	Discourage insect bites
Wire-mesh or SAM splint	1	Cervical collar or splint
Sawyer Extractor	1	Removal of venom from insect/snake bites

SUGGESTED ITEMS	QUANTITY	USE
Rx. Cavit (obtain from dentist)	7 mg tube	Temporary tooth filling
Rx. Acetazolamide (**Diamox**),	14	Prevention of acute
250 mg tablets		mountain sickness
Rx. Promethazine (**Phenergan**,	4	Treat nausea & vomiting
25 mg suppository)		
Imodium, 2 mg tablets	12/person/week	Treat diarrhea
Corticosteroid cream (**Cortaid**) 1%	15 mg tube	Treat rashes swelling & itching from plant contact or insect bites

*Rx. indicates prescription from physician required.
Discuss possible side effects with your physician.
First drug name is the generic and parentheses or bold type indicates a brand name.

Additional Items for First-Aid Use
Swiss army knife, tweezers, duct tape, magnifying glass (plastic), electrolyte replacement drink, sanitary napkins (good to absorb bleeding from cuts), latex or other protective gloves. Empty your first-aid kit annually and check for expired medications and deteriorated bandaging supplies.

Figure 16-1: *First-aid kit. What you need in your first-aid kit depends on the length of trip, level of medical training, time to evacuation, size of party, and climate.*

After gaining some experience, you may become aware of additional items that are appropriate for different types of trips.

If you purchase a packaged first-aid kit, you'll probably want to eliminate some items and add others to suit your needs. Repackage items in a lightweight, sealed container to decrease bulk and weight. The list shown in Figure 16-1 contains items suitable for a group of four traveling into remote areas for up to one week. These supplies, of course, would not be adequate for the long-term treatment of people with serious injuries or illnesses. After first aid is rendered, evacuation from the wilderness and treatment at a hospital is the appropriate course of action. Before offering any medication (even over the counter ones), ask recipient if they are allergic to it. If yes, **Do not give the medication to them.**

Women may want to add certain supplies to their medical kit such as vaginal suppositories for yeast infections and antibiotics for urinary-tract infections. Vaginal suppositories need to be kept cool, so pack them where they will be least exposed to heat.

FIRST AID IN THE FIELD

Despite the best planning, injuries and unexpected illnesses do occur on trips. Although it is hoped that these difficulties can be quickly remedied and the trip continued, sometimes a trip has to be aborted. The participants may need to devote all their efforts to returning to the trailhead (or other exit point) quickly and safely. A careful plan to assess the extent and nature of the illness or injury is needed in order to determine whether or not the trip can continue, and what future course of action to take.

Assessment of an Injured Person

If a victim is conscious, obtain his consent for treatment. Identify yourself as someone who is able to help, using a simple statement such as, "I'm Mary. I'm trained in first aid and I want to help you." This can help decrease the anxiety of the seriously ill or injured person. If the victim can be moved to a safer environment without causing further injury, do so as soon as possible.

The history of events leading to the accident or illness should be obtained if possible. Questions—Where do you hurt? Are you having difficulty breathing? What happened? What do you think is wrong?—can bring out useful information not only about what happened, but also about the current state of the victim.

If the victim is unconscious, consent for treatment is implied. First assess for breathing and a pulse. If either are absent, begin the ABC procedure of basic life support:

A—Airway. Check the airway and open it by placing your hand on the forehead, applying gentle pressure to tilt the head back and lifting the chin up using two fingers. Often, proper positioning is all that is needed to clear the airway and restart breathing. Remove visible debris from the mouth. If the victim suffered a fall he may have a neck fracture, so manipulation of the head must be minimal. Clearing the airway is best accomplished using the jaw thrust maneuver and supporting the neck. If there is a possible neck injury do not bend the neck forward or backward.

B—Breathing. If the victim does not breathe spontaneously after the airway has been cleared, start rescue breathing by pinching the nose closed, placing your mouth over the victim's mouth and giving 1 breath every 5 seconds. It is advisable to use some kind of protection such as a disposable breathing mask.

C—Cardiopulmonary resuscitation. If there is no carotid pulse, begin CPR with 2 breaths for every 15 compressions. This is a skill that should be learned and practiced before you have to use it. The ABC procedure is described in American Red Cross and American Heart Association courses. CPR for a victim of hypothermia or near drowning may be required for an extended period of time to be successful. In all other cases in remote settings, if CPR fails to return spontaneous heartbeat and respirations within 15 minutes, it will not do so, and may be discontinued.

For a conscious victim, a complete survey should be undertaken to determine the extent of injury or the severity of illness. This is the focused physical exam described in several of the references listed in the Appendix. Communicate with and calm the victim by explaining what you are going to do before you start. Check the pupil size and response to light, feel the neck for tenderness, and observe the chest motion as the victim takes a deep breath. All tender areas should be examined for fractures or bleeding. Strength, pulse, and sensation in all extremities should be assessed. Before offering any medication, make sure the person is not allergic to it.

All information, especially breathing rate, pulse rate, and responsiveness, should be written down so changes over time can be observed. Keep the victim warm, stop any bleeding with direct pressure, and splint all fractures to prevent any further motion.

In general, evacuation is necessary for any victim who is unconscious, has spine or lower extremity fractures, difficulty breathing, a serious eye injury, or pain that does not respond to simple measures such as taking aspirin or ibuprofen.

The following list summarizes the proper sequence of action in the event of a serious accident or illness suffered by a member or members of your party:

1. Approach the victim safely without jeopardizing your own safety.
2. Restore and/or maintain breathing and heartbeat.
3. Control any heavy bleeding.
4. Examine the victim carefully (focused exam) after the above problems are controlled.
5. Decide where and how you (or others in your group) will obtain help.
6. Write down the following information to take along when you go, or send someone, for help: name of the person or group reporting the accident (if a sponsored trip, include the phone number of the parent or organization); name, address, and home phone number of victim(s); date, time, and nature of the accident; condition of the victim; first-aid treatment rendered; and exact location of the victim (it may be best to mark this location on a map).
7. When you reach help (by telephone, radio, or in person), find out to whom you are talking.
8. Convey all the pertinent information listed in number 6, taking special care to give explicit map directions to the site of the victim, including any information about where rescuers could get lost.
9. Give an estimate of how many rescuers you think may be required and the expected difficulty of the rescue.
10. If you have notified any other agencies, reveal that information.
11. Have the person to whom you gave the information repeat it back to ensure it was understood. And finally, if you're on the phone, let the other party end the conversation. Never hang up first.

While waiting for help at the site of the accident, the person(s) remaining with the victim should do the following:

- Continually monitor the victim's condition.
- Protect the victim from the environment and from further injury.
- Supply any necessary liquids, foods, or further first-aid treatments, as applicable.
- Provide emotional support in a tactful way.
- Maintain a written log of any changes in the victim's condition and of any treatment given.

In any emergency situation, one person should take charge. This person can be the leader of the group or the person with the most medical knowledge or experience in first aid. This person designates responsibilities and assigns tasks. Everyone should stick to her plan. Only changes in the victim's condition or the weather should alter that plan.

Shock

Shock occurs when the circulatory system fails to provide enough blood and oxygen to vital parts of the body. It can occur as a result of trauma, bleeding, burns, heart attack, breathing difficulties, spinal cord damage, infection, diabetes, and extreme allergic reactions. In the wilderness, early recognition of shock is essential because shock can progress rapidly and treatment is limited. Early signs of shock include a feeling of anxiety; a rapid, weak pulse; altered consciousness; lethargy; stupor; and slurred speech.

The best treatment for shock is the correction of the cause, if possible. Stabilize suspected neck fractures (see photo), perform rescue breathing, administer CPR, control bleeding, splint fractures, and treat allergic reactions, as necessary. Severe shock requires aggressive medical treatment often not available in a wilderness situation.

Whether the cause is treatable or not, provide first aid for shock by keeping the victim warm and comfortable. A victim in shock may lose body heat even in warm weather conditions and needs to be insulated from the ground to prevent further heat loss. Victims should be kept flat, except those with heart and breathing problems, who should sit up. Reassure and comfort the victim. Avoid any rough handling, and monitor the victim's condition by frequent physical evaluations. Only give fluids if medical assistance will not arrive shortly, or as long as the victim is not unconscious, having convulsions, vomiting, or clearly has an injury requiring surgery.

A severe allergic reaction known as anaphylactic shock can occur from insect bites, medications, or foods. The symptoms are itching or burning skin (especially on the face and chest), flushed skin, hives,

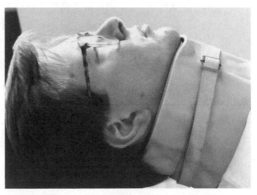

Improvised cervical collar. (Photo by Carol Murdock.)

swelling of the face and tongue, blue lips, a tight feeling or pain in the chest, and breathing difficulties. There may be a weak pulse, dizziness, faintness, or even coma. The treatment is to maintain an open airway. If available, give an antihistamine, such as diphenhydramine (Benadryl) orally while the victim is still able to swallow. Those known to be allergic to specific substances should carry a prescription injection kit, such as EpiPen® or Anakit, and should let someone in the group know where the kit is kept.

MEDICAL PROBLEMS IN THE WILDERNESS
Abdominal Pain

Abdominal pain can be encountered in the wilderness and often resolves spontaneously. The objective in assessment is to decide which types will go away and identify those for which the victim should be evacuated. Constant pain is usually more significant than intermittent pain. Pain around the umbilicus, or a pain that shifts from one place to another, is generally less significant than pain located at one of the corners of the abdomen.

Vomiting is usually an attempt by the body to rid itself of toxins. Give nothing by mouth for the first hour and then 1 ounce of clear fluids every 15 minutes. If available, antiemetic suppositories such as Phenergan or compazine (see fig. 16-1) will help. Persistent vomiting and vomiting associated with a head injury requires evacuation. If several people on an outing start to vomit at the same time, think food poisoning, which usually resolves itself, or altitude sickness. Diarrhea may occur in the wilderness, especially if the water supply is impure, or if the food is spoiled or contaminated. Most diarrhea can be treated with a bland, low fat, low bulk diet, increased fluid intake, and possibly an antidiarrheal. If there is fever or blood in the stool, the condition is more serious and the victim should be evacuated. Diarrhea causes dehydration, so large amounts of fluid may be needed to restore the fluids lost in watery stools.

Appendicitis is always a feared cause of abdominal pain. There is usually a history of vague discomfort or pain around the umbilicus, which then moves to the lower-right part of the abdomen. A low-grade fever, constipation, loss of appetite, and nausea are common symptoms. These victims should be evacuated as soon as possible.

Stroke

Stroke is a name applied to a group of disorders that disrupt the blood supply to a part of the brain. It can be caused by either a ruptured or a blocked blood vessel in the brain. Signs and symptoms occur suddenly. The specific symptoms depend on which part of the brain is involved. A victim's face may be flushed and warm, with perhaps a grayish pallor. Their pupils may be unequal in size; often one eyelid droops. There may be weakness or paralysis on one side of the body. The victim may lose the ability to talk. Breathing can be slow and of a snoring type. The victim may be unconscious and lose control of bowels and bladder.

Treatment is supportive. Keep the airway open and anticipate the need for CPR. Handle the victim gently and don't move him more than necessary. Keep him warm and, if unconscious, position the victim on his affected side with an arm supporting the head, so secretions drain from the side of the mouth. See photo of recovery position (below). Send for help, but do not move the victim.

Heart Attack

Heart attack (myocardial infarction) is caused by lack of blood and oxygen to the heart and results in tissue death of a portion of the heart. There are other conditions that can cause chest pain, but this condition is the most life-threatening. Victims may describe the pain as aching, squeezing, crushing, or as a heaviness in the center of the chest behind the breastbone. The pain may radiate to the arm, shoulders, neck, or jaw. It lasts longer than 2 minutes and is not relieved by rest. Other symptoms may include sweating, nausea, weakness, light headedness, and shortness of breath. Sometimes heart pain may masquerade as indigestion or upper abdominal pain.

Treat by having the victim stop what he is doing and rest quietly. Rescue personnel must be notified as soon as possible. If the person has a history of heart disease or angina, he should have medications,

Proper positioning of an unconscious person. (Photo by Carol Murdock.)

most importantly nitroglycerine, to treat the chest pain. Nitro tabs are always placed under the tongue every 3 to 5 minutes for a maximum of 3 doses. Heart attacks may be accompanied by heart rhythm disturbances, which may lead to cardiac arrest and may require CPR.

Diabetes

Diabetes is a chronic disease resulting from a relative lack of insulin. Two major problems can happen with diabetics. One is diabetic coma (too much sugar) and the other is insulin shock (too much insulin or too little sugar).

Signs and symptoms of diabetic coma happen slowly. The victim may complain of a dry mouth and thirst, or experience excessive urination, abdominal pain, and/or vomiting. The skin is dry, red, and warm. Pulse may be weak and rapid. The victim's breath may smell fruity or sickeningly sweet. If left untreated, confusion and then coma result. Treatment consists of keeping the victim warm, encouraging copious amounts of fluids, and evacuating the victim to a medical facility.

Insulin shock occurs rapidly when a diabetic skips a meal or overexercises. Signs and symptoms include dizziness and headache; complaints of intense hunger; pale, cold, and clammy skin; profuse perspiration, and possibly, aggressive behavior abnormal for the victim (similar to alcohol intoxication). Symptoms can progress to fainting, convulsions, and finally coma.

Insulin shock must be treated immediately. If the victim is conscious, give fluids containing sugar, such as fruit juice, sports drinks, or sugar water. If unavailable, then give hard candy, dried fruit, or plain sugar. The symptoms should improve in about 20 or 30 minutes. If they don't, give another dose of sugar. If the victim becomes unconscious, sprinkle sugar under the tongue or use one of the commercially prepared gels made for this purpose. If you're unsure that the condition is diabetic coma or insulin shock, give sugar. It treats insulin shock, may be life-saving, and won't aggravate the symptoms of diabetic coma much.

Women's Health Concerns

Whether you're expecting your menstrual cycle or not, pack in the usual supply of sanitary products and pain medications. Pack out used tampons or pads in a plastic zipper-lock bag with one or two aspirins in it to dissipate odor.

Vaginal infections can be prevented by wearing loose-fitting nylon or cotton underwear and wiping front to back. Daily cleaning of the perineal area with soap and water and decreasing intake of sugar, alcohol, and caffeine helps. Woman prone to vaginal yeast infections should carry a supply of medication for treatment.

Menopause can bring on a different set of considerations for the outdoorswoman. Until the menstrual cycle has been absent for a full year, there's always the possibility of having an unexpected episode. Estrogen therapy can result in a return of menstrual-like cycles.

If you're troubled by hot flashes during menopause, getting overheated only makes the problem worse. Avoid hiking in hot weather if you can, make use of shade during rest breaks, and stay well hydrated by drinking plenty of liquid. On group trips, inform the leader of your needs.

Bone thinning (osteoporosis) is a health problem for many aging people. For women, a high rate of bone loss seems to be associated with menopause. Thinner bones are more likely to break, possibly in rugged areas that might be far from medical facilities. If you know you have osteoporosis, you can adapt by keeping your pack weight to a minimum and perhaps foregoing trips to remote areas. If carrying a backpack causes lower back or hip pain, you can still continue to enjoy the wilderness by day hiking.

ENVIRONMENTAL HAZARDS IN THE WILDERNESS

Attacks by crawling, flying, biting, or stinging creatures can range from irritating to life threatening. Exposure to allergens in certain plants or overexposure to the sun can be incapacitating or at least misery inducing. These and other environmental hazards can usually be avoided by being aware of the potential dangers.

Bites

Poisonous snakes. Few snakebite victims in the United States actually die from the effects of the venom, primarily because most reach help relatively quickly. The seriousness of a poisonous snakebite depends on the amount of venom injected (some bites are actually "dry"), the species of the snake, the condition of the victim, and other factors.

Where venom has been injected, there is immediate swelling, warmth, and pain. Tingling or numbness around the victim's mouth may develop later and nausea and vomiting may occur. The victim may become weak, feel faint, sweat, and have a weak, rapid pulse. Breathing difficulties, muscle twitching, and paralysis can follow. The use of a suction device (such as a Sawyer Extractor) to remove some of the venom is most effective if done within the first 5 minutes of the bite. After that, it does little good. The only further treatment is antivenom, given in the hospital.

While being evacuated, or awaiting rescue, a snakebite victim should be kept at rest to prevent the venom from spreading throughout the body. Some physicians advise the use of a constriction band 2–4 inches above the bite to prevent the spread of venom. A constriction band is not a tourniquet—it is tied loosely enough so your fingers can fit underneath it. An arm can be splinted and kept at heart level for comfort. Do not use ice or pressure dressings, or make incisions around the bite. Any rings or jewelry worn near the site of the bite should be removed, since a great deal of swelling can occur.

Ticks. Ticks are common in wooded areas and attach themselves to a victim's skin, usually under clothing, in order to draw blood. They can transmit diseases such as Rocky Mountain spotted fever, Colorado tick fever, and Lyme disease. The best method of removal is to use a pair of tweezers to grasp the tick close to the skin and pull gently. Avoid crushing or puncturing the tick and do not grasp it with your bare hands. After removal, disinfect the site and wash your hands. If parts of the tick break off in the skin, or if symptoms of any of the above diseases appear (fever, headache, spreading redness around the bite, or a red-spotted rash over much of the body), evacuate and seek advice from a physician.

Poisonous spiders. A black widow spider bite produces pain similar to a pinprick, slight burning, and redness at the site. Local tissue reactions vary, with some victims exhibiting an immediate 1- or 2-inch area of blanching around puncture wounds surrounded by redness. Other victims have no significant reaction at all. If a large amount of venom has been injected, the victim develops painful muscle cramps that rapidly spread to the entire body. The victim may be anxious and restless, and may complain of weakness and sweating. Most people recover over the course of 1 or 2 days. However, children and the elderly are more likely to have serious reactions. Treatment consists of applying ice to the bite and immediately transporting any victim with symptoms to the hospital.

Initially, brown recluse spider bites cause very little pain. The victim often develops a characteristic red blister surrounded by a bull's-eye of whitish-blue discoloration within 1 to 5 hours. Generalized reactions include itching, rash, chills, fever, nausea, vomiting, and headache. The damage from the bite is caused by tissue destruction, which can take place weeks or months after the bite. A physician may either give drugs or remove the tissue surgically.

Bees, wasps, and hornets. The immediate reactions to stings by bees, wasps, and hornets include pain, swelling, redness, warmth at the site, and itching. Some victims may experience a severe allergic reaction called anaphylactic shock. To remove the stinger place the dull side of a knife-edge or a credit card next to the stinger and push it out from the skin, or use the Sawyer Extractor to remove the stinger and attached venom sac left by bees. Take care not to squeeze the venom sac. Applying a cool compress to the sting site brings relief.

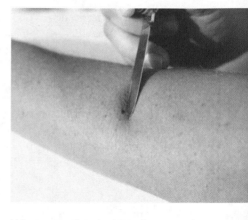

When removing a stinger by scraping with a knife, be sure not to squeeze the poison sac. (Photo by Carol Murdock.)

Other insects. Several kinds of flies, mosquitoes, and fleas can cause irritating bites with local skin reactions. You can relieve the discomfort with a product called After Bite, a hydrocortisone cream, or a simple cold application. In situations with heavy insect populations, try to keep all skin covered with thick clothing or netting. Chemical repellents containing a 40 to 60 percent concentration of DEET (N,N-diethyl-meta-toluamide) applied sparingly to skin and liberally on clothing work best. Some adults may experience skin irritation or rare severe side effects. Do not use concentrations of DEET stronger than 15 percent on children under age 6. In those cases, protective clothing and netting may be the best defenses. Another product that is less toxic is Permethrin, which is derived from chrysanthemums.

Scorpions. Scorpions attack with a thin tail that has a stinger on the end. Most scorpions in North America are nonlethal and produce a reaction similar to a wasp or a hornet sting. To treat stings apply an ice pack or chill the bite area in some way. One species lethal to humans is found in northern Mexico and less commonly in parts of the Southwest. The sting from a lethal species may initially go unnoticed, but in 5 to 60 minutes, pain develops and may be severe. Lightly tapping the area produces a tingling or prickly feeling, and the affected area becomes quite sensitive to touch. Children, who are most susceptible to the reaction, experience elevated blood pressure. Any victim experiencing these symptoms should be transported to a hospital as quickly as possible.

Rodents. Rodents such as mice, squirrels, chipmunks, raccoons, and marmots occasionally carry rabies as well as fleas that can spread other diseases to humans. Avoid any wild animal even if it appears tame or friendly. If you are bitten, clean the wound with soap and water and seek medical attention. This also applies to bats, which are more likely to carry rabies than most other mammals. Don't attempt to befriend or feed any animal in the wild. Hantavirus is spread in the fecal droppings, saliva, and urine of deer and cotton mice in the Southwest and is frequently fatal. Anyone who has been around these droppings and has a fever, muscle aches, cough, breathing problems, or mottled skin on the limbs should seek medical attention immediately.

Rashes

Poison oak is a three-leafed bush, and poison ivy and poison sumac are three-leafed vines. All are found throughout North America. Sap from these plants contains a resin that causes an irritating allergic reaction on the skin of susceptible individuals. The onset of a rash may appear anywhere from 1 hour to 2 or 3 days after exposure. Many favorite treatments abound, but all serve only to relieve the irritation. Lotions or creams such as calamine or hydrocortisone are soothing and help dry the rash and control itching. Antihistamines taken orally control itching but can cause drowsiness. Severe involvement may require the use of oral corticosteroids prescribed by a physician.

Susceptibility to poison oak/ivy/sumac rash varies widely among individuals. Those who are particularly allergic should become familiar with and avoid contact with the plant. If contact cannot be avoided, barrier creams such as IvyBlock can be used before contact on hands and any other body parts not covered by clothing. After contact, the resin must be removed from the skin usually within 30 minutes to prevent the reaction. If possible, wash the skin with plain soap and water or with a specially formulated soap, and remove contaminated clothing. If the resin stays on the skin, scratching can spread the rash from one area of the body to another. It helps to cover the exposed area with a light gauze wrap to keep from spreading the resin. The rash can last up to 6 weeks.

Overexposure To Ultraviolet Radiation

Sunburn. Sunburn is caused by overexposure to the ultraviolet radiation of the sun. Overexposure can occur quite rapidly whenever the sun is high in the sky and at high altitudes, where the atmosphere is thinner. UV radiation penetrates thin clouds easily, and it readily reflects off of rock, soil, water, and especially snow. In most wilderness situations, everyone (children especially) needs protection from the sun in the form of clothing and sunscreen lotions.

Sunburned skin becomes red and sensitive, and the affected individual may experience chills, fatigue, and nausea a few hours after the exposure. Besides the immediate damage, repeated overexposure to the sun produces degenerative changes in the skin and can eventually lead to skin cancer.

Treatment consists of relieving the discomfort and avoiding any further sun exposure. Apply cold, wet dressings to the affected areas if the skin is unbroken. Hydrocortisone preparations are also effective if applied early, but sparingly. Aspirin or ibuprofen may prevent or relieve some of the pain and inflammation.

Snow blindness. This is a sunburn of the cornea, typically brought on at high altitudes where intense ultraviolet light reflects from snow and strikes the surface of the eye. Symptoms include excessive tearing, intense light sensitivity, severe pain and redness of the eyes, and swelling of the lids. About 8 to 12 hours after exposure, the victim may complain that the eyes feel irritated and gritty. There may also be headache and a decrease in vision.

Don't let the victim rub his eyes. Have him keep his eyes closed and cover them with cold compresses. The eyes will be photosensitive and will need to be at rest. Frequent application of ophthalmic ointment or drops help relieve pain. Recheck the eyes in 24 hours, and if the light sensitivity and pain are not too severe, a trial of activity using dark sunglasses or at night may be attempted.

Burns

Burns are damage to the skin caused by heat, chemicals, or radiation. The signs and symptoms depend on the degree of burn sustained. With a first-degree burn, the skin appears red, as in a mild sunburn. A second-degree burn is red with blisters and may be swollen for several days. The blisters usually contain clear fluid. A third-degree burn involves several layers of skin and is white or charred in appearance with broken blisters and evidence of damage to underlying structures. There may be no pain associated with a third-degree burn if nerve endings in the skin have been destroyed.

The severity of burns can also be described in terms of the percentage of the body affected. To estimate the percentage of body surface involved, use the palm of your hand—it represents about 1 percent of your body's surface area.

First- and second- degree burns are treated by cooling with cold-water applications over the area for 20 to 30 minutes for first-degree and 1½ to 2 hours with second-degree burns. A cool, wet tee shirt or clean cloth can be applied to a burn that does not have a broken skin surface. Second- and third-degree burns have broken skin; do not use ointment, spray, or any home remedy on them.

With a third-degree burn, do not remove adherent clothing or apply water. Instead, cover the burn with any clean dressings (sterile, if available). Elevate hands, feet, or legs if involved. When the face is involved, maintain an open airway with the victim sitting up. Apply cold packs to burn areas, but not directly on the burns. If the victim is conscious and not vomiting, give one of the commercially prepared electrolyte fluid replacements (e.g., Gookinaid, Gatorade) slowly in small amounts. If burns cover a joint, are near the eyes or genitals, are deep, or if the victim is over age 50 or under age 5, evacuate immediately. Burn victims have a high risk of going into shock from fluid loss.

Lightning

Lightning injuries can occur from direct strikes, secondarily after another object has been hit, or from ground currents. Many people can be struck at once, causing multiple victims.

The first assessment is to check for breathing and heartbeat. The victim may need prolonged CPR before you can check for further injuries. Other common problems include spiderlike burns, fractures, and temporary paralysis. These should be treated accordingly.

Blisters

Blisters are caused by friction, which results in an accumulation of fluid under the skin. The most common place is on the feet from poorly fitting boots or shoes or from tender, unaccustomed feet.

The first sign of a blister is a "hot spot" that appears red and is tender to touch. If untreated, fluid pools and the skin covering the fluid may break and leave an irritated, open, bleeding area.

Treat blisters early in their formation by covering with tape or moleskin. Products such as New-Skin or Second Skin can be used to coat the friction area and protect it from further rubbing. Do not pop a blister unless there is a danger of it rupturing or if it interferes with walking. Before popping a blister, wash your hands and clean the skin with soap and water or disinfectant. Sterilize a pin over a flame, holding the end of the pin with a cloth. Puncture the edge of the blister, not the top, and drain. Cut a hole in a piece of moleskin and apply it to the skin around the blister.

For further protection from friction, you may want to put a piece of molefoam over the blister itself. Some people prefer duct tape because its slick outer surface is less likely to grip the sock and pull off or produce friction.

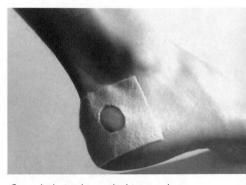

Cut a hole in the moleskin patch to relieve pressure on the blister site. (Photo by Carol Murdock.)

Overheating

Heat cramps. Heat cramps are caused by the loss of electrolytes (sodium, potassium, magnesium, and chloride) from the body during heavy exertion. Cramps often occur in warm weather or after prolonged strenuous physical activity. They are usually characterized by severe, spasmodic contractions in one or more of the large muscles of the legs.

Treat heat cramps with rest, gentle massage, and stretching, and by drinking a lot of fluids containing electrolytes. For a cramp in a calf muscle, straighten leg forward and support the affected leg, grasp the foot at the toes, and pull slowly and gently. Never pound or twist a cramped or sore muscle.

Heat exhaustion. Heat exhaustion is caused by the inability of the body to dissipate heat, and by the loss of electrolytes during strenuous exercise in a hot, humid environment. Heat exhaustion and heat stroke are thought to be the same phenomenon but of different severity.

Signs and symptoms of heat exhaustion include fatigue, faintness, dizziness, and nausea which may lead to vomiting. The victim's skin becomes pale and moist. The heart rate and temperature are normal, however. Immediate treatment includes rest and removal to a cooler environment such as a shady area if possible. Give the victim electrolyte fluid replacement, or water if that is all that is available. Apply wet cloths to the victim and fan vigorously. When the victim is rested, activity can resume.

Heat stroke. Heat stroke is a very serious condition caused by dehydration and the loss of the body's ability to dissipate enough heat in a hot environment. The onset of heat-stroke symptoms can be rapid. The victim becomes confused, loses coordination, and may become unconscious. The skin becomes hot and dry, and the body temperature rises to 102° F or higher. There may be shortness of breath, diarrhea, and seizures.

Begin treatment at once. Stop all activity and seek a cooler environment. To provide shade you may have to place the victim under some vegetation, or make your own shade by holding a tarp or ground cover above him. Remove the victim's clothing, wet him down, and fan vigorously if there is no wind. If water is limited, sponge the victim, especially under the armpits, behind the neck, and in the groin. Give liquids only if he is conscious and able to swallow. Recheck the victim's temperature every 30 minutes and continue cooling until his temperature is down to normal. Do not give aspirin products or stimulants. After the victim's condition has stabilized, seek medical help.

Chilling

Frostbite. Frostbite is an injury produced by severe cold in which flesh freezes. It is caused by exposure of a body part to cold air, wind, or snow. The extent of injury is categorized as simple, superficial, or deep, depending on the symptoms and on the depth of tissue damage. Treatment depends on the depth of the frozen tissue.

Simple frostbite (or frostnip) commonly affects the hands, feet, face, and ears. The earliest signs include a sensation of cold or pain, with redness of the affected skin. As freezing progresses, the tissues become whiter and all sensation is lost. The victim may not be aware of the problem until someone indicates that there is something unusual about his skin color.

Simple frostbite is treated by slowly warming the affected area with your own bare hands, by blowing warm air on the site, or, if fingers are involved, holding them in your armpits. Complaints of tingling or a burning sensation during recovery is normal. Never rub snow on frostbitten areas; it damages tissue. Never expose frostbitten flesh to a source of extreme heat, such as directly above a campfire.

Superficial frostbite affects deeper tissues and the skin appears white and waxy. The area will feel like a half-frozen steak. Begin rapid warming of the area *only* if there is no chance of refreezing. The entire body should be kept warm during and after the treatment. Rapid warming procedures are described in *Medicine for the Outdoors* (see the Appendix). Protect the superficial frostbitten area by covering it and handling the affected part gently. As soon as possible, transport the victim to a medical facility with the affected limb slightly elevated. Remember to remove rings if the fingers are affected, as swelling may make this impossible later.

Deep frostbite or frozen limbs have a wooden feel and no resilience when touched. The skin turns mottled or blotchy and is white, then grayish yellow, and finally grayish blue.

Deep or severe frostbite should not be treated under field conditions. Walking out on frozen feet does less damage than inadequate warming and subsequent refreezing. Carry the victim if he is unable to walk, and get him to a medical facility as soon as possible.

Hypothermia. Hypothermia is a generalized cooling of the body's core temperature to a point where the body can no longer generate its own heat. It can happen within a matter of minutes in the case of immersion in cold water, or over a period of hours following the onset of cold, wet weather conditions. Even in temperatures well above freezing, hypothermia can result from inadequate or improper clothing, or from a lack of shelter from wind and precipitation. Physical exhaustion, inadequate food, and wet clothing accelerate the process. Children and the elderly are particularly predisposed to hypothermia.

To avoid serious stages of hypothermia, be alert for early signs and symptoms, such as fatigue, weakness, slowness, apathy, forgetfulness, and confusion. Others may recognize these changes, but the victim may not be aware of them.

Hypothermia is classified as either mild or profound. The victim of mild hypothermia usually experiences little or no change in mental ability, with either normal or slightly impaired coordination for activities such as walking. The victim may be shivering and typically has difficulty manipulating buttons, zippers, and bootlaces. The victim may also be somewhat lethargic, and his speech may be vague, slow, and slurred.

It is important to recognize these signs and to begin treatment immediately. Get the victim out of the wind, rain, or cold environment, and remove any wet clothing. Protect him from further heat loss, especially from the head and neck. Give him warm liquids and a hot meal (but no alcohol). Complications from mild hypothermia are minimal, and he can resume his activities when warmed up.

A victim who advances to profound hypothermia experiences a definite change in mental status. The victim may be apathetic and uncooperative; shivering is replaced by muscle rigidity. All movements become erratic and jerky. As the victim's core temperature falls further, he becomes irrational, loses contact with his surroundings, and falls into a stupor. If untreated, the victim eventually lapses into unconsciousness and then dies from cardiac arrest or other complications.

In addition to the treatments given for mild hypothermia, handle the victim gently when removing clothing and giving care. Do not rub the extremities to stimulate circulation. Instead, place wrapped warmed rocks or hot water bottles around the victim to accelerate the warming process. If possible, place the victim in a sleeping bag in contact with two other people who are nonhypothermic. Continue warming the victim until evacuation to a medical facility is possible.

In practice, such treatments in the field can be problematic, since other members of a party may be afflicted by varying degrees of hypothermia as well. In bad weather it is essential that all members of a party stick together so that they can look after each others' welfare.

Altitude Illnesses

High-altitude illnesses have been recognized for many years, but they've become more common as more people experience rapid ascents into the mountains. These illnesses range from mild conditions of headache, nausea, and fatigue to the truly life-threatening conditions of high-altitude pulmonary edema (HAPE) and high-altitude cerebral edema (HACE). As with most conditions, prevention is much better than any of the current treatments.

The development of acute mountain sickness (AMS) is related to a person's physical activity, past acclimatization, rate of ascent, and altitude reached. It is uncommon below 8000 feet but occurs in 30 percent of people abruptly exposed to 10,000 feet, and 70 percent of people abruptly exposed to 14,800 feet. The most effective preventive measure is to remain at 8000 to 10,000 feet for a few days and then gradually ascend to the planned altitude. If ascent is less than 1000 feet per day above 10,000 feet, the condition is not likely to occur. Another preventive measure is to avoid alcohol and sleeping pills.

The symptoms of AMS vary in severity in different individuals but tend to be constant for a given person with each reexposure to altitude. Symptoms usually begin from 12 to 24 hours after ascent. A throbbing, generalized headache, decreased appetite, nausea and vomiting, and general fatigue characterize this relatively mild illness. The symptoms have been compared to that of a hangover from an alcohol binge. They tend to gradually decrease as long as further ascent is postponed. A high-carbohydrate diet begun a few days before ascent may help to prevent or decrease these symptoms.

While most persons with AMS do well and can remain at 8000 to

10,000 feet, some have more severe symptoms or symptoms that begin at higher altitudes. These may include cough, shortness of breath, intermittent breathing, and difficulty with coordination. (To check for coordination, have the person walk a straight line putting the heel of the forward foot to the toe of the back foot.) Individuals with these symptoms should descend at least 1000 feet to prevent further complications. Conditions that may mimic AMS include dehydration, hypothermia, carbon monoxide poisoning, and severe infections.

HAPE is less common than AMS, but much more serious and potentially fatal. It strikes 1 or 2 percent of climbers above 12,000 feet and is most common on the second night at these altitudes. It too, is related to rate of ascent, exertion, use of alcohol or sleeping pills, and cold. Early symptoms may include a dry cough, increased pulse rate, and decreased exercise performance. Shortness of breath, bluish skin color, and a cough producing pink-tinged phlegm occur as the condition progresses. In some cases, a victim of HAPE can lapse into coma or suddenly die without any warning signs at all. Although several forms of medication, including diuretics and oxygen have been used, descent is the only uniformly successful form of treatment.

HACE represents a markedly more severe form of high-altitude illness. There is a progression of symptoms such as lack of coordination, changes in consciousness, severe headache, bizarre behavior, and coma. Descent is the only successful treatment.

Although slow ascent is the best prevention for high-altitude illnesses of all types, there are medications that can help when this is not possible. Acetazolamide (Diamox) in doses of 250 milligrams twice a day beginning 24 hours before ascent and continuing 24 to 48 hours at altitude decreases the likelihood of AMS. (Acetazolamide is a sulfonamide; people who have reacted in the past to sulfa drugs should not take it. Side effects include tingling of the lips and fingers and an altered sense of taste. Because it is a diuretic, water consumption should be increased after taking this medication.)

Dexamethasone (Decadron), a cortisone-type drug, can also be used at a dosage of 4 milligrams taken every 6 hours starting 24 hours before ascent and continuing for several days. Because there may be some serious side effects to this drug, it should not be taken unless under the direction of a medical professional in the group.

High-altitude illness is a preventable condition. Mild forms are inconvenient, but the more severe forms can be fatal. Slow ascent, especially above 10,000 feet with sleep at a lower altitude, use of

Diamox, and avoidance of alcohol and sleeping pills helps to make your trip pleasant and safe.

TRAUMA

Bleeding

Uncontrolled bleeding can quickly lead to shock. It can occur internally or be visible externally. The first step in controlling bleeding is the application of direct pressure to the bleeding site. A clean or sterile dressing is preferred, but, if unavailable, use your hand. If bleeding has been difficult to stop, don't remove the dressing but add more on top of the first ones. If you don't suspect a fracture, elevate the extremity above the heart. Pressure points (places where an artery crosses a bone) can also be used to control bleeding but are not usually effective when used alone. Tourniquets should only be used when the loss of a limb is necessary to save a life. The presence of the tourniquet should be clearly indicated on the victim's forehead with a marker.

A bruised, swollen, tender, or rigid abdomen is a sign of internal bleeding. Penetrating chest or abdominal wounds, fracture of the pelvis, and bleeding from the rectum or vagina are also likely to indicate internal bleeding. These victims should be evacuated immediately.

Small bruises can be treated with cold compresses or cold-water immersion for the first 48 hours, along with a mild compression dressing.

Wounds such as lacerations should be cleaned with soap and water or a disinfectant. Grossly contaminated wounds can be irrigated with cooled boiled water or water disinfected using iodine or chlorine. Closing wounds with sutures should be avoided, but adhesive tape or sterile cloth strips may be used. Highly contaminated wounds should be observed for signs of infection (swelling, redness, warmth around the wound, and foul-smelling drainage). These wounds should be treated at a medical facility.

Scalp wounds bleed profusely and may prove to be small. Gentle direct pressure using your fingertips can stop this bleeding. Instead of cutting the hair around the cut, try wrapping around one of your fingers a few strands of the victim's hair on either side of the cut and then tying the twisted hairs together to close the cut.

Nosebleed

To stop most nosebleeds, apply pressure on the soft cartilage at the bridge of the nose and have the victim sit upright and lean with his head slightly forward. This prevents the blood from leaking down the throat and into the stomach causing nausea and vomiting. If bleeding doesn't stop in 10 minutes, roll up a small piece of cloth or cotton and insert it into the nostril.

Fracture

Fractures are classified as either closed (no broken skin) or open (bone protrudes through the skin). Signs and symptoms are pain, swelling, deformity, bruising, tenderness over the area, and inability to move the injured limb. The victim may also report a "snapping" sound at the time of injury.

Treat fractures with splints to prevent movement. If it is a compound (open) fracture, you may also have to place a dressing and bandage over the open area. Splints should be carefully padded and improvised from whatever is available. Practice splinting on an uninjured individual before apply-

For nosebleeds, apply pressure to the soft cartilage at the bridge of the nose. Have the victim sit upright and lean with the head slightly forward. (Photo by Carol Murdock.)

ing the splint to a victim. Splint one extremity against an uninjured one if necessary. Improvise, using items such as high-density foam and pack waist bands (as cervical collars), wire splints, ice axes, camera tripods, and parts of pack frames.

Sprains, Strains, and Dislocations

Sprains are stretched or torn tendons, ligaments, and blood vessels around joints. The ankle is the most common site of a sprain. Signs and symptoms are pain, tenderness, discoloration, and swelling at the joint.

Treat a mild or moderate sprain by wrapping the joint with an elastic bandage in a figure-eight pattern and applying cold—snow or stream water. A more severe sprain (blue-purple discoloration below the ankle bone after 12 to 24 hours) should be elevated, wrapped with an elastic bandage, and not used to bear weight. The boot may be kept on as long as it does not interfere with circulation from swelling.

Strains are stretched or torn muscles and often occur in the back. Improperly lifting a heavy object causes them. Signs and symptoms

Splinting with available materials.
(Photo by Carol Murdock.)

include sharp pain, stiffness, and swelling. Treatment consists of applying cold over the area for 24 hours, rest, and use of pain-control medicines.

If there is doubt about an injury being a sprain, strain, or dislocation, treat it as a fracture.

Foreign Body in the Eye

To remove an irritating object from the eye, try grasping the lashes of the upper eyelid and pulling the lid down over the lower lid. If this does not solve the problem, with the head tilted down so fluid drains from the nose area to the outside of the eye, gently pour clean water to wash out the eye. If still unsuccessful, place the flat stick of a cotton swab against the upper eyelid, grasp the lashes and "snap" the upper eyelid inside out. You can then see the object better and gently lift it off the surface of the eye using the edge of a soft cloth.

BUG IN THE EAR

An insect buzzing around in your ear can be very irritating, and the insect may sting if you try to retrieve it. Instead, apply a few drops of oil (any kind will do). This suffocates the insect, and then you can wash it out of your ear with water.

Search and Rescue

Jeff Marchand and Donald B. Stouder

If everyone who ventured into the wilderness was prepared to do so, there would be less need for a chapter like this. But for many circumstances—some avoidable and some unavoidable—people do get lost or injured in the outdoors. Thoughtful planning can often prevent these occurrences.

People accustomed to living in remote places for several days at a stretch are usually well prepared to deal with adverse circumstances. Those who run into difficulty in the wilderness are often casual users—day hikers, anglers, hunters—who don't travel very far from the nearest road or civilized place. With too little equipment and too little knowledge, they risk getting into situations they can't handle.

Thoughtful planning, even for day trips, greatly reduces the risk of being stranded without help. Below are some ways to implement that planning.

First, leave a detailed itinerary with someone you trust. Agree on a time of return (allowing plenty of room for changes in your schedule), and then do your best to meet that intended itinerary. Instruct your contact person to call for help if you do not return, and provide a list of emergency contacts in the area where you will be. If you get into a situation where you need help and can't get out, at least someone will be aware of your predicament and help will come eventually.

Second, never go into an unfamiliar area without the basic tools of navigation—map and compass—and the competence to use both effectively.

Third, carry the essential safety and survival items appropriate for your trip. Ask yourself, "What would I need to survive the worst conditions I could realistically encounter?" Always carry the Ten Essentials (see Chapter 5, Outfitting, "The Foundation"). There is always the possibility of getting stuck out overnight if you or someone with you becomes lost or injured; or if you get caught out after dark and it is not safe to continue.

BEING LOST, AND DEALING WITH IT

If you become lost, admit it to yourself early and start dealing with it in a rational manner. Stop moving and think. If you stop before you become completely disoriented, you can usually find your way back to a known location. If you are lost, don't wander about without a coherent plan.

If you've gotten separated from your group and become disoriented, stop and listen for them. They may be signaling you. Call to them, or, better yet, use your whistle. Make some tentative movements toward where you think they went, or climb to a nearby high point for a better view. Don't go far from the point where you became aware you were lost. When your companions realize you are missing, they will begin looking for you from where they last saw you.

If you aren't successful, then remember the cardinal rule: Don't panic. If you've absorbed all the information contained in this book and are reasonably well equipped, then you know everything you need in order to survive. The most important thing you need now is the patience to sit down and think clearly and calmly about your choices.

Should you sit still, make yourself comfortable, and wait to be found? Should you attempt to find your way out? The alternative you choose depends, of course, on many factors. Will the weather hold up? How long until sunset? How prepared are you for a bivouac (emergency overnight stay)? Do you have the proper navigational tools, and if so, can you locate yourself on the map and navigate to a position of safety or possible rescue? What obstacles lie along the way? How long before someone reports you as missing?

You may decide to stay put and let the searchers find you. If so, take care of yourself. Find shelter; conserve your strength; protect yourself as best you can from wind and rain, heat or cold, and excess sunlight.

Then, make yourself as conspicuous as possible. If the sun is up, build a smoky fire (but think very carefully about how you'll do this safely in wildfire-prone areas). To catch the attention of aerial searchers, lay out bright-colored clothing or camping gear on a hilltop or in a clearing. Rearrange the natural features of the landscape (rocks, branches, etc.) into some unnatural geometric form (if that doesn't take too much energy). Remember, three of anything (whistle blasts, gunshots, rock piles) is the universal signal for distress. Use a signal mirror if you have one. At night, build a fire both to keep warm and to attract attention. Above all, know that when you are missed, you'll be looked for. Relax, all you have to do is survive until you are found.

If you're certain you can reach help by your own muscles and know-how, then be reasonable about it. Take the time to think it through. Don't stumble through unknown terrain in the dark. Don't hurry across the desert in the midday heat if you need to conserve your water supply. If you reach civilization before rescuers find you, your first order of business is to make sure that fact is communicated to anyone who may be out looking for you.

DEALING WITH A MISSING HIKER

Discovering that a friend, relative, or member of your party is missing is a terribly unnerving experience. But again, that's never an excuse to panic. You may be able to locate the missing person with a quick search of the immediate area, or you may need to contact the authorities to launch an organized search. Take into consideration who is missing, and that person's experience, age, and health status. Also consider whether or not the person has the proper equipment and how long he has been unaccounted for. The appropriate time to initiate a search may depend on current or anticipated weather conditions and the time of day.

First, try to establish where the person was last seen ("point last seen," or PLS, in rescuer's parlance). It's very important that the area near the PLS remain undisturbed so that future searchers can examine it carefully for clues such as tracks and scents. Shout or make other noises first to see if the lost person responds. This should be followed by a brief search of the trails (being careful not to disturb footprints) or other possible places a person could have gone in the area around the PLS. Those who are searching should stay in pairs and keep communicating with others as much as possible. Each searcher should be on the lookout for clues such as footprints or personal belongings. If there's no indication of success after about 2 hours, then it's time to call for outside help.

Fortunately for outdoor enthusiasts, most areas are served by search and rescue teams. Most teams are volunteers; some are part of the sheriff's or parks department, while others are independent groups. All operate under the authority of a local agency, usually the county sheriff or the National Park Service. As a rule, the individual rescuers are required to participate in extensive training.

You can expect the searchers to respond as quickly as possible once they know someone is missing, however, it may take 2–24 hours for them to mobilize. They consider all the possibilities of how this person became missing and what the missing person might do. Then the search effort concentrates on the most likely areas first. They start with the PLS and try to determine the direction the lost person went. Using a variety of search tactics—including trackers, search dogs, aircraft and four-wheel-drive vehicles—the area where the missing person is believed to be is confined and systematically searched. Searchers are looking not only for the lost person, but also for clues that the lost person may have left. A clue can be a track, a piece of discarded gear, or any sign that the lost person has been there. By finding and following clues, the searchers can find the lost person much faster than if they were only looking for the lost person.

Sending for Help

Self-reliance should be your goal, but you need to know how to contact the proper authorities when there is an emergency that requires outside help.

If you find yourself in a situation that requires sending someone out for help, you must decide how to divide the group and your resources. When determining who should go for help and who should stay, consider leadership, the skills of each person (such as navigation and first aid), physical strength, equipment, water supply, and how long it will take for rescuers to reach you.

If the distance to the nearest source of help is long, send at least two well-equipped persons. They must carry detailed information about what the problem is and the location, what equipment and experience the group has, the condition of any injured person (for a detailed list of information messengers should carry about injured persons, see Chapter 16, Wilderness First Aid, "First Aid in the Field"), what kind of help is needed, as well as the group's plans. Those going for help should mark their route so rescuers can quickly follow their trail back and find the location. When the search and rescue team arrives, let them take over. Allay your considerable anxiety with the knowledge that they know their business better than anyone else.

To summon help to find a lost person or to evacuate an injured person, notify the local law-enforcement authority, be it the county sheriff, park ranger, or other authority. (Where applicable, the emergency telephone number 911 is the fastest way to reach the right agency).

Cell Phones

More people are carrying cell phones in the wilderness these days, with the false idea that they can call for help from anywhere. A cell phone *may* aid in summoning help, but it cannot be counted on in the wilderness, where cell phone coverage is limited and rugged terrain can block signals. A cell phone is not a substitute for the proper survival skills and equipment. It may be a good idea to bring your cell phone with you, but only in addition to what you should otherwise carry for safety and survival.

(Photo by Jerry Schad.)

If you plan to carry a cell phone, find out where you can expect to have service. Before making the call, organize all the information you need to give to the authorities (as you would for sending someone out for help). If you have a poor signal, you may be able to improve it by moving to a different location. Try to find an open area free from obstructions or move to higher ground. You have a better chance of a good signal on a ridge top than you do at the bottom of a canyon. Cell phone battery life is limited, so consider carrying extra batteries.

chapter
18

Mountain Biking

Bob Feuge and Ian Wickson

Mountain biking is riding a crest of popularity all over North America and Europe. Men and women of all ages are taking up the sport. For some, a bicycle is a sightseeing platform. For the more adventurous, mountain biking is a means of getting out for some vigorous exercise. Competitive types may opt to participate in cross-country and downhill races. Competitive biking requires advanced skills and is, therefore, beyond the scope of this book.

Before getting into the sport itself, it might be useful to describe the features of a mountain bike that distinguish it from a road bike. Mountain bikes have stronger and more durable frames that are designed and constructed to take the punishment of riding on rugged terrain. They feature wide, knobby tires that are capable of maintaining traction in a variety of trail conditions. Most have some form of suspension that absorbs the shock created by obstacles in the trail. Mountain bikes have more powerful braking systems than road bikes and a wider range of gearing. Collectively, these features enhance control of the bike in rough conditions and make the ride more comfortable. Road bikes, on the other hand, are built for speed. They are light, have thin tires that create little rolling resistance, and rarely have suspension.

While mountain bikes are gaining wider acceptance, they are still not welcome everywhere. In fact, they are banned from all federally designated wilderness and other ecologically sensitive areas. Other areas permit off-road vehicles (ORVs) such as mountain bikes on trails or on off-road areas expressly designated for their use, or on all dirt roads but not on trails. On most national forest lands, mountain bikes can be ridden almost without restrictions. Still, mountain bikes should be ridden only on trails designated for their use by the appropriate land management agency. They shouldn't be ridden off-trail or on hikers-only trails. Even with these restrictions, the possibilities of mountain-bike travel are almost endless. There are hundreds of thousands of miles of dirt roads and trails open to mountain biking.

It is the responsibility of all mountain bikers to adhere to these restrictions.

THE SPORT OF MOUNTAIN BIKING

Some say the sport began in 1974, when Gary Fisher equipped his vintage klunker with motorcycle brakes and rode down Mount Tamalpais in Marin, California. Others dispute this claim, insisting mountain biking is an evolution of the European sport of cyclocross. Regardless of who spawned the sport or when, Americans were ready

Mountain biking in Arizona. (Photo by Bob Feuge.)

for a new way to travel the backcountry. Soon, mountain bikes were being mass produced and bikers literally took to the hills, freed from the confines of pavement and competition with automobiles.

The Single Track Experience

While mountain bikers ride dirt roads and jeep trails, riding single-track trails is the most exhilarating experience! It is this experience that sets the sport apart from other forms of bicycling. Single-track trails generally have only one narrow path whereas a forest service road, for example, might provide two parallel paths to ride on. Riding a good single-track trail is somewhat like riding a roller coaster. There are occasional steep climbs followed by rapid descents. There are twists and turns, ups and downs. Of course, there are straight sections where some speed is possible. Occasionally, there are sharp bends or curves in the path that challenge your ability to maintain momentum and balance. Along the trail, you may encounter a variety of trail surfaces from deep sand to mud to slick rock. Single-track trails occasionally will be smooth but most are fraught with rocks, roots, small ledges, limbs, and other obstacles. Negotiating such a trail requires technical skill to maneuver the bike safely. And yes, it is possible to ride bikes enjoyably on such trails.

Many of the single-track trails that mountain bikers ride are the same ones that hikers and equestrians use. As an alternative to hiking or horseback riding, the sport of mountain biking has some unique advantages and disadvantages to consider.

Pros and Cons of Mountain Biking

You might ask, "Why take up mountain biking when I already hike?" To answer this question, mountain biking will be contrasted with hiking. As you might suspect, both have their niche and the choice is not either/or—you can do both! In the end, it's a matter of personal preference.

What draws so many people to mountain biking?

Mountain biking is fun. Relative to hiking, mountain biking just might be more fun! The wind in your face . . . the feeling of speed . . . none of that's changed since the last time you rode a bike. Speed compresses the time interval between successive events such as turns, drops, and climbs, and you are forced to think ahead while controlling the bike. The combined mental and physical challenge makes mountain biking fun.

Because of the mechanical advantages, bikers can cover more terrain than hikers. It's not uncommon to travel 20 or 30 miles on a bike outing, and take only part of a day to do so. Hiking the same distance might require an overnight trip.

Mountain biking as exercise. Mountain biking is a great low-impact, cardiovascular exercise. Aerobic activity, which increases your metabolism, is the best way to burn calories. Aerobic activity also strengthens your heart, lungs, and leg muscles. Your blood's capacity to carry oxygen and nutrients is increased, producing stamina. In this regard, cycling is similar to running.

To a certain extent, you can use the bike's gears to regulate the intensity of your cardiovascular workout. Using lower gears for an easy spin brings your heart and respiration rates up to sustainable levels for long periods. Or, use the big gears and feel the burn on short, intense rides.

Because of cardiovascular benefits, some have discovered that biking makes an excellent adjunct sport to other activities, such as hiking and backpacking.

Mountain biking and your joints. Compared to hiking and running, biking creates little repetitive impact on leg joints and the spine (provided you stay upright on the bike). Some physicians recommend cycling as an alternative to high-impact exercise for those with chronic pain caused by leg injuries or damaged cartilage. By caring for your joints through low-impact activities, you may prolong your career in backcountry travel. Proper bike size and fit is critical to keeping the stress off these joints, so when selecting a bike, ensure that its features are adjusted to fit you.

Mountain biking as a challenge. Once the sole province of young daredevils, men and women of all ages are now getting into the sport. It is not uncommon to see riders in their 50s, 60s, or even 70s. Part of the attraction is the challenge that comes from the interaction between bike and rider. If you accept this challenge and work at it, your skills will improve. Everyone has personal limits, but practice and tenacity will soon have you riding trails that you once found intimidating. Overcoming these challenges produces a lot of thrills and also provides a sense of accomplishment.

Why do some people shy away from mountain biking?

Fear of injury. Mountain biking involves risk. Backcountry trails are fraught with loose rocks, roots, ledges, overhanging limbs, and sometimes cacti. Failing to negotiate these menaces, you fall. There is a theory suggesting there are two types of riders—those who *have* fallen, and those who are *about* to! It happens when you least expect it, especially while learning. Bumps, bruises, and scrapes (or worse) are part of the sport. Each person must decide whether the risk is worth the thrill, challenge, and cardiovascular benefit.

Too strenuous. The sport is not for everyone. Some people simply don't want to exert the energy required to mountain bike. They prefer to travel slower, taking in the wonders of the backcountry on a more stable platform. Other people assume they could never achieve the fitness and stamina required to ride any distance on a mountain bike. Unfortunately, this assumption is often made without ever trying the sport. They overlook the fact that everyone starts at an elemental level and develops skill and endurance incrementally.

High cost. Some never take up cycling for financial reasons. Mountain biking is a money sink, just like golfing, boating, photography, and other diversions. To outfit yourself with a new entry-level bike, apparel, safety gear, and basic tools, you may easily spend $1000 or more. Compare that to the cost of hiking boots!

If you are at all inclined to try mountain biking, borrow or rent before you invest. Strap on a helmet, and try the bike out on some easy trails. If you're thrilled, go ahead and hock the house to buy a good one. You won't regret it!

ETHICAL ISSUES

For years, trails were the sole territory of hikers and horseback riders. The established etiquette involving hikers and equestrians now has been modified to include mountain bikers as well. To help standardize riding practices, the National Off-Road Bicycle Association (NORBA) has developed the following riding code:

1. I will yield the right-of-way to other nonmotorized recreationalists.
2. I will use caution when overtaking another and will make my presence known well in advance.
3. I will maintain control of my speed at all times.
4. I will stay on designated trails.
5. I will not disturb wildlife or livestock.
6. I will not litter.
7. I will respect public and private property.
8. I will always be self-sufficient.
9. I will not travel solo when bike-packing in remote areas.
10. I will observe the practice of minimum-impact bicycling.
11. I will always wear a helmet whenever I ride.

Bikes and wilderness. Bicycles—and all other mechanical forms of transportation, such as all-terrain vehicles (ATV) and hang gliders—are expressly prohibited in areas protected by the Wilderness Act of 1964.

Wilderness is land set aside from human development because of rare or sensitive geological, biological, hydrological, or ecological features that exist within it. The goal is to preserve those features in pristine condition, unmarred by human use. Congress has established these areas to be explored by primitive means, such as hiking, backpacking, or horseback riding.

In the opinion of the U.S. Forest Service, bicycles are no worse than hikers in terms of erosion and trail damage. But bicycles are simply not considered a primitive means of travel.

Topographical maps outline wilderness boundaries. Additionally, most trails leading into wilderness areas are marked with signs similar to the ones shown in the photo below. You may be fined as much as $300 for the first offense and up to $500 for subsequent offenses, plus your bike may be confiscated. Worse, you mar the reputation of responsible mountain bikers and diminish the experience of other wilderness travelers.

Wilderness boundary sign: it is illegal to have a bike in your possession beyond this point. (Photo by Bob Feuge.)

Ultimately, it's your responsibility to know which trails are legal to ride. If in doubt, consult the local land management agency that has jurisdiction over the trails in question.

National park policy. Mountain bikes are allowed in some national parks. Policy requires that each park conduct an analysis to make a determination regarding environmental impact. Some parks allow bikes but only on certain trails; others prohibit them. Again, check with park rangers to be sure.

Preservation. Cyclists are subject to the same code of conduct as hikers and equestrians. Stay on established trails. Never cut switchbacks, and never ride immediately after precipitation. Riding in the mud not only creates large ruts, but also leads to increased erosion. Don't modify trails to suit your skill level. Removing rocks and roots may increase erosion as well as spoil the challenge for more experienced riders.

Control your speed to avoid skidding, especially on descents. Skidding not only damages the trail, but also unnerves others using the trail. Try not to leave tire marks on rocks—they will remain there a long time. Paraphrasing the Sierra Club motto, take only photographs, leave only tire tracks (in the sand).

Your opportunities to aid in preservation of trails are not limited to on-trail activities. Consider doing volunteer work to help create and maintain your local trails. Many communities and bike shops sponsor clubs that take part in regular trail-maintenance activities. Contact the International Mountain Bike Association (IMBA) at *www.imba.com* for links to local clubs.

BIKING ETIQUETTE

Backcountry trails are shared by bikers, hikers, backpackers, equestrians, and, in some areas, motorized traffic.

Etiquette owed to other trail users. Cyclists have the lowest priority in terms of right-of-way and must yield to all other non-motorized trail users—especially equestrians. There are two reasons for such low status. One is safety. Since bikes are capable of traveling faster than most other trail users, the responsibility is on bikers to control their speed and avoid collisions. The second is tradition. Being the newest form of backcountry transportation, it's only natural that bikes are last in the pecking order.

If you encounter an equestrian on the trail, you should stop, dismount, and move your bike away from the trail to allow easy passage for the horse. Because horses are potential prey animals, they are often leery of unfamiliar objects perched above them. They are less leery if

Yielding the trail: dismount and give equestrians plenty of room. (Photo by Cheryl Victory.)

you are on their downhill side. This position may not always be safe for you. If the trail follows an escarpment and you are on the downhill side, a spooked horse might cause you to fall. If necessary, move to another place or backtrack to a safer area.

As the horse approaches, speak softly to identify yourself as a human. Don't touch the animal unless encouraged to do so by the rider. If you are the first in a line of bikers, tell the horse rider how many are in your group so further encounters can be anticipated.

When overtaking hikers, slow down and give an audible signal by voicing your presence or ringing a bell. Be polite. Most hikers are happy to step aside (even though they technically have the right-of-way) if you treat them with respect. Acknowledge their compliance. If they elect to stay on the trail, be prepared to walk your bike around them. Again, inform them of your group size so that subsequent riders won't startle them.

Etiquette owed to other bikers. When encountering another biker head-on, both riders should slow down and move to the right, just as you would when driving a car down a narrow lane.

On a hill, the ascending rider has priority over the descending rider because of the effort required to get restarted. The descending rider has the advantage of gravity, so stopping and starting up again is less troublesome. However, if another rider has already committed to a steep descent, it may be best to allow that rider the right-of-way. Don't risk a collision, especially if the other rider appears out of control.

When overtaking, slow down and communicate. Let the rider know how you are going to pass (e.g., on your left). Make your pass in a safe spot, but be prepared to stop if something unexpected happens. Never startle unsuspecting riders by zooming by unannounced. It is both rude and unsafe.

When riding in a group, be considerate by maintaining a safe distance between you and the rider ahead. If you get well ahead of the other rider(s), stop and wait a bit to ensure that all is well before proceeding. Always stop at trail intersections to ensure that everyone knows the way.

Motorized traffic. On backcountry roads and trails, you may encounter everything from family sedans to motorcycles and ATVs. Technically the same rules apply on dirt roads as in normal city traffic. Stay to the right, signal for turns, etc. Areas open to ATVs may or may not prioritize bicycles in terms of right-of-way. Again, check with local land management agencies for specifics.

From a practical standpoint, don't count on others to see you. They may be distracted while looking at the sights, or traveling too fast for the conditions. Chances are, you will see and hear motorized vehicles before they see you. Give the vehicle plenty of room, regardless of right-of-way rules that might apply.

BASIC TECHNIQUE

Obviously, no written instruction can teach you to be a proficient rider. Technique is learned mostly through trial and error. More detailed instruction is contained in *Mountain Bike Like a Champion* by Ned Overend (Rodale Press, 1999). For humorous instruction, consult *Mountain Bike! A Manual of Beginning to Advanced Technique* by William Nealy (Menasha Ridge Press, 1992).

Technique, simply put, is interacting with your bike. It involves maintaining balance, shifting weight, pedaling efficiently, braking and shifting gears smoothly. According to Overend, the basic goal of mountain biking is to create and maintain momentum. Master the following techniques, and you are on your way.

Pedaling. Overend recommends that beginners learn to pedal in circles. By this he means exerting force on the pedals throughout the entire crank rotation. Using a clock analogy and looking at the bike from the right side, beginners tend to push down on the pedals only from the one o'clock to the five o'clock position. In contrast, pushing the pedals over the top and then dragging them up through the bottom of the circle will result in more efficient pedaling. Pedals that attach to your biking shoes make this process easier and allow you to pull up on the back side of the stroke as well.

When coasting, keep your cranks horizontal to the ground (pedals at nine and three o'clock positions). This arrangement puts you in the best position to rise from the saddle to absorb bumps, keeps your pedals clear of obstacles, and helps you maintain balance.

Balance. Once a bike achieves some speed, it gains some semblance of balance through gyroscopic forces. Therefore, you want to maintain speed as much as possible in order to maintain balance. Backcountry trails, however, are rarely smooth and you are occasionally forced to slow down and wobble a bit. To maintain balance, shift your body weight in response to trail conditions. Overend suggests that you visualize these movements as occurring in an inverted 3-D cone. This upside down cone extends upward from your feet on the pedals (the narrowest point) to a wide circle at the top that encompasses your body and shoulder movements.

In rough terrain, stay light in the saddle and concentrate your weight on your feet. This allows the bike to move freely beneath you without upsetting your balance. Look ahead and choose a reasonable line of travel through trail obstacles. Follow that imaginary line with your eyes, and allow the bike to bounce and flow over the rocks and roots. Practice improves your balance and helps you ride with more confidence.

Climbing. Maintaining traction is the key to successful climbing. Stay in the saddle as much as possible to keep weight on the rear tire. Keep your arms slightly bent and away from your rib cage to allow efficient breathing (see photo opposite). Avoid bending too far forward and leaning on the handlebar. This transfers weight to the front tire, interferes with your breathing, and makes it difficult to keep your head up to scan the trail ahead.

Often a steep incline requires you to stand and pedal. If you do stand, make the transition smoothly to avoid losing traction on the rear tire and spinning out. Standing moves your center of gravity forward, off of the rear tire. Compensate by maintaining an even, upward pull on the handlebar to put force back on the rear tire. If your biking shoes are attached to the pedals, try to exert more force on the pedals during the climb by pulling up through the back of the pedal circle.

Braking and descending. Mountain bikes have handlebar-mounted brake levers. Normally, the right-hand lever controls the rear brake, and the left controls the front. It's extremely important to remember

Good climbing technique: weight centered over pedals, arms away from body, head up, and eyes scanning ahead. (Photo by Mark Trainor.)

which is which, especially on steep descents. Hard braking on the front wheel during a descent can cause the bike to flip, ejecting you over the bars. In biking parlance, this is called an "endo," and it is not good for you or the bike! With practice, you will discover that the front brake can be quite useful.

It's also important to apply brakes smoothly and evenly to avoid lockup (skidding). A locked front wheel causes dangerous loss of control, while a locked rear brake causes a skid and damages the trail. On level ground, it is best to apply both brakes with equal pressure. Other situations will require that you modulate braking pressure between front and rear wheels.

On steep descents, it may be necessary to shift your body far to the rear—sometimes behind the saddle—to maintain proper weight distribution between the front and rear wheels. In anticipation of long downhill sections, you may want to lower the saddle to make this movement easier. A quick-release seat-post clamp facilitates lowering and raising the saddle.

Even if you shift your body behind the saddle, decelerating (braking) transfers most of your weight forward onto the front wheel, giving it better traction than the rear wheel. Therefore, you have more braking control with the front brake than the back brake. It takes experience to know how much front braking you can apply without risking an endo. Work up to riding severe terrain and use judgment when tackling steep descents.

Shifting gears. Using the appropriate gear combination helps you to create and maintain momentum. To change gears, operate one or both of the shift control levers on your handlebar. These levers are connected to the derailleurs via cables. The left lever controls the front derailleur while the right lever controls the rear. Derailleurs are the components that guide the chain onto the various chain rings and cogs. Most mountain bikes today are equipped with three front chain rings and nine rear cogs, for a total of twenty-seven possible gear combinations. Gears amplify the force you apply on the pedals through leverage. Shifting the front gears makes large or coarse changes in leverage while the rear gears make finer adjustments.

There is at least one combination of front and back gears that will give you the correct mechanical advantage for any given situation. For example, climbing steep hills generally calls for the use of the small front ring and larger rear cogs. Conversely, using the large front ring and the smaller rear cogs allows you to maintain force on the pedals while descending.

To ride efficiently, survey the trail ahead, calculate the proper gearing, and anticipate when to shift up or down. Shifts must be executed quickly and smoothly. When encountering a hill, downshift before you begin to climb. Pedal through the shift, but with feather force. Overloading the pedals while shifting prematurely wears or damages components in the shifting system. With practice, you'll learn good shifting technique.

Other techniques. Look where you want to go, not at hazards. Riders are often amazed when the bike "magnetically" tracks toward an object on the trail that they were staring at and wanting to avoid. This problem is called "target fixation" among bikers. You unconsciously steer where you look. To solve this problem, keep your head up and scan 20 to 50 feet ahead instead of immediately in front of the bike. If you see an obstacle coming, don't fixate on it. Instead, concentrate on finding a clear route around the obstacle and then look beyond it. One cycling proverb says, "If you look down, you'll go down!"

As much as possible, stay relaxed. If you're tense and tightly gripping the bars, you will be more easily knocked off balance as the bike reacts to the terrain underneath it. Work to develop a smooth, fluid riding style that allows you to roll with the terrain and conserve energy for pedaling.

When possible, ride with more experienced riders. Observe their line of travel and note where they apply brakes, when they change gears, and how they shift their weight. Allow them to challenge you to ride more difficult terrain, but always reserve the option to dismount if you get in over your head.

Above all, ride for enjoyment. Don't expect to become an expert mountain biker overnight. As your skills increase you will be able to ride more confidently and take in more of the scenery around you. After all, that's why you go to the backcountry.

SAFETY

What is the most important *safety* item in mountain biking? Most people would answer, "The helmet, of course!" They would be generally correct. You should never get on any bike without one. However, it's what's inside the helmet that's most important—**your brain!** Use it.

Use your head. The cognitive functions of preparation, planning, and judgment go a long way toward ensuring that you won't put undue stress on your helmet and other safety equipment.

Preparation is the long-term aspect of the safety equation. It refers to the skills you need to be safe in the backcountry—first aid, navigation, bike repair, etc. Learn these skills ahead of time. It does no good to carry gear unless you know how to use it. See Chapter 9, Wilderness Travel, and Chapter 16, Wilderness First Aid, for more on these topics.

Planning means accounting for safety before each ride. Be sure you carry the Ten Essentials when biking as well as when hiking (see Chapter 5, Outfitting.) In group situations, choose routes that are within everyone's ability. Plan to ride at a comfortable pace and punctuate the ride with periodic rest stops. Once on the trail, be flexible. If the planned route becomes too demanding, change routes or turn back.

Before you depart, inform a responsible person of your intended route, possible alternates, and when you expect to return. Riding alone may be unavoidable at times, but if you plan to travel far into the backcountry, away from help, then it's not advisable to ride alone.

Judgment is staying safe in the moment. It's the little voice in your head that says, "Slow down!" or "Don't try that." Listen to that little voice! Learn to assess your own skill accurately and ride within it. Don't let peers pressure you into trying something you're not comfortable doing. Never assume that once you have "cleaned" a trail (ridden it without walking or falling), you can always do so. Everyone has off days. If you're having one, don't hesitate to walk your bike. There is no shame in walking the bike.

Safety equipment. You are only as safe as the quality of safety equipment allows. In other words, don't scrimp on safety gear. As the saying goes, "Dress for the crash, not the ride!"

A **helmet** is not an accessory—it's a necessity. Notice that all riders captured in this chapter's photos are wearing helmets. On a mountain bike, you can attain relatively high speed on long, downhill runs. Falling at these speeds may cause the rider to strike the ground or nearby objects (such as rocks) with tremendous force. Such accidents can occur even when you are using good judgment, so you need to be protected.

The helmet protects your head by attenuating, or absorbing, energy. It does this through partial destruction of the helmet's core structure. The core is constructed of expanded polystyrene that crushes during an impact. The flashy plastic shell may provide additional puncture protection against tree limbs, but it does little to attenuate energy.

If your helmet has received any impact during a fall, damage to the core may have already occurred. Such damage may be internal and not readily detectable. If such damage has occurred, the helmet's ability to absorb further impacts has been compromised. It's best to replace it rather than risk total failure and head injury on the next fall.

Buy a helmet designed for mountain biking. Look for a sticker inside the helmet that bears the words "Complies with US CPSC Safety Standard for Bicycle Helmets." This indicates the design has undergone rigorous testing and meets criteria specific to cycling. Choose a current design because it provides more protection than older designs for the occipital (rear) area of your skull.

Some helmets offer greater ventilation than others (i.e., have more air holes). You will probably pay more for these models because the manufacturer reinforces the helmet to compensate for the reduced amount of protective core material around the air holes.

Proper fit is critical to the helmet's ability to protect you. Each manufacturer provides detailed fitting instructions that must be followed carefully. If you're not sure how to make your helmet fit, don't guess—ask for assistance at your local bike shop.

During a ride, use **eye protection.** Sunglasses with shatter-resistant, polycarbonate lenses protect your eyes from insects, overhanging branches, as well as dust and rocks thrown up by those knobby tires.

Look for designs that cover the entire eye orbit, not just the eyeball. They should fit snugly and stay in place while riding. Glasses that slide down your nose are both irritating and unsafe. If your glasses do slip, it is best to stop and adjust them rather than taking one hand off of the handlebar while riding.

Additional safety gear includes gloves to protect your hands from trailside vegetation and blisters. They also provide a first line of defense during a fall. Full-finger gloves, while somewhat warmer than fingerless designs, provide the best protection.

You may also want guards to protect your elbows and knees during a fall. Good guards are lightweight, well ventilated, and don't impede motion. Most designs incorporate a hard plastic outer shell and comfortable padding inside.

Starting out, you may choose to ride in running shoes, but they do not protect your feet. Good riding shoes have stiffer soles that are designed for pedaling. Since you may occasionally walk your bike, you need shoes with cleated soles that bite into dirt surfaces and maintain traction on surfaces such as slick rock. Rubber soles are safer and more comfortable on such surfaces than soles made of other material.

MOUNTAIN BIKES

Trade-offs. Considering your established needs and the basic bike information above, it is possible to select the style of bike that is appropriate for you. If you plan to take short to medium-length rides on smooth but hilly trails or jeep roads and comfort isn't paramount, you should opt for a front suspension (hard-tail) bike. The hard-tail design is light, easy to maintain, and reliable. It is also the best design for climbing hills. With a hard-tail bike, however, you will feel the bumps caused by rocks, roots, and other obstacles. If comfort does become an issue, swap your seat post for one with a built-in shock absorber. Hard-tail bikes are also the most economical design.

If you take longer rides on rough trails in the backcountry, ride more difficult trails, and consider comfort an issue, then you should select a full-suspension bike with a rugged frame. Opt for higher-quality components that are more reliable and repairable in the field. It is important to remember, however, that either style of bike can be ridden almost anywhere.

Accessories

Repair equipment. On any ride, you may encounter flat tires, broken chains, broken spokes, or maladjusted brakes and shifters. To make

repairs in the backcountry, carry some basic tools. It is generally recommended that your repair items include a patch kit and spare tube, tire levers, inflation device, chain tool and spare links, spoke wrench, and a set of Allen wrenches. There are some clever all-in-one tools available that reduce the number of things you have to carry.

You also need to know how to use these tools, so a basic understanding of bicycle repair is crucial. Practice repairs at home, before you have a real emergency. And don't be afraid to improvise. Try anything to get your bike rolling again.

Take local conditions into account when outfitting your repair kit. For instance, installing liquid sealant into your tubes may be advisable if thorns are prevalent. If you ride in wooded areas, limbs have a nasty habit of flipping up through wheels and playing havoc with delicate spokes. Carry extra spokes and a spoke tool if you plan to ride in areas littered with deadfall.

Hydration packs. Carry plenty of water or electrolyte replacement drinks with you on each ride. A quality hydration pack is the best way to do this. A hydration pack looks like a small backpack with a plastic bladder inside. The bladder is equipped with a hose and bite valve to facilitate fluid intake while riding. Extra pockets provide additional storage space for repair items, clothing, and snacks.

Bikes may be equipped with one or two holders for water bottles. If you plan lengthy trips where there is no water, don't rely solely on water bottles for your hydration needs. Even two bottles may not contain enough fluid to get you home—especially if something goes wrong and you are forced to spend more time on the trail than planned.

Clothing. Biking shorts come in two designs—single or double layer. Single-layer designs are made of tight-fitting Lycra, with padding in the seat to reduce chafing. Double-layer designs incorporate a Lycra short inside, and a loose-fitting, nylon layer outside. While not as cool as single-layer designs, they provide extra protection and a casual appearance.

In cold weather, layer synthetic garments (such as polypropylene) underneath, and top with a nylon shell. Shed or add layers to suit changing conditions just as you would if you were hiking or skiing.

SUMMARY

Mountain biking is an excellent way to experience the backcountry and get exercise. To enjoy the sport fully, you will need to buy or rent a bike (and a helmet), practice technique, and equip yourself to handle climatic conditions and equipment problems. Be sure to respect other trail users!

Opposite: *The adventure of mountain biking. (Photo by Ian Wickson.)*

Appendix: Resources

CHAPTER 2

Hampton, Bruce, and David Cole. *Soft Paths: How to Enjoy the Wilderness without Harming It.* Mechanicsburg, PA: Stackpole Books, 1988. (An excellent account of specific dos and don'ts, covering a wide range of outdoor activities.)

McGivney, Annette. *Leave No Trace: A Guide to the New Wilderness Etiquette,* 2nd ed. Seattle: The Mountaineers Books, 2003.

Meyer, Kathleen. *How to Shit in the Woods: An Environmentally Sound Approach to a Lost Art.* Berkeley, CA: Ten Speed Press, 1994. (A lighthearted but serious account of how to take care of toilet needs while enjoying the outdoors.)

Tilton, Buck, and Rick Bennett. *Don't Get Sick.* Seattle: The Mountaineers Books, 2002.

CHAPTER 3

American College of Sports Medicine. *Resource Manual for Guidelines for Exercise Testing and Prescription,* 4th ed. Edited by Jeffrey L. Roitman. Philadelphia: Lippincott, Williams, and Wilkins, 2001.

Anderson, Bob. *Stretching: 20th Anniversary Edition.* Bolinas, CA: Shulter Publications, 2000. (A well-illustrated reference with stretching exercises for various activities.)

Bowers, Richard W., and Edward L. Fox. *Sports Physiology,* 3rd ed. Dubuque, IA: Wm. C. Brown Publishers, 1992.

Cooper, Kenneth H. *Aerobics.* New York: M. Evans, 1968. (A classic work on aerobic testing and conditioning.)

Cox, Steven M., and Kris Fulsaas. *Mountaineering: The Freedom of the Hills,* 7th ed. Seattle: The Mountaineers Books, 2003.

Fixx, James F. *The Complete Book of Running.* New York: Random House, 1997. (Well-researched, practical, and easy-to-read advice on running and sports performance.)

Mann, Don, and Kara Schaad. *The Complete Guide to Adventure Racing: The Insider's Guide to the Greatest Sport on Earth.* New York: Hatherleigh Press, 2001.

Shangold, Mona M., and Gabe Mirkin. *The Complete Sports Medicine Book for Women.* New York: Simon and Schuster, Inc., 1992.

Tinley, Scott, and Ken Alpine. *Scott Tinley's Winning Guide to Sports Endurance: How to Maximize Speed, Strength and Stamina.* Emmaus, PA: Rodale Press, 1994.

Wilmore, Jack H., and David L. Costill. *Training for Sport and Activity: The Physiological Basis of the Conditioning Process.* Champaign, IL: Human Kinetics Publishers, 1993.

CHAPTER 5

To keep current on equipment and manufacturers, read equipment articles and reviews in magazines such as *Backpacker* or *Outside.* Back issues may be available at your local library, and hiking clubs may have publications with equipment articles as well. To buy equipment locally, check your telephone directory for backpacking, camping, and sports outfitting stores. Or search for articles, reviews, and suppliers on the Internet.

CHAPTER 6

Applegate, Elizabeth. *Eat Smart, Play Hard*. Emmaus, PA: Rodale, Inc., 2001. (Good overall advice on nutrition for athletes. Includes extensive information on new hiking foods such as sports drinks, energy bars, and gels.)

————. *Encyclopedia of Sports and Fitness Nutrition*. Roseville, CA: Prima Publishing, 2002. (Liz Applegate's articles are regularly featured in *Runner's World* magazine. This comprehensive work is an overview on the nutritional needs of athletes and people of all ages.)

Berger, Karen. *Hiking and Backpacking: A Complete Guide*. New York: W. W. Norton and Company, 1995. (Includes tips on how to walk, what to wear, what to carry, food, no-trace camping, backcountry safety and rescue, and navigation.)

Braaten, Brenda L., Ph.D., R.D. *Pack Light, Eat Right*. www.frc.mass.edu/bbraate/packlite (An Internet site devoted to nutrition for backpacking and other endurance sports.)

Coleman, Ellen. *Eating for Endurance*. Boulder, CO: Bull Publishing Company, 2000. (A nutrition guide for endurance athletes. Good information on your body's use of glycogen and fat, protein in the diet, hydration, and eating for performance.)

Cox, Steven M., and Kris Fulsaas. *Mountaineering: The Freedom of the Hills*, 7th ed. Seattle: The Mountaineers Books, 2003. (The classic guide for mountaineers.)

Curtis, Rick. *The Backpacker's Field Manual*. New York: Three Rivers Press, 1998. (A good overall guide for trip planning, equipment, cooking, nutrition, first aid, navigation, wilderness travel, safety, and weather observation.)

Jacobson, Cliff. *Camping's Top Secrets*. Guilford, CT: Globe Pequot Press, 1998. (Topics are organized alphabetically and range from Anchor to Yard Goods.)

Townsend, Chris. *The Advanced Backpacker*. Camden, ME: Ragged Mountain Press, 2001. (Good advice for long-distance trips, preparation and planning, food and resupply methods, feet and footwear, and equipment.)

Cookbooks

Barker, Harriett. *Supermarket Backpacker*. Chicago: Contemporary Books, Inc., 1977.

Bunnelle, Hasse, and the editors of *Backpacker* magazine. *The Backpacker's Food Book*. New York: Simon and Schuster, 1981.

Conners, Tim, and Christine Conners. *Lipsmackin' Backpackin'*. Helena, MT: Falcon Publishing, 2000.

Fleming, June. *The Well-Fed Backpacker*. New York: Random House, 1985.

Franz, Carl, and Lorena Havens. *The On and Off Road Cookbook*. Santa Fe: John Muir Publications, 1982.

Gray, Melissa, and Buck Tilton. *Cooking the One-Burner Way*. Guilford, CT: Globe Pequot Press, 2000.

Jacobson, Don. *The One-Pan Gourmet: Fresh Food on the Trail*. Camden, ME: Ragged Mountain Press, 1993.

Kesselheim, Alan S. *Trail Food: Drying and Cooking Food for Backpackers and Paddlers*, rev. ed. Camden, ME: Ragged Mountain Press, 1998.

Kinmont, Vikki, Claudia Axcell, and Diana Cooke. *Simple Foods for the Pack*. San Francisco: Sierra Club Books, 1986.

Latimer, Carole. *Wilderness Cuisine*. Berkeley: Wilderness Press, 1991.

McHugh, Gretchen. *Hungry Hiker's Book of Good Cooking*. New York: Alfred A. Knopf, Inc., 1982.

Miller, Dorcas. *Backcountry Cooking: From Pack to Plate in 10 Minutes*. Seattle: The Mountaineers Books, 1998.

———. *More Backcountry Cooking*. Seattle: The Mountaineers Books, 2002.

Pearson, Claudia, ed. *NOLS Cookery*. Mechanicsburg, PA: Stackpole Books, 1997.

Prater, Yvonne, and Ruth Dyar Mendenhall. *Gorp, Glop, and Glue Stew: Favorite Foods from 165 Outdoor Experts*. Seattle: The Mountaineers Books, 1982.

Yaffe, Linda Frederick. *Backpack Gourmet*. Mechanicsburg, PA: Stackpole Books, 2002.

CHAPTER 7

USGS topographic maps and many other maps useful for hikers can be purchased at outdoor equipment stores, map stores, on the Internet, or through the USGS.

For areas west of the Mississippi River: Branch of Distribution, U.S. Geological Survey, Box 25286, Federal Center, Denver, CO 80225.

For areas east of the Mississippi River: Branch of Distribution, U.S. Geological Survey, 1200 South Eads Street, Arlington, VA 22202.

mapping.usgs.gov.

Ferguson, Michael. *GPS Land Navigation: A Complete Guidebook for Backcountry Users of the NAVSTAR Satellite System*. Boise, ID: Glassford Publishing, 1997. (A useful GPS navigation book that also includes map-and-compass instruction.)

Fleming, June. *Staying Found: The Complete Map and Compass Handbook*, 3rd ed. Seattle: The Mountaineers Books, 2001.

Letham, Lawrence. *GPS Made Easy: Using Global Positioning Systems in the Outdoors*, 4th ed. Seattle: The Mountaineers Books, 2003.

CHAPTER 8

Lockhart, Gary. *The Weather Companion: An Album of Meteorological History, Science, Legend, and Folklore*. New York: Wiley Press, 1988.

Schaefer, Vincent J., and John A. Day. *A Field Guide to the Atmosphere*. Boston: Houghton Mifflin Co., 1981.

Scorer, R. S. *Clouds of the World: A Complete Color Encyclopedia*. Harrisburg, PA: Stackpole Books, 1972.

Weather-Related Websites

www.weather.com (Provides current weather reports for cities and zip codes.)

www.wunderground.com (Displays a variety of different types of weather maps.)

www.weather-photography.com/gallery.php?cat=clouds (Provides a photographic gallery of clouds, atmospheric optics, and lightning.)

asd-www.larc.nasa.gov/SCOOL/cldchart.html (Features an online cloud chart.)

weather.unisys.com/surface/sfc_front.html (Displays a map that shows the current and recent positions of weather fronts across North America.)

www.lightningsafety.noaa.gov (Focuses on lightning weather phenomena and provides information, safety tips, and a display of photographs.)

weather.uwyo.edu (Maintained by the University of Wyoming Department of Atmospheric Science, and offers a huge array of weather-related information and charts.)

www.theweatherprediction.com/habyhints/index.html (Has more than three hundred different forecasting hints and articles about weather.)

CHAPTER 9

Brainerd, John W. *The Nature Observer's Handbook: Learning to Appreciate Our Natural World.* Guilford, CT: Globe Pequot, 1986.

Fletcher, Colin, and Chip Rawlins. *The Complete Walker IV.* New York: Alfred A. Knopf, 2002.

Maughan, Jackie Johnson, and Ann Puddicombe. *Hiking the Backcountry: A Do-It-Yourself Guide for the Adventurous Woman.* Harrisburg, PA: Stackpole Books, 1981. (Now out of print. Excellent, in-depth treatment.)

Meyer, Kathleen. *How to Shit in the Woods: An Environmentally Sound Approach to a Lost Art.* Berkeley: Ten Speed Press, 1994. (A lighthearted but serious account of how to take care of toilet needs while enjoying the outdoors.)

Niemi, Judith. *The Basic Essentials of Women in the Outdoors.* Merrillville, IN: ICS Books, Inc., 1990. (Encouraging and practical.)

CHAPTER 10

Herrero, Stephen. *Bear Attacks: Their Causes and Avoidance.* New York: Nick Lyons Books, 1985. (A good blend of anecdotal and research information. Highly recommended for those planning backcountry trips in the grizzly territories of the United States and Canada.)

CHAPTER 11

Burton, Joan. *Best Hikes with Children in Western Washington,* 2nd ed. Seattle: The Mountaineers Books, 1999.

Cornell, Joseph. *Sharing Nature with Children: The Classic Parents' and Teachers' Nature Awareness Guidebook.* Nevada City, CA: Dawn Publications, 1998.

———. *Sharing Nature with Children II: A Sequel to the Classic Parents' and Teachers' Nature Awareness Guidebook.* Nevada City, CA: Dawn Publications, 1999.

Doan, Marlyn. *Starting Small in the Wilderness.* San Francisco: Sierra Club Books, 1989. (A good introduction for the beginning family hiker.)

Foster, Lynne. *Take a Hike: The Sierra Club Kid's Guide to Hiking and Backpacking.* New York: Little, Brown & Co., 1991.

Henderson, Bonnie. *Best Hikes with Children in Western and Central Oregon,* 2nd ed. Seattle: The Mountaineers Books, 1999.

Keilty, Maureen. *Best Hikes with Children in Colorado.* Seattle: The Mountaineers Books, 1998.

———. and Thomas J. Lewis. *Best Hikes with Children in Connecticut, Massachusetts, and Rhode Island,* 2nd ed. Seattle: The Mountaineers Books, 1998.

———. and Thomas J. Lewis. *Best Hikes with Children in the Catskills and Hudson River Valley,* 2nd ed. Seattle: The Mountaineers Books, 2002.

Lewis, Cynthia C., and Thomas J. Lewis. *Best Hikes with Children in Vermont, New Hampshire, and Maine,* 2nd ed. Seattle: The Mountaineers Books, 2000.

McMillon, Bill, and Kevin McMillon. *Best Hikes with Children around Sacramento.* Seattle: The Mountaineers Books, 1993.

————. *Best Hikes with Children in the San Francisco Bay Area*, 2nd ed. Seattle: The Mountaineers Books, 2002.

Mooers, Robert L. *Finding Your Way in the Outdoors: Compass Navigation, Map Reading, Route Finding, Weather Forecasting*. New York: Outdoor Life, 1972. (Easy reading, and many diagrams.)

Silverman, Goldie. *Backpacking with Babies and Small Children*. Berkeley: Wilderness Press, 1998. (Practical information, with answers to questions you usually forget to ask.)

Zatz, Arline. *Best Hikes with Children in New Jersey*. Seattle: The Mountaineers Books, 1992.

Outfitters for Children

Eastern Mountain Sports (gear for kids): *www.ems.com*
Kelty Kids (child carriers): *www.kelty.com*
Merrell (hiking boots): *www.merrell.com*
Outdoor Kids (all gear for kids): *www.outdoorkids.com*
Patagonia: *www.patagonia.com*
Recreational Equipment Inc. (gear for kids): *www.rei.com*
Tough Traveler KidSYSTEMS (child carriers): *www.toughtraveler.com*
VauDe (child carriers): *www.vaude.com*
Wildernet Gear Store (gear for kids): *www.wildernet.com*

CHAPTER 12

Brandon, Jeffrey L., and Frank J. Rikop. *Life between the Tides: The Natural History of the Common Seashore Life of Southern California*. San Diego: American Southwest Publishing Company, 1985. (Best of all field guides to the intertidal zone.)

California Coastal Commission. *California Coastal Access Guide,* 6th ed. Berkeley: University of California Press, 2003. (Information on all the scenic and recreational facilities of the California coast, including descriptions of several hundred public accessways.)

Coulombe, Deborah A. *The Seaside Naturalist: A Guide to Study at the Seashore*. New York: Simon and Schuster, 1992. (Excellent review of intertidal inhabitants. Good diagrams.)

Hinton, Sam D. *Seashore Life of Southern California*, rev. ed. Berkeley: University of California Press, 1988. (This popular guide to intertidal life in southern California also includes a "Selected References" list of books about other areas along the Pacific coast.)

Kozloff, Eugene N. *Seashore Life of the Northern Pacific Coast: An Illustrated Guide to Northern California, Oregon, Washington, and British Columbia*. Seattle: University of Washington Press, 1983.

Miller, Arthur, and Marjorie Miller. *Park Ranger Guide to Seashores: Discover Sea Life along the Coasts, Marshes, Bays, and Beaches*. Harrisburg, PA: Stackpole Books 1992. (Good book dealing with the natural history of coastlines of the United States.)

Russo, Ron, and Pam Olhausen. *Pacific Intertidal Life: A Guide to Organisms of Rocky Reefs and Tide Pools of the Pacific Coast*. Rochester, NY: Nature Study Guild, 1981. (Good inexpensive field guide.)

CHAPTER 14

Abbey, Edward. *Desert Solitaire: A Season in the Wilderness.* New York: McGraw-Hill, 1968.

Hogue, Lawrence. *All the Wild and Lonely Places: Journeys in a Desert Landscape.* Washington, D.C.: Island Press, 2000.

Larson, Peggy Pickering. *The Deserts of the Southwest: A Sierra Club Naturalist's Guide,* 2nd ed. San Francisco: Sierra Club Books, 2000.

Schad, Jerry. *California Deserts.* Helena, MT: Falcon Press, 1988.

Shelton, Richard. *Going Back to Bisbee.* Tucson: University of Arizona Press, 1992.

Zwinger, Ann. *The Mysterious Lands: A Naturalist Explores the Four Great Deserts of the Southwest.* Tucson: University of Arizona Press, 1996.

CHAPTER 15

Beck, Dave. *Ski Touring in California.* Berkeley: Wilderness Press, 1980. (Contains instructional material as well as a collection of Sierra Nevada ski tours for beginning to advanced skiers.)

Cox, Steven M., and Kris Fulsaas. *Mountaineering: The Freedom of the Hills,* 7th ed. Seattle: The Mountaineers Books, 2003. (Includes extensive coverage of snow and glacier travel. A classic in its field.)

Curtis, Sam. *Harsh Weather Camping.* Birmingham, AL: Menasha Ridge Press, 1987. (If you are a fair-weather camper, this book will either convert you or kill you. Curtis has experienced all the joys and hardships of winter camping.)

Ferguson, Sue and Edward R. LaChapelle. *The ABCs of Avalanche Safety,* 3rd ed. Seattle: The Mountaineers Books, 2003. (The classic pocket guide to avoiding avalanches—updated with the latest in technology and technique.)

Prater, Gene. *Snowshoeing: From Novice to Master,* 5th ed. Seattle: The Mountaineers Books, 2002. (Includes a well-illustrated section on snow camping.)

Randall, Glenn. *Cold Comfort: Keeping Warm in the Outdoors.* New York: The Lyons Books, 1987. (No other book addresses the issue of avoiding cold so succinctly and completely.)

Additional Reading

Bein, Vic. *Mountain Skiing.* Seattle: The Mountaineers Books, 1982.

Brady, Michael. *Cross-Country Ski Gear.* Seattle: The Mountaineers Books, 1987.

Daffern, Tony. *Avalanche Safety for Skiers and Climbers.* Seattle: The Mountaineers Books, 1992.

Fredston, Jill, and Doug Fesler. *Snow Sense,* 4th ed. Anchorage: Alaska Mountain Safety Center, 1994.

Gillette, Ned, and John Dostal. *Cross-Country Skiing,* 3rd ed. Seattle: The Mountaineers Books, 1988.

Hall, William. *The Professional Ski Instructors of America Present Cross-Country Skiing Right.* San Francisco: Harper and Row, 1985.

Parker, Paul. *Free-Heel Skiing: Telemark and Parallel Techniques,* 3rd ed. Seattle: The Mountaineers Books, 2001.

Tejada-Flores, Lito. *Backcountry Skiing: The Sierra Club Guide to Skiing off the Beaten Track.* San Francisco: Sierra Club Books, 1981.

U.S. Department of Agriculture. *Avalanche Handbook.* USDA Publication 489. Washington, D.C., 1978.

Watters, Ron. *Ski Camping: A Guide to the Delights of Backcountry Skiing.* Pocatello, ID: The Great Rift Press, 1989.

Wilkerson, James. *Hypothermia, Frostbite and Other Cold Injuries: Prevention, Recognition, and Prehospital Treatment.* Seattle: The Mountaineers Books, 1986.

CHAPTER 16

Auerbach, Paul S. *Medicine for the Outdoors: The Essential Guide to Emergency Medical Procedures and First Aid.* New York: Nick Lyons Press, 2003. (Comprehensive and easily understood by the layman. However, procedures for CPR and choking are outdated.)

Darvill, Fred T. *Mountaineering Medicine and Backcountry Medical Guide.* Berkeley: Wilderness Press, 1998. (Concise and easily understood. This should be carried in every backpacker's first-aid kit.)

Isaac, Jeffrey. *The Outward Bound Wilderness First-Aid Handbook.* New York: Lyons Press, 1998. (Easily understandable with case studies as examples.)

Morrissey, Jim. *Wilderness Medical Associates Field Guide,* 3rd ed. Bryant Pond, ME: Wilderness Medical Associates, 2000. (Handy field reference.)

Schimelpfenig, Tod, and Linda Lindsey. *NOLS Wilderness First Aid.* Mechanicsburg, PA: Stackpole Books, 2000. (Comprehensive with good illustrations.)

CHAPTER 17

Cooper, Donald C., Patrick "Rick" LaValla, and Robert "Skip" Stoffel. *Search and Rescue Fundamentals,* 3rd ed. Olympia, WA: Emergency Response Institute, 1996. (Basic skills and knowledge to perform wilderness, inland, search and rescue).

Setnicka, Tim J. *Wilderness Search and Rescue.* AMC Books, 1980. (The bible of search and rescue techniques.)

CHAPTER 18

Nealy, William. *Mountain Bike! A Manual of Beginning to Advanced Technique.* Birmingham, AL: Menasha Ridge Press, 1992.

Overend, Ned. *Mountain Bike Like a Champion.* Emmaus, PA: Rodale Press, Inc, 1999. (Contains many valuable tips for improving biking technique.)

Sloane, Eugene A. *Eugene A. Sloane's Complete Guide to All-Terrain Bicycles.* New York: Simon and Schuster, 1985. (Helpful guide to all aspects of mountain bikes.)

Van der Plas, Rob. *The Mountain Bike Book.* San Francisco: Bicycle Books, 1993. (Helpful information about choosing, riding, and maintaining off-road bicycles.)

Index

About the Authors

Barbara Amato

Barbara Amato was certified as an aerobics instructor through the YMCA in 1983. As an avid ocean swimmer, she moved easily into triathlon sports. She enjoyed marathon running and ultra-distance trail running while training as a triathlete between 1989 and 1999. She enjoys hiking, backpacking, and camping through the Sierra Club's Wilderness Basics Course and Outings programs. She is also an active environmental advocate in San Diego County.

Kristi Anderson

Kristi Anderson spent the first half of her life not hiking and camping, until she took the Wilderness Basics Course in 1996 and was hooked! Since then, she has been hiking and leading camps for the Wilderness Basics Course and the Sierra Club as a Chapter Outing Leader. She is currently training to climb San Gorgonio (11,500 feet) and wants to eventually climb Mount Whitney—and spend the rest of her days hiking and camping.

Hal Brody

Hal Brody has been exploring the Southwestern deserts since 1980. Since becoming a Sierra Club trip leader in 1981, he has served as a Wilderness Basics Course leader, specializing in desert outings. For more than seven years, he has carefully prepared and led qualified adventurers on summer desert trips. He shares his love and knowledge of the desert with his trip members in order to help them gain a deep appreciation of the desert, and to create environmentalists whose votes and political actions may help safeguard the remaining desert wilderness.

Nelson Copp

A geologist by training, Nelson Copp has been hiking and backpacking in the Southwest since the early 1960s. His many interests include bicycling, backpacking, cross-country skiing, surfing, and chasing solar eclipses all over the globe. He is the co-author of *Cycling San Diego* and a popular lecturer. Nelson enjoys teaching map and compass and GPS classes for the Sierra Club and other groups and loves to help people "find themselves," so to speak. He is a frequent Sierra Club outing leader.

Bob Feuge

Robert L. (Bob) Feuge has lived in the Southwest all of his 62 years. During childhood, he developed an interest in American Indian cultures and spent much of his time hiking to ancient archaeological sites and exploring near his home in Fredericksburg, Texas. Interest in backpacking, skiing, and canoeing eventually followed. He joined the staff of the Wilderness Basics Course in 1991 and has served as snow camp coordinator, lecture coordinator, and vice chair. Bob served as WBC chair in 1997 and 1998. In 1998, he moved to Sedona, Arizona, where he took up mountain biking while still actively interested in hiking and backpacking. Bob reports on Sedona Westerner hikes for the *Red Rock News*.

Mike Fry

Mike Fry started backpacking with the Boy Scouts in the late 1950s, but that primitive experience was not worth continuing. He discovered the Sierra Club and REI in 1968, and has been a wilderness traveler ever since. He is an outing leader for the San Diego Chapter and is chair of the ski section and the Bus Trip program. In his spare time he backpacks and skis, and he enjoys the heavy labor of trail construction on the Fry/Koegel Trail on Mount Woodson in the city of Poway.

David M. Gottfredson

David M. Gottfredson has been hiking and camping since he was a child growing up in the foothills of southern California. Formally introduced to hiking in the desert through what was then the Sierra Club San Diego Chapter's Basic Mountaineering Course (now Wilderness Basics) in 1986, he went on to serve as an instructor and treasurer of the course for the next sixteen years. He is an avid hiker who splits his time between the desert and the mountains and particularly enjoys hiking in the Southwest, especially in Utah and Arizona.

Alfred F. Hofstatter

As a Boy Scout, Alfred F. Hofstatter embraced the experience of camping and hiking, and has continued to pursue his outdoor adventures to this day. He introduced his passion to his sons and grandchildren and now goes camping in the Sierra and Alaska with them. He has been on the staff of the Wilderness Basics Course since 1999 and was instrumental in introducing the Leave No Trace concepts into the curriculum. As a chapter outing leader, he leads training outings for the WBC in the Anza-Borrego Desert State Park. He and his wife have traveled the world extensively.

Inner City Outings

Ellen Feeney, Liz Gabrych, Paul Kater, Denise McClellan, and Heather Tatton are volunteers and leaders for the San Diego Sierra Club Chapter of Inner City Outings (ICO). Through ICO, all five have been a part of leading youth outings in the wilderness. ICO volunteers believe that the wilderness exists as a resource for everyone and that wildlands should be accessible to all. With the guidance of ICO volunteers, local youth discover the beauty of wildlands and how to enjoy these areas without causing them harm. Young people learn valuable survival skills and strengthen their abilities to face challenges, both inside and outside their urban environments. Through active involvement with nature, the ICO program increases participants' environmental awareness. Interpersonal skills and self-esteem develop as a natural result of teamwork and an active relationship with the outdoors.

Pauline Jimenez

Pauline Jimenez discovered backpacking and the Sierra Club when she took their Basic Mountaineering (now Wilderness Basics) Course in 1976. She became a Chapter Outings Leader in 1993. She also delivers the course's food and nutrition module and enjoys trail-testing new recipes. In addition to leading backpacks in the Anza-Borrego Desert State Park and longer summer trips in the Sierra Nevada, she is one of the editors for the *Hi Sierran,* the San Diego Chapter's bimonthly newsletter, chair of the *Hi Sierran* Committee, and secretary to the Chapter's Outing Committee. Pauline's trail avocations include ethnobotany, astronomy, and harmonica concerts under the stars.

Jeff Marchand

Jeff Marchand is an avid hiker, biker, skier and sea kayaker, who grew up in the Pacific Northwest. His interest in outdoor education and search and rescue began in the late 1970s. He became an active member on the San Diego Mountain Rescue Team when he moved to southern California fourteen years ago. He has been involved with the North County Group of the San Diego Chapter of the Sierra Club since 1991 and has been the chair of their Wilderness Basics Course for seven years.

Jim Matlock

Jim Matlock is a long-time member of the Sierra Club and has been an outing leader for the San Diego Chapter of the Sierra Club for ten years. He is currently WBC program coordinator and is responsible for the ten-week program that is offered each winter; he also leads backpacks for the WBC each year. Jim is involved with the chapter's Family Program and is currently chair of the Outing Committee.

Mark Mauricio

Mark Mauricio was born and raised in northern California. He has explored not only the United States but also parts of Mexico, Europe, central India, the Tibetan Plateau region of northern India, and he took a brief peek at Thailand. He is a Sierra Club Chapter Outings Leader and has been involved with San Diego's Wilderness Basics Course since 1992.

Carol P. Murdock

Carol P. Murdock is a retired registered nurse, a former Red Cross first-aid instructor, and a former member of the Wilderness Medical Society. She has been a Sierra Club outing leader for more than thirty years and has lead day hikes, backpacks in remote areas, mule trips, and bicycle rides. For more than twenty years she organized and taught an annual weekend wilderness first-aid seminar for the San Diego Chapter. She was responsible for coordinating and teaching first aid for San Diego Chapter outing leaders and trainees and also led Sierra backpacks as a national leader. She still leads day hikes, and she car camps.

Jerry Schad

Jerry Schad introduces his students at San Diego Mesa College to the wonders of the natural world by way of courses in the physical sciences. He also guides hikers and bicyclists along thousands of miles of California roads and trails by way of his several guidebooks and columns written for various publications. Jerry enjoys trips to the celebrated parks and wilderness areas around the West, as well as to the "vest-pocket wildernesses" that lie very near some of California's most populated areas.

Marty Stevens

Ever since his father took him on canoe trips as a young boy in the Boundary Waters Canoe Area, Marty Stevens has been an outdoor enthusiast. Marty is an avid backpacker and cross-country skier, who spends much of his free time in the high Sierra, the backcountry of San Diego County, or on the snowy slopes of California, Utah, and Colorado. In the course of his career, Marty has visited many places that have offered opportunities for outdoor adventure. He has rafted the rivers of the Northwest, hiked New Zealand and Bavaria, and spent two seasons in the Antarctic and at the South Pole. Marty has organized backpacking trips and leadership seminars for the San Diego Chapter and is a leader for the chapter's Wilderness Basics Course.

Bob Stinton

Bob Stinton was introduced to backpacking in the Boy Scouts, where each troop member had to make their own backpack and other equipment items. After participating in the Basic Mountaineering (now Wilderness Basics) Course in 1975, he became an outing leader for the San Diego Chapter of the Sierra Club. He and his wife Marcy, also an outing leader, enjoy leading backpacking trips and introducing individuals to backcountry travel.

Arleen Tavernier

Arleen Tavernier was introduced to the deserts and mountains of the Southwest by her dad. With his never-ending curiosity to explore new areas, the family would take off to some remote area in search of either the perfect mineral or the largest fish. Over the years this led to many adventures in the outdoors, but it was not until she signed up as a student of the Wilderness Basics Course in 1991 that she was able to put it all together. From that time on, she has been on the staff of WBC, currently as its chair. She recently completed more than 800 miles of the Pacific Crest Trail, with hopes of someday completing the rest of the trail.

Emily B. Troxell

Emily B. Troxell recently retired from her position as an interpretative ranger at Cabrillo National Monument. Her responsibility as education coordinator led to the development and coordination of programs for elementary, middle, and high school students in the study of intertidal habitats. As an interpretative ranger, she often related the story of the Pacific gray whale, but her most enjoyable task was wading into the intertidal area while telling about the life patterns of the creatures found there. She believes that courses in outdoor education and wilderness appreciation for adults will help people better use and appreciate the world's natural places.

Eugene A. Troxell

Eugene A. Troxell is an associate professor of philosophy at San Diego State University. He has taught there continuously since receiving his Ph.D. in philosophy in 1966 from the University of Chicago. He is co-author of *Making Sense of Things*, published in 1976 by St. Martin's Press. His academic specialties include the philosophy of Wittgenstein, and ethics—particularly environmental ethics. He has served as president of the San Diego Ecology Centre, is an aikido instructor, and counts among his avocations hiking, camping, and backpacking.

Ian Wickson

Ian Wickson was born in Vancouver, Canada, in 1964. In 1972 his family relocated to Arizona, where he has lived ever since. Mild winters in Arizona fostered a passion for cycling and rock climbing while summer trips were spent sailing, hiking, and whitewater kayaking. He was introduced to wilderness travel and mountaineering through a Colorado Outward Bound program in 1981. After a stint in aviation, Ian shared his knowledge of the outdoors as a professional rock climbing, canyoneering, and backpacking guide. He currently resides in Sedona, Arizona, where he designs custom mountain bikes and writes a weekly column for the *Red Rock News*.

Ted Young

A native southern Californian, Ted Young has long enjoyed visiting California's deserts in winter and the mountains in summer. His favorite kind of summer vacation is backpacking to a base camp above timberline in the Sierra Nevada and then spending the days hiking cross-country—ideal circumstances for refining wilderness navigation skills.

Other Contributors

Priscilla Anderson, Scott Anderson, Jan Craven, Mary Engles, Skip Forsht, Keith Gordon, David Moser, Marianne Kinghoff, Donald B. Stouder, Carl W. Trygstad, Dave Ussell, Olive Wenzel.

THE MOUNTAINEERS, founded in 1906, is a nonprofit outdoor activity and conservation club whose mission is "to explore, study, preserve, and enjoy the natural beauty of the outdoors. . . . " Based in Seattle, Washington, the club is now the third-largest such organization in the United States, with seven branches throughout Washington State.

The Mountaineers sponsors both classes and year-round outdoor activities in the Pacific Northwest, which include hiking, mountain climbing, ski-touring, snowshoeing, bicycling, camping, kayaking and canoeing, nature study, sailing, and adventure traveling. The club's conservation division supports environmental causes through educational activities, sponsoring legislation, and presenting informational programs. All club activities are led by skilled, experienced volunteers who are dedicated to promoting safe and responsible enjoyment and preservation of the outdoors.

If you would like to participate in these organized outdoor activities or the club's programs, consider a membership in The Mountaineers. For information and an application, write or call The Mountaineers, Club Headquarters, 300 Third Avenue West, Seattle, WA 98119; 206-284-6310.

The Mountaineers Books, an active, nonprofit publishing program of the club, produces guidebooks, instructional texts, historical works, natural history guides, and works on environmental conservation. All books produced by The Mountaineers Books fulfill the club's mission.

Send or call for our catalog of more than 500 outdoor titles:

The Mountaineers Books
1001 SW Klickitat Way, Suite 201
Seattle, WA 98134
800-553-4453
mbooks@mountaineersbooks.org
www.mountaineersbooks.org

The Mountaineers Books is proud to be a corporate sponsor of Leave No Trace, whose mission is to promote and inspire responsible outdoor recreation through education, research, and partnerships. The Leave No Trace program is focused specifically on human-powered (nonmotorized) recreation.

Leave No Trace strives to educate visitors about the nature of their recreational impacts, as well as offer techniques to prevent and minimize such impacts. Leave No Trace is best understood as an educational and ethical program, not as a set of rules and regulations.

For more information, visit *www.LNT.org,* or call 800-332-4100.

OTHER TITLES YOU MIGHT ENJOY FROM
THE MOUNTAINEERS BOOKS

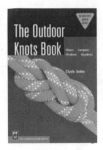

The Outdoor Knots Book: Hikers, Campers, Climbers, Kayakers, *Clyde Soles*
A guide to the ropes and knots used in the outdoors by hikers, campers, paddlers, and climbers.

Staying Found: The Complete Map & Compass Handbook,
June Fleming
An easy-to-understand handbook for learning map and compass skills.

GPS Made Easy: Using Global Positioning Systems in the Outdoors, *Lawrence Letham*
Learn all you need to know about using handheld Global Positioning System receivers for accurate navigation.

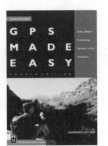

Backpacker Adventure Journal,
Kristin Hostetter
Inspiration and a perfect format for chronicling your outdoor adventure.

Don't Forget the Duct Tape,
Kristin Hostetter
Don't Get Sick, *Buck Tilton, M.S. &*
Rick Bennett, Ph.D.
Don't Get Bitten, *Buck Tilton*
Don't Get Eaten, *Dave Smith*

Available at fine bookstores and outdoor stores, by phone at 800-553-4453 or on the Web at *www.mountaineersbooks.org*

THE MOUNTAINEERS BOOKS